Simulation

Second Edition

This is a volume in
STATISTICAL MODELING AND DECISION SCIENCE
Gerald J. Lieberman and Ingram Olkin, editors
Stanford University, Stanford, California

A list of titles in this series appears at the end of this volume.

Simulation
Second Edition

Sheldon M. Ross
DEPARTMENT OF INDUSTRIAL ENGINEERING AND OPERATIONS RESEARCH
UNIVERSITY OF CALIFORNIA
BERKELEY, CALIFORNIA

San Diego London Boston
New York Sydney Tokyo Toronto

Copyright © 1997 by Academic Press

Academic Press
A Harcourt Science and Technology Company
525 B Street, Suite 1900, San Diego, California 92101-4495, U.S.A.
http://www.apnet.com

Academic Press
24-28 Oval Road, London NW1 7DX, UK
http://www.hbuk.co.uk/ap/

Harcourt/Academic Press
A Harcourt Science and Technology Company
200 Wheeler Road, Burlington, Massachusetts 01803
http://www.harcourt-ap.com

Library of Congress Cataloging-in-Publication Data

Ross, Sheldon M.
  Simulation / Sheldon M. Ross.—2nd ed.
    p. cm.—(Statistical modeling and decision science)
  Rev. ed. of: A course in simulation. c1990.
  Includes bibliographical references and index.
  ISBN 0-12-598410-3 (alk. paper)
    1. Random variables. 2. Probabilities. 3. Computer
simulation.
  I. Ross, Sheldon M. Course in simulation. II. Title.
  III. Series.
  QA273.R82   1996
  519.2—dc20   96-30669
                                                           CIP

Printed in the United States of America
    00 01 02 03 MM 9 8 7 6 5 4 3

Contents

Chapter 3   Random Numbers

Chapter 4   Generating Discrete Random Variables

Chapter 5   Generating Continuous Random Variables

Chapter 6   The Discrete Event Simulation Approach

Chapter 7   Statistical Analysis of Simulated Data

Chapter 8   Variance Reduction Techniques

Chapter 9   Statistical Validation Techniques

Chapter 10   Markov Chain Monte Carlo Methods

Chapter 11   Some Additional Topics

Preface

In formulating a stochastic model to describe a real phenomenon, it used to be that one compromised between choosing a model that is a realistic replica of the actual situation and one whose mathematical analysis is tractable. That is, there did not seem to be any payoff in choosing a model that faithfully conformed to the phenomenon under study if it were not possible to mathematically analyze that model. Similar considerations have led to the concentration on asymptotic or steady-state results as opposed to the more useful ones on transient time. However, the relatively recent advent of fast and inexpensive computational power has opened up another approach—namely, to try to model the phenomenon as faithfully as possible and then to rely on a simulation study to analyze it.

In this text we show how to analyze a model by use of a simulation study. In particular, we first show how a computer can be utilized to generate random (more precisely, pseudorandom) numbers, and then how these random numbers can be used to generate the values of random variables from arbitrary distributions. Using the concept of discrete events we show how to use random variables to generate the behavior of a stochastic model over time. By continually generating the behavior of the system we show how to obtain estimators of desired quantities of interest. The statistical questions of when to stop a simulation and what confidence to place in the resulting estimators are considered. A variety of ways in which one can improve on the usual simulation estimators are presented. In addition, we show how to use simulation to determine whether the stochastic model chosen is consistent with a set of actual data.

The successive chapters in this text are as follows. Chapter 1 is an introductory chapter which presents a typical phenomenon that is of interest to study. Chapter 2 is a review of probability. Whereas this chapter is self-contained and does not assume the reader is familiar with probability, we imagine that it will indeed be a review for most readers. Chapter 3 deals with random numbers and how a variant of them (the so-called pseudorandom numbers) can be generated on a computer. The use of random numbers to generate discrete and then continuous random variables is considered in Chapters 4 and 5.

Chapter 6 presents the discrete event approach to track an arbitrary system as it evolves over time. A variety of examples—relating to both single and multiple server queueing systems, to an inventory system, to a machine repair model, and to the exercising of a stock option—are presented. Chapter 7 introduces the subject matter of statistics. Assuming that our average reader has not previously studied this subject, the chapter starts with very basic concepts and ends by introducing the bootstrap statistical method, which is quite useful in analyzing the results of a simulation.

Chapter 8 deals with the important subject of variance reduction. This is an attempt to improve on the usual simulation estimators by finding ones having the same mean and smaller variances. The chapter begins by introducing the technique of using antithetic variables. We note (with a proof deferred to the chapter's appendix) that this always results in a variance reduction along with a computational savings when we are trying to estimate the expected value of a function that is monotone in each of its variables. We then introduce control variables and illustrate their usefulness in variance reduction. For instance, we show how control variables can be effectively utilized in analyzing queueing systems, reliability systems, a list reordering problem, and blackjack. We also indicate how to use regression packages to facilitate the resulting computations when using control variables. Variance reduction by use of conditional expectations is then considered. Its use is indicated in examples dealing with estimating π, and in analyzing finite capacity queueing systems. Also, in conjunction with a control variate, conditional expectation is used to estimate the expected number of events of a renewal process by some fixed time. The use of stratified sampling as a variance reduction tool is indicated in examples dealing with queues with varying arrival rates and evaluating integrals. The relationship between the variance reduction techniques of conditional expectation and stratified sampling is explained and illustrated in the estimation of the expected return in video poker. The technique of importance sampling is next considered. We indicate and explain how this can be an extremely powerful variance reduction technique when estimating small probabilities. In doing so, we introduce the concept of tilted distributions and show how they can be utilized in an importance sampling estimation of a small convolution tail probability. Applications of importance sampling to queueing, random walks, and random permutations, and to computing conditional expectations when one is conditioning on a rare event, are presented. The final variance reduction technique of Chapter 8 relates to the use of a common stream of random numbers.

Chapter 9 is concerned with statistical validation techniques, which are statistical procedures that can be used to validate the stochastic model when some real data are available. Goodness of fit tests such as the chi-square test and the Kolmogorov–Smirnov test are presented. Other sections in this chapter deal with the two-sample and the n-sample problems and with ways of statistically testing the hypothesis that a given process is a Poisson process.

Chapter 10 is concerned with Markov chain Monte Carlo methods. These are techniques that have greatly expanded the use of simulation in recent years. The standard simulation paradigm for estimating $\theta = E[h(\mathbf{X})]$, where $\mathbf{X}$ is a random vector, is to simulate independent and identically distributed copies of $\mathbf{X}$ and then use the average value of $h(\mathbf{X})$ as the estimator. This is the so-called "raw" simulation estimator, which can then possibly be improved upon by using one or more of the variance reduction ideas of Chapter 8. However, in order to employ this approach it is necessary both that the distribution of $\mathbf{X}$ be specified and also that we be able to simulate from this distribution. However, as we see in Chapter 10, there are many examples where the distribution of $\mathbf{X}$ is known but we are not able to directly simulate the random vector $\mathbf{X}$, and other examples where the distribution is not completely known but is only specified up to a multiplicative constant. Thus, in either case, the usual approach to estimating θ is not available. However, a new approach, based on generating a Markov chain whose limiting distribution is the distribution of $\mathbf{X}$, and estimating θ by the average of the values of the function h evaluated at the successive states of this chain, has become widely used in recent years. These Markov chain Monte Carlo methods are explored in Chapter 10. We start, in Section 10.2, by introducing and presenting some of the properties of Markov chains. A general technique for generating a Markov chain having a limiting distribution that is specified up to a multiplicative constant, known as the Hastings–Metropolis algorithm, is presented in Section 10.3, and an application to generating a random element of a large "combinatorial" set is given. The most widely used version of the Hastings–Metropolis algorithm is known as the Gibbs sampler, and this is presented in Section 10.4. Examples are discussed relating to generating random points in a region subject to a constraint that no pair of points are within a fixed distance of each other, to analyzing product form queueing networks, and to analyzing a hierarchical Bayesian statistical model for predicting the numbers of home runs that will be hit by certain baseball players. An application of the methods of this chapter to deterministic optimization problems, called simulated annealing, is presented in

Section 10.5, and an example concerning the traveling salesman problem is presented. The final section of Chapter 10 deals with the sampling importance resampling algorithm, which is a generalization of the acceptance rejection technique of Chapters 4 and 5. The use of this algorithm in Bayesian statistics is indicated.

Chapter 11 deals with some additional topics in simulation. In Section 11.1 we learn of the alias method which, at the cost of some setup time, is a very efficient way to generate discrete random variables. Section 11.2 is concerned with simulating a two-dimensional Poisson process. In Section 11.3 we present an identity concerning the covariance of the sum of dependent Bernoulli random variables and show how its use can result in estimators of small probabilities having very low variances. Applications relating to estimating the reliability of a system, which appears to be more efficient that any other known estimator of a small system reliability, and to estimating the probability that a specified pattern occurs by some fixed time, are given. Section 11.4 introduces random hazards. These quantities can be used as control variables when estimating the mean time until a given Markov process reaches a specified set of states. In addition, in situations where it is not guaranteed that the set of states will ever be reached, the random hazard can be used as an estimator of the probability of this event. It will be a particularly effective estimator when the probability of ever reaching the set of states is small.

Chapter 1 | Introduction

Consider the following situation faced by a pharmacist who is thinking of setting up a small pharmacy where he will fill prescriptions. He plans on opening up at 9 A.M. every weekday and expects that, on average, there will be about 32 prescriptions called in daily before 5 P.M. His experience indicates that the time that it will take him to fill a prescription, once he begins working on it, is a random quantity having a mean and standard deviation of 10 and 4 minutes, respectively. He plans on accepting no new prescriptions after 5 P.M., although he will remain in the shop past this time if necessary to fill all the prescriptions ordered that day. Given this scenario the pharmacist is probably, among other things, interested in the answers to the following questions:

1. What is the average time that he will depart his store at night?
2. What proportion of days will he still be working at 5:30 P.M.?
3. What is the average time it will take him to fill a prescription (taking into account that he cannot necessarily immediately begin working on a newly arrived prescription but rather it must wait for him to complete work on all earlier ones)?
4. What proportion of prescriptions will be filled within 30 minutes?
5. If he changes his policy on accepting all prescriptions between 9 A.M. and 5 P.M., but rather only accepts new ones when there are fewer than five prescriptions still needing to be filled, how many prescriptions, on average, will be lost?
6. How would the conditions of limiting orders affect the answers to questions 1 through 4?

In order to employ mathematics to analyze this situation and answer the questions, we first construct a probability model. To do this it is necessary to make some reasonably accurate assumptions concerning the above scenario. For instance, we must make some assumptions about the probabilistic mechanism that describes the arrivals of the daily average of 32 customers. One possible assumption might be that the arrival rate is, in a probabilistic sense, constant over the day, whereas a second (probably more realistic) possible assumption is that the arrival rate depends on the time of day. We must then specify a probability distribution (having mean 10 and standard deviation 4) for the time it takes to service a prescription, and we must make assumptions about whether or not the service time of a given prescription always has this distribution or whether it changes as a function of other variables (e.g., the number of waiting prescriptions to be filled or the time of day). That is, we must make probabilistic assumptions about the daily arrival and service times. We must also decide if the probability law describing a given day changes as a function of the day of the week or whether it remains basically constant over time. After these assumptions, and possibly others, have been specified, a probability model of our scenario will have been constructed.

Once a probability model has been constructed, the answers to the questions can, in theory, be analytically determined. However, in practice, these questions are much too difficult to determine analytically, and so to answer them we usually have to perform a simulation study. Such a study programs the probabilistic mechanism on a computer, and by utilizing "random numbers" it simulates possible occurrences from this model over a large number of days and then utilizes the theory of statistics to estimate the answers to questions such as those given. In other words, the computer program utilizes random numbers to generate the values of random variables having the assumed probability distributions, which represent the arrival times and the service times of prescriptions. Using these values, it determines over many days the quantities of interest related to the questions. It then uses statistical techniques to provide estimated answers—for example, if out of 1000 simulated days, there are 122 in which the pharmacist is still working at 5:30 we would estimate that the answer to question 2 is 0.122.

In order to be able to execute such an analysis, one must have some knowledge of probability so as to decide on certain probability distributions and questions such as whether appropriate random variables are to be assumed independent or not. A review of probability is provided in Chapter 2. The bases of a simulation study are so-called random numbers. A discussion of these quantities and how they are computer generated is presented in Chapter 3. Chapters 4 and 5 show

how one can use random numbers to generate the values of random variables having arbitrary distributions. Discrete distributions are considered in Chapter 4 and continuous ones in Chapter 5. After completing Chapter 5, the reader should have some insight into the construction of a probability model for a given system and also how to use random numbers to generate the values of random quantities related to this model. The use of these generated values to track the system as it evolves continuously over time—that is, the actual simulation of the system—is discussed in Chapter 6, where we present the concept of "discrete events" and indicate how to utilize these entities to obtain a systematic approach to simulating systems. The discrete event simulation approach leads to a computer program, which can be written in whatever language the reader is comfortable in, that simulates the system a large number of times. Some hints concerning the verification of this program—to ascertain that it is actually doing what is desired—are also given in Chapter 6. The use of the outputs of a simulation study to answer probabilistic questions concerning the model necessitates the use of the theory of statistics, and this subject is introduced in Chapter 7. This chapter starts with the simplest and most basic concepts in statistics and continues toward the recent innovation of "bootstrap statistics," which is quite useful in simulation. Our study of statistics indicates the importance of the variance of the estimators obtained from a simulation study as an indication of the efficiency of the simulation. In particular, the smaller this variance is, the smaller is the amount of simulation needed to obtain a fixed precision. As a result we are led, in Chapter 8, to ways of obtaining new estimators that are improvements over the raw simulation estimators because they have reduced variances. This topic of variance reduction is extremely important in a simulation study because it can substantially improve its efficiency. Chapter 9 shows how one can use the results of a simulation to verify, when some real-life data are available, the appropriateness of the probability model (which we have simulated) to the real-world situation. Chapter 10 introduces the important topic of Markov chain Monte Carlo methods. The use of these methods has, in recent years, greatly expanded the class of problems that can be attacked by simulation. Chapter 11 considers a variety of additional topics.

Exercises

1. The following data yield the arrival times and service times that each customer will require, for the first 13 customers at a single server system.

Upon arrival, a customer either enters service if the server is free or joins the waiting line. When the server completes work on a customer, the next one in line (i.e., the one who has been waiting the longest) enters service.

Arrival Times: 12 31 63 95 99 154 198 221 304 346 411 455 537
Service Times: 40 32 55 48 18 50 47 18 28 54 40 72 12

(a) Determine the departure times of these 13 customers.

(b) Repeat (a) when there are two servers and a customer can be served by either one.

(c) Repeat (a) under the new assumption that when the server completes a service, the next customer to enter service is the one that has been waiting the least time.

2. Consider a service station where customers arrive and are served in their order of arrival. Let A_n, S_n, and D_n denote, respectively, the arrival time, the service time, and the departure time of customer n. Suppose there is a single server and that the system is initially empty of customers.

(a) Argue that $D_0 = 0$, and for $n > 0$

$$D_n - S_n = \text{Maximum}\{A_n, D_{n-1}\}$$

(b) Determine the corresponding recursion formula when there are two servers.

(c) Determine the corresponding recursion formula when there are k servers.

(d) Write a computer program to determine the departure times as a function of the arrival and service times and use it to check your answers in parts (a) and (b) of Exercise 1.

Chapter 2 | Elements of Probability

2.1 Sample Space and Events

Consider an experiment whose outcome is not known in advance. Let S, called the sample space of the experiment, denote the set of all possible outcomes. For example, if the experiment consists of the running of a race among the seven horses numbered 1 through 7, then

$$S = \{\text{all orderings of } (1, 2, 3, 4, 5, 6, 7)\}$$

The outcome $(3, 4, 1, 7, 6, 5, 2)$ means, for example, that the number 3 horse came in first, the number 4 horse came in second, and so on.

Any subset A of the sample space is known as an event. That is, an event is a set consisting of possible outcomes of the experiment. If the outcome of the experiment is contained in A, we say that A has occurred. For example, in the above, if

$$A = \{\text{all outcomes in } S \text{ starting with } 5\}$$

then A is the event that the number 5 horse comes in first.

For any two events A and B we define the new event $A \cup B$, called the union of A and B, to consist of all outcomes that are either in A or B or in both A and B. Similarly, we define the event, AB, called the intersection of A and B, to consist of all outcomes that are in both A and B. That is, the event $A \cup B$ occurs if either A or B occurs, whereas the event AB occurs if both A and B occur. We can also define unions and intersections of more than two events. In particular, the union of the events $A_1, \ldots, A_n$—designated by $\cup_{i=1}^{n} A_i$—is defined to consist of all outcomes that are in any of the A_i. Similarly, the intersection of the events $A_1, \cdots, A_n$—designated by $A_1A_2 \cdots A_n$—is defined to consist of all outcomes that are in all of the A_i.

For any event A we define the event A^c, referred to as the complement of A, to consist of all outcomes in the sample space S that are not in A. That is, A^c occurs if and only if A does not. Since the outcome of the experiment must lie in the sample space S, it follows that S^c does not contain any outcomes and thus cannot occur. We call S^c the null set and designate it by $\varnothing$. If $AB = \varnothing$ so that A and B cannot both occur (since there are no outcomes that are in both A and B), we say that A and B are mutually exclusive.

2.2   Axioms of Probability

Suppose that for each event A of an experiment having sample space S there is a number, denoted by $P(A)$ and called the probability of the event A, which is in accord with the following three axioms:

Axiom 1 $0 \leq P(A) \leq 1$

Axiom 2 $P(S) = 1$

Axiom 3   *For any sequence of mutually exclusive events* $A_1, A_2, \ldots$

$$P\left(\bigcup_{i=1}^{n} A_i\right) = \sum_{i=1}^{n} P(A_i), \qquad n = 1, 2, \ldots, \infty$$

Thus, Axiom 1 states that the probability that the outcome of the experiment lies within A is some number between 0 and 1. Axiom 2 states that with probability 1 this outcome is a member of the sample space; and Axiom 3 states that for any set of mutually exclusive events, the probability that at least one of these events occurs is equal to the sum of their respective probabilities.

These three axioms can be used to prove a variety of results about probabilities. For instance, since A and A^c are always mutually exclusive, and since $A \cup A^c = S$, we have from Axioms 2 and 3 that

$$1 = P(S) = P(A \cup A^c) = P(A) + P(A^c)$$

or equivalently

$$P(A^c) = 1 - P(A)$$

In words, the probability that an event does not occur is 1 minus the probability that it does.

2.3   Conditional Probability and Independence

Consider an experiment that consists in flipping a coin twice, noting each time whether the result was heads or tails. The sample space of this experiment can be taken to be the following set of four outcomes:

$$S = \{(H, H), (H, T), (T, H), (T, T)\}$$

where (H, T) means, for example, that the first flip lands heads and the second tails. Suppose now that each of the four possible outcomes is equally likely to occur and thus has probability ¼. Suppose further that we observe that the first flip lands on heads. Then, given this information, what is the probability that both flips land on heads? To calculate this probability we reason as follows: Given that the initial flip lands heads, there can be at most two possible outcomes of our experiment, namely, (H, H) or (H, T). In addition, as each of these outcomes originally had the same probability of occurring, they should still have equal probabilities. That is, given that the first flip lands heads, the (conditional) probability of each of the outcomes (H, H) and (H, T) is ½, whereas the (conditional) probability of the other two outcomes is 0. Hence the desired probability is ½.

If we let A and B denote, respectively, the events that both flips land on heads and the event that the first flip lands on heads, then the probability obtained above is called the conditional probability of A given that B has occurred and is denoted by

$$P(A|B)$$

A general formula for $P(A|B)$ that is valid for all experiments and events A and B can be obtained in the same manner as given previously. Namely, if the event B occurs, then in order for A to occur it is necessary that the actual occurrence be a point in both A and $B;$ that is, it must be in AB. Now since we know that B has occurred, it follows that B becomes our new sample space and hence the probability that the event AB occurs will equal the probability of AB relative to the probability of B. That is,

$$P(A|B) = \frac{P(AB)}{P(B)}$$

As indicated by the coin flip example, $P(A|B)$, the conditional probability of A, given that B occurred, is not generally equal to $P(A)$, the unconditional probability of A. In other words, knowing that B has occurred generally changes the probability that A occurs (what if they were mutually exclusive?). In the special case where $P(A|B)$ is equal to $P(A)$, we say that A and B are independent. Since $P(A|B) = P(AB)/P(B)$, we see that A is independent of B if

$$P(AB) = P(A)P(B)$$

Since this relation is symmetric in A and B, it follows that whenever A is independent of B, B is independent of A.

2.4   Random Variables

When an experiment is performed we are sometimes primarily concerned about the value of some numerical quantity determined by the result. These quantities of interest that are determined by the results of the experiment are known as random variables.

The cumulative distribution function, or more simply the distribution function, F of the random variable X is defined for any real number x by

$$F(x) = P\{X \leq x\}$$

A random variable that can take either a finite or at most a countable number of possible values is said to be discrete. For a discrete random variable X we define its probability mass function $p(x)$ by

$$p(x) = P\{X = x\}$$

If X is a discrete random variable that takes on one of the possible values x_1, x_2 . . . , then, since X must take on one of these values, we have

$$\sum_{i=1}^{\infty} p(x_i) = 1$$

Example 2a   Suppose that X takes on one of the values 1, 2, or 3. If

$$p(1) = \frac{1}{4}, \qquad p(2) = \frac{1}{3}$$

then, since $p(1) + p(2) + p(3) = 1$, it follows that $p(3) = \frac{5}{12}$. ∎

Whereas a discrete random variable assumes at most a countable set of possible values, we often have to consider random variables whose set of possible values is an interval. We say that the random variable X is a continuous random variable if there is a nonnegative function $f(x)$ defined for all real numbers x and having the property that for any set C of real numbers

$$P\{X \in C\} = \int_C f(x)\, dx \qquad (2.1)$$

The function f is called the probability density function of the random variable X.

The relationship between the cumulative distribution $F(\cdot)$ and the probability density $f(\cdot)$ is expressed by

$$F(a) = P\{X \in (-\infty, a]\} = \int_{-\infty}^{a} f(x)\, dx$$

Differentiating both sides yields

$$\frac{d}{da} F(a) = f(a)$$

That is, the density is the derivative of the cumulative distribution function. A somewhat more intuitive interpretation of the density function may be obtained from Equation (2.1) as follows:

$$P\left\{a - \frac{\epsilon}{2} \le X \le a + \frac{\epsilon}{2}\right\} = \int_{a-\epsilon/2}^{a+\epsilon/2} f(x)\, dx \approx \epsilon f(a)$$

when ϵ is small. In other words, the probability that X will be contained in an interval of length ϵ around the point a is approximately $\epsilon f(a)$. From this, we see that $f(a)$ is a measure of how likely it is that the random variable will be near a.

In many experiments we are interested not only in probability distribution functions of individual random variables, but also in the relationships between two or more of them. In order to specify the relationship between two random variables, we define the joint cumulative probability distribution function of X and Y by

$$F(x, y) = P\{X \le x, Y \le y\}$$

Thus, $F(x, y)$ specifies the probability that X is less than or equal to x and simultaneously Y is less than or equal to y.

If X and Y are both discrete random variables, then we define the joint probability mass function of X and Y by

$$p(x, y) = P\{X = x, Y = y\}$$

Similarly, we say that X and Y are jointly continuous, with joint probability density function $f(x, y)$, if for any sets of real numbers C and D

$$P\{X \in C, Y \in D\} = \iint_{\substack{x \in C \\ y \in D}} f(x, y)\, dx\, dy$$

The random variables X and Y are said to be independent if for any two sets of real numbers C and D

$$P\{X \in C, Y \in D\} = P\{X \in C\}P\{Y \in D\}$$

That is X and Y are independent if for all sets C and D the events $A = \{X \in C\}$, $B = \{Y \in D\}$ are independent. Loosely speaking, X and Y are independent if knowing the value of one of them does not affect the probability distribution of the other. Random variables that are not independent are said to be dependent.

Using the axioms of probability, we can show that the discrete random variables X and Y will be independent if and only if, for all x, y,

$$P\{X = x, Y = y\} = P\{X = x\}P\{Y = y\}$$

Similarly, if X and Y are jointly continuous with density function $f(x, y)$, then they will be independent if and only if, for all x, y,

$$f(x, y) = f_X(x)f_Y(y)$$

where $f_X(x)$ and $f_Y(y)$ are the density functions of X and Y, respectively.

2.5   Expectation

One of the most useful concepts in probability is that of the expectation of a random variable. If X is a discrete random variable that takes on one of the possible values $x_1, x_2, \ldots$, then the *expectation* or *expected value* of X, also called the mean of X and denoted by $E[X]$, is defined by

$$E[X] = \sum_i x_i P\{X = x_i\} \tag{2.2}$$

In words, the expected value of X is a weighted average of the possible values that X can take on, each value being weighted by the probability that X assumes it. For example, if the probability mass function of X is given by

$$p(0) = \frac{1}{2} = p(1)$$

then

$$E[X] = 0\left(\frac{1}{2}\right) + 1\left(\frac{1}{2}\right) = \frac{1}{2}$$

is just the ordinary average of the two possible values 0 and 1 that X can assume. On the other hand, if

$$p(0) = \frac{1}{3}, \qquad p(1) = \frac{2}{3}$$

then

$$E[X] = 0\left(\frac{1}{3}\right) + 1\left(\frac{2}{3}\right) = \frac{2}{3}$$

is a weighted average of the two possible values 0 and 1 where the value 1 is given twice as much weight as the value 0 since $p(1) = 2p(0)$.

Example 2b   If I is an indicator random variable for the event A, that is, if

$$I = \begin{cases} 1 & \text{if } A \text{ occurs} \\ 0 & \text{if } A \text{ does not occur} \end{cases}$$

then

$$E[I] = 1P(A) + 0P(A^c) = P(A)$$

Hence, the expectation of the indicator random variable for the event A is just the probability that A occurs.   ■

If X is a continuous random variable having probability density function f, then, analogous to Equation (2.2), we define the expected value of X by

$$E[X] = \int_{-\infty}^{\infty} x f(x) \, dx$$

Example 2c If the probability density function of X is given by

$$f(x) = \begin{cases} 3x^2 & \text{if } 0 < x < 1 \\ 0 & \text{otherwise} \end{cases}$$

then

$$E[X] = \int_0^1 3x^3 \, dx = \frac{3}{4}$$
∎

Suppose now that we wanted to determine the expected value not of the random variable X but of the random variable $g(X)$, where g is some given function. Since $g(X)$ takes on the value $g(x)$ when X takes on the value x, it seems intuitive that $E[g(X)]$ should be a weighted average of the possible values $g(x)$ with, for a given x, the weight given to $g(x)$ being equal to the probability (or probability density in the continuous case) that X will equal x. Indeed, the preceding can be shown to be true and we thus have the following result.

Proposition *If X is a discrete random variable having probability mass function $p(x)$, then*

$$E[g(X)] = \sum_x g(x)p(x)$$

whereas if X is continuous with probability density function $f(x)$, then

$$E[g(X)] = \int_{-\infty}^{\infty} g(x)f(x) \, dx$$

A consequence of the above proposition is the following.

Corollary *If a and b are constants, then*

$$E[aX + b] = aE[X] + b$$

Proof In the discrete case

$$E[aX + b] = \sum_x (ax + b)p(x)$$

$$= a \sum_x xp(x) + b \sum_x p(x)$$

$$= aE[X] + b$$

Since the proof in the continuous case is similar, the result is established. ∎

It can be shown that expectation is a linear operation in the sense that for any two random variables X_1 and X_2

$$E[X_1 + X_2] = E[X_1] + E[X_2]$$

which easily generalizes to give

$$E\left[\sum_{i=1}^{n} X_i\right] = \sum_{i=1}^{n} E[X_i]$$

2.6 Variance

Whereas $E[X]$, the expected value of the random variable X, is a weighted average of the possible values of X, it yields no information about the variation of these values. One way of measuring this variation is to consider the average value of the square of the difference between X and $E[X]$. We are thus led to the following definition.

Definition   *If X is a random variable with mean μ, then the variance of X, denoted by Var(X), is defined by*

$$\text{Var}(X) = E[(X - \mu)^2]$$

An alternative formula for Var(X) is derived as follows:

$$\begin{aligned}
\text{Var}(X) &= E[(X - \mu)^2] \\
&= E[X^2 - 2\mu X + \mu^2] \\
&= E[X^2] - E[2\mu X] + E[\mu^2] \\
&= E[X^2] - 2\mu E[X] + \mu^2 \\
&= E[X^2] - \mu^2
\end{aligned}$$

That is,

$$\text{Var}(X) = E[X^2] - (E[X])^2$$

A useful identity, whose proof is left as an exercise, is that for any constants a and b

$$\text{Var}(aX + b) = a^2 \text{Var}(X)$$

Whereas the expected value of a sum of random variables is equal to the sum of the expectations, the corresponding result is not, in general, true for variances.

It is, however, true in the important special case where the random variables are independent. Before proving this let us define the concept of the covariance between two random variables.

Definition *The covariance of two random variables X and Y, denoted Cov(X, Y), is defined by*

$$\text{Cov}(X, Y) = E[(X - \mu_x)(Y - \mu_y)]$$

where $\mu_x = E[X]$ *and* $\mu_y = E[Y]$.

A useful expression for Cov(X, Y) is obtained by expanding the right side of the above equation and then making use of the linearity of expectation. This yields

$$\begin{aligned}
\text{Cov}(X, Y) &= E[XY - \mu_x Y - X\mu_y + \mu_x \mu_y] \\
&= E[XY] - \mu_x E[Y] - E[X]\mu_y + \mu_x \mu_y \qquad (2.3) \\
&= E[XY] - E[X]E[Y]
\end{aligned}$$

We now derive an expression for Var(X + Y) in terms of their individual variances and the covariance between them. Since

$$E[X + Y] = E[X] + E[Y] = \mu_x + \mu_y$$

we see that

$$\begin{aligned}
\text{Var}(X + Y) &= E[(X + Y - \mu_x - \mu_y)^2] \\
&= E[(X - \mu_x)^2 + (Y - \mu_y)^2 + 2(X - \mu_x)(Y - \mu_y)] \\
&= E[(X - \mu_x)^2] + E[(Y - \mu_y)^2] + 2E[(X - \mu_x)(Y - \mu_y)] \\
&= \text{Var}(X) + \text{Var}(Y) + 2 \, \text{Cov}(X, Y) \qquad (2.4)
\end{aligned}$$

We end this section by showing that the variance of the sum of independent random variables is equal to the sum of their variances.

Proposition *If X and Y are independent random variables then*

$$\text{Cov}(X, Y) = 0$$

and so, from Equation (2.4),

$$\text{Var}(X + Y) = \text{Var}(X) + \text{Var}(Y)$$

Proof From Equation (2.3) it follows that we need to show that $E[XY] = E[X]E[Y]$. Now in the discrete case,

$$E[XY] = \sum_j \sum_i x_i y_j P\{X = x_i, Y = y_j\}$$

$$= \sum_j \sum_i x_i y_j P\{X = x_i\} P\{Y = y_j\} \qquad \text{by independence}$$

$$= \sum_j y_j P\{Y = y_j\} \sum_i x_i P\{X = x_i\}$$

$$= E[Y]E[X]$$

Since a similar argument holds in the continuous case, the result is proved. ∎

2.7 Chebyshev's Inequality and the Laws of Large Numbers

We start by a result known as Markov's inequality.

Proposition: Markov's Inequality *If X takes on only nonnegative values, then for any value a > 0*

$$P\{X \geq a\} \leq \frac{E[X]}{a}$$

Proof We give a proof for the case where X is a continuous random variable having density function f.

$$E[X] = \int_0^\infty x f(x)\, dx$$

$$= \int_0^a x f(x)\, dx + \int_a^\infty x f(x)\, dx$$

$$\geq \int_a^\infty x f(x)\, dx$$

$$\geq \int_a^\infty a f(x)\, dx \qquad \text{since } x f(x) \geq a f(x) \text{ when } x \geq a$$

$$= a \int_a^\infty f(x)\, dx = a P\{X \geq a\}$$

and the result is proved. ∎

As a corollary we have the so-called Chebyshev's inequality, which states that the probability that a random variable differs from its mean by more than k of its standard deviations is bounded by $1/k^2$, where the standard deviation of a random variable is defined to be the square root of its variance.

Corollary: Chebyshev's Inequality   *If X is a random variable having mean μ and variance σ^2, then for any value $k > 0$,*

$$P\{|X - \mu| \geq k\sigma\} \leq \frac{1}{k^2}$$

Proof   Since $(X - \mu)^2/\sigma^2$ is a nonnegative random variable whose mean is

$$E\left[\frac{(X - \mu)^2}{\sigma^2}\right] = \frac{E[(X - \mu)^2]}{\sigma^2} = 1$$

we obtain from Markov's inequality that

$$P\left\{\frac{(X - \mu)^2}{\sigma^2} \geq k^2\right\} \leq \frac{1}{k^2}$$

The result now follows since the inequality $(X - \mu)^2/\sigma^2 \geq k^2$ is equivalent to the inequality $|X - \mu| \geq k\sigma$.   ∎

We now use Chebyshev's inequality to prove the weak law of large numbers, which states that the probability that the average of the first n terms of a sequence of independent and identically random variables differs from its mean by more than ϵ goes to 0 as n goes to infinity.

Theorem: The Weak Law of Large Numbers   *Let $X_1, X_2, \ldots$ be a sequence of independent and identically distributed random variables having mean μ. Then, for any $\epsilon > 0$,*

$$P\left\{\left|\frac{X_1 + \cdots + X_n}{n} - \mu\right| > \epsilon\right\} \rightarrow 0 \qquad \text{as } n \rightarrow \infty$$

Proof   We give a proof under the additional assumption that the random variables X_i have a finite variance σ^2. Now

$$E\left[\frac{X_1 + \cdots + X_n}{n}\right] = \frac{1}{n}(E[X_1] + \cdots + E[X_n]) = \mu$$

and

$$\text{Var}\left(\frac{X_1 + \cdots + X_n}{n}\right) = \frac{1}{n^2}[\text{Var}(X_1) + \cdots + \text{Var}(X_n)] = \frac{\sigma^2}{n}$$

where the above equation makes use of the fact that the variance of the sum of independent random variables is equal to the sum of their variances. Hence, from Chebyshev's inequality, it follows that for any positive k

$$P\left\{\left|\frac{X_1 + \cdots + X_n}{n} - \mu\right| \geq \frac{k\sigma}{\sqrt{n}}\right\} \leq \frac{1}{k^2}$$

Hence, for any $\epsilon > 0$, by letting k be such that $k\sigma/\sqrt{n} = \epsilon$, that is, by letting $k^2 = n\epsilon^2/\sigma^2$, we see that

$$P\left\{\left|\frac{X_1 + \cdots + X_n}{n} - \mu\right| \geq \epsilon\right\} \leq \frac{\sigma^2}{n\epsilon^2}$$

which establishes the result. ■

A generalization of the weak law is the strong law of large numbers, which states that, with probability 1,

$$\lim_{n \to \infty} \frac{X_1 + \cdots + X_n}{n} = \mu$$

That is, with certainty, the long-run average of a sequence of independent and identically distributed random variables will converge to its mean.

2.8   Some Discrete Random Variables

There are certain types of random variables that frequently appear in applications. In this section we survey some of the discrete ones.

BINOMIAL RANDOM VARIABLES

Suppose that n independent trials, each of which results in a "success" with probability p, are to be performed. If X represents the number of successes that occur in the n trials, then X is said to be a binomial random variable with parameters (n, p). Its probability mass function is given by

$$p_i \equiv P\{X = i\} = \binom{n}{i} p^i(1 - p)^{n-i}, \qquad i = 0, 1, \ldots, n \qquad (2.5)$$

where $\binom{n}{i} = n!/[(n - i)!i!]$ is the binomial coefficient, equal to the number of different subsets of i elements that can be chosen from a set of n elements.

The validity of Equation (2.5) can be seen by first noting that the probability of any particular sequence of outcomes that results in i successes and $n - i$ failures is, by the assumed independence of trials, $p^i(1 - p)^{n-i}$. Equation (2.5) then follows since there are $\binom{n}{i}$ different sequences of the n outcomes that result in i successes and $n - i$ failures—which can be seen by noting that there are $\binom{n}{i}$ different choices of the i trials that result in successes.

A binomial $(1, p)$ random variable is called a Bernoulli random variable.

Since a binomial (n, p) random variable X represents the number of successes in n independent trials, each of which results in a success with probability p, we can represent it as follows:

$$X = \sum_{i=1}^{n} X_i \tag{2.6}$$

where

$$X_i = \begin{cases} 1 & \text{if the } i\text{th trial is a success} \\ 0 & \text{otherwise} \end{cases}$$

Now

$$E[X_i] = P\{X_i = 1\} = p$$

$$\text{Var}(X_i) = E[X_i^2] - E([X_i])^2$$

$$= p - p^2 = p(1 - p)$$

where the above equation uses the fact that $X_i^2 = X_i$ (since $0^2 = 0$ and $1^2 = 1$). Hence the representation (2.6) yields that, for a binomial (n, p) random variable X,

$$E[X] = \sum_{i=1}^{n} E[X_i] = np$$

$$\text{Var}(X) = \sum_{i=1}^{n} \text{Var}(X_i) \quad \text{since the } X_i \text{ are independent}$$

$$= np(1 - p)$$

The following recursive formula expressing p_{i+1} in terms of p_i is useful when computing the binomial probabilities:

$$p_{i+1} = \frac{n!}{(n - i - 1)! \, (i + 1)!} \, p^{i+1}(1 - p)^{n-i-1}$$

$$= \frac{n!(n - i)}{(n - i)!i! \, (i + 1)} \, p^i(1 - p)^{n-i} \, \frac{p}{1 - p}$$

$$= \frac{n - i}{i + 1} \frac{p}{1 - p} p_i$$

POISSON RANDOM VARIABLES

A random variable X that takes on one of the values 0, 1, 2, . . . is said to be a Poisson random variable with parameter λ, $\lambda < 0$, if its probability mass function is given by

$$p_i = P\{X = i\} = e^{-\lambda} \frac{\lambda^i}{i!}, \qquad i = 0, 1, \ldots$$

The symbol e, defined by $e = \lim_{n \to \infty}(1 + 1/n)^n$, is a famous constant in mathematics that is roughly equal to 2.7183.

Poisson random variables have a wide range of applications. One reason for this is that such random variables may be used to approximate the distribution of the number of successes in a large number of trials (which are either independent or at most "weakly dependent") when each trial has a small probability of being a success. To see why this is so, suppose that X is a binomial random variable with parameters (n, p)—and so represents the number of successes in n independent trials when each trial is a success with probability p—and let $\lambda = np$. Then

$$P\{X = i\} = \frac{n!}{(n - i)!i!} p^i(1 - p)^{n-i}$$

$$= \frac{n!}{(n - i)!i!} \left(\frac{\lambda}{n}\right)^i \left(1 - \frac{\lambda}{n}\right)^{n-i}$$

$$= \frac{n(n - 1) \cdots (n - i + 1)}{n^i} \frac{\lambda^i}{i!} \frac{(1 - \lambda/n)^n}{(1 - \lambda/n)^i}$$

Now for n large and p small,

$$\left(1 - \frac{\lambda}{n}\right)^n \approx e^{-\lambda}, \qquad \frac{n(n - 1) \cdots (n - i + 1)}{n^i} \approx 1, \qquad \left(1 - \frac{\lambda}{n}\right)^i \approx 1$$

Hence, for n large and p small,

$$P\{X = i\} \approx e^{-\lambda} \frac{\lambda^i}{i!}$$

Since the mean and variance of a binomial random variable Y are given by

$$E[Y] = np, \qquad \text{Var}(Y) = np(1 - p) \approx np \qquad \text{for small } p$$

it is intuitive, given the relationship between binomial and Poisson random variables, that for a Poisson random variable X, having parameter λ,

$$E[X] = \text{Var}(X) = \lambda$$

An analytic proof of the above is left as an exercise.

To compute the Poisson probabilities we make use of the following recursive formula:

$$\frac{p_{i+1}}{p_i} = \frac{\dfrac{e^{-\lambda}\lambda^{i+1}}{(i+1)!}}{\dfrac{e^{-\lambda}\lambda^{i}}{i!}} = \frac{\lambda}{i+1}$$

or, equivalently,

$$p_{i+1} = \frac{\lambda}{i+1}\, p_i, \qquad i \geq 0$$

GEOMETRIC RANDOM VARIABLES

Consider independent trials, each of which is a success with probability p. If X represents the number of the first trial that is a success, then

$$P\{X = n\} = p(1 - p)^{n-1}, \qquad n \geq 1 \tag{2.7}$$

which is easily obtained by noting that in order for the first success to occur on the nth trial, the first $n - 1$ must all be failures and the nth a success. Equation (2.7) now follows since the trials are independent.

A random variable whose probability mass function is given by (2.7) is said to be a geometric random variable with parameter p. The mean of the geometric is obtained as follows:

$$E[X] = \sum_{n=1}^{\infty} np(1 - p)^{n-1} = \frac{1}{p}$$

where the above equation made use of the algebraic identity, for $0 < x < 1$,

$$\sum_{n=1}^{\infty} nx^{n-1} = \frac{d}{dx}\left(\sum_{n=0}^{\infty} x^n\right) = \frac{d}{dx}\left(\frac{1}{1-x}\right) = \frac{1}{(1-x)^2}$$

It is also not difficult to show that

$$\mathrm{Var}(X) = \frac{1 - p}{p^2}$$

THE NEGATIVE BINOMIAL RANDOM VARIABLE

If we let X denote the number of trials needed to amass a total of r successes when each trial is independently a success with probability p, then X is said to be a negative binomial, sometimes called a Pascal, random variable with parameters p and r. The probability mass function of such a random variable is given by the following:

$$P\{X = n\} = \binom{n - 1}{r - 1} p^r(1 - p)^{n-r}, \qquad n \geq r \qquad (2.8)$$

To see why Equation (2.8) is valid note that in order for it to take exactly n trials to amass r successes, the first $n - 1$ trials must result in exactly $r - 1$ successes— and the probability of this is $\binom{n-1}{r-1} p^{r-1}(1 - p)^{n-r}$—and then the nth trial must be a success—and the probability of this is p.

If we let X_i, $i = 1, \ldots, r$, denote the number of trials needed after the $(i - 1)$st success to obtain the ith success, then it is easy to see that they are independent geometric random variables with common parameter p. Since

$$X = \sum_{i=1}^{r} X_i$$

we see that

$$E[X] = \sum_{i=1}^{r} E[X_i] = \frac{r}{p}$$

$$\text{Var}(X) = \sum_{i=1}^{r} \text{Var}(X_i) = \frac{r(1 - p)}{p^2}$$

where the above made use of the corresponding result for geometric random variables.

HYPERGEOMETRIC RANDOM VARIABLES

Consider an urn containing $N + M$ balls, of which N are light colored and M are dark colored. If a sample of size n is randomly chosen [in the sense that each of the $\binom{N+M}{n}$ subsets of size n is equally likely to be chosen] then X, the number of light colored balls selected, has probability mass function

$$P\{X = i\} = \frac{\binom{N}{i}\binom{M}{n - i}}{\binom{N + M}{n}}$$

A random variable X whose probability mass function is given by the preceding equation is called a hypergeometric random variable.

Suppose that the n balls are chosen sequentially. If we let

$$X_i = \begin{cases} 1 & \text{if the } i\text{th selection is light} \\ 0 & \text{otherwise} \end{cases}$$

then

$$X = \sum_{i=1}^{n} X_i \tag{2.9}$$

and so

$$E[X] = \sum_{i=1}^{n} E[X_i] = \frac{nN}{N + M}$$

where the above equation uses the fact that, by symmetry, the ith selection is equally likely to be any of the $N + M$ balls, and so $E[X_i] = P\{X_i = 1\} = N/(N + M)$.

Since the X_i are not independent (why not?), the utilization of the representation (2.9) to compute $\text{Var}(X)$ involves covariance terms. The end product can be shown to yield the result

$$\text{Var}(X) = \frac{nNM}{(N + M)^2} \left(1 - \frac{n - 1}{N + M - 1} \right)$$

2.9   Continuous Random Variables

In this section we consider certain types of continuous random variables.

UNIFORMLY DISTRIBUTED RANDOM VARIABLES

A random variable X is said to be uniformly distributed over the interval (a, b), $a < b$, if its probability density function is given by

$$f(x) = \begin{cases} \dfrac{1}{b - a} & \text{if } a < x < b \\ 0 & \text{otherwise} \end{cases}$$

In other words, X is uniformly distributed over (a, b) if it puts all its mass on that interval and it is equally likely to be "near" any point on that interval.

The mean and variance of a uniform (a, b) random variable are obtained as follows:

$$E[X] = \frac{1}{b-a} \int_a^b x \, dx = \frac{b^2 - a^2}{2(b-a)} = \frac{b+a}{2}$$

$$E[X^2] = \frac{1}{b-a} \int_a^b x^2 \, dx = \frac{b^3 - a^3}{3(b-a)} = \frac{a^2 + b^2 + ab}{3}$$

and so

$$\mathrm{Var}(X) = \frac{1}{3}(a^2 + b^2 + ab) - \frac{1}{4}(a^2 + b^2 + 2ab) = \frac{1}{12}(b-a)^2$$

Thus, for instance, the expected value is, as one might have expected, the midpoint of the interval (a, b).

The distribution function of X is given, for $a < x < b$, by

$$F(x) = P\{X \leq x\} = \int_a^x (b-a)^{-1} \, dx = \frac{x-a}{b-a}$$

NORMAL RANDOM VARIABLES

A random variable X is said to be normally distributed with mean μ and variance σ^2 if its probability density function is given by

$$f(x) = \frac{1}{\sqrt{2\pi}\,\sigma} e^{-(x-\mu)^2/2\sigma^2}, \qquad -\infty < x < \infty$$

The normal density is a bell-shaped curve that is symmetric about μ (see Figure 2.1).

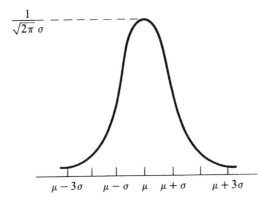

Figure 2.1 The normal density function

It is not difficult to show that the parameters μ and σ^2 do indeed equal the expectation and variance of the normal. That is,

$$E[X] = \mu \quad \text{and} \quad \text{Var}(X) = \sigma^2$$

An important fact about normal random variables is that if X is normal with mean μ and variance σ^2, then for any constants a and b, $aX + b$ is normally distributed with mean $a\mu + b$ and variance $a^2\sigma^2$. It follows from this that if X is normal with mean μ and variance σ^2, then

$$Z = \frac{X - \mu}{\sigma}$$

is normal with mean 0 and variance 1. Such a random variable Z is said to have a standard (or unit) normal distribution. Let ϕ denote the distribution function of a standard normal random variable; that is,

$$\phi(x) = \frac{1}{\sqrt{2\pi}} \int_{-\infty}^{x} e^{-x^2/2} \, dx, \quad -\infty < x < \infty$$

The result that $Z = (X - \mu)/\sigma$ has a standard normal distribution when X is normal with mean μ and variance σ^2 is quite useful because it allows us to evaluate all probabilities concerning X in terms of ϕ. For example, the distribution function of X can be expressed as

$$F(x) = P\{X \le x\}$$
$$= P\left\{ \frac{X - \mu}{\sigma} \le \frac{x - \mu}{\sigma} \right\}$$
$$= P\left\{ Z \le \frac{x - \mu}{\sigma} \right\}$$
$$= \phi\left(\frac{x - \mu}{\sigma} \right)$$

The value of $\phi(x)$ can be determined either by looking it up in a table or by writing a computer program to approximate it.

For a in the interval $(0, 1)$, let z_a be such that

$$P\{Z > z_a\} = 1 - \phi(z_a) = a$$

That is, a standard normal will exceed z_a with probability a (see Figure 2.2). The values of z_a can be obtained from a table of the values of ϕ. For example, since

$$\phi(1.64) = 0.95, \qquad \phi(1.96) = 0.975, \qquad \phi(2.33) = 0.99$$

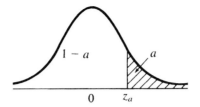

Figure 2.2 $P\{Z > z_a\} = a$

we see that

$$z_{.05} = 1.64, \qquad z_{.025} = 1.96, \qquad z_{.01} = 2.33$$

The wide applicability of normal random variables results from one of the most important theorems of probability theory—the central limit theorem, which asserts that the sum of a large number of independent random variables has approximately a normal distribution. The simplest form of this remarkable theorem is as follows.

The Central Limit Theorem *Let* $X_1, X_2, \ldots$ *be a sequence of independent and identically distributed random variables having finite mean* μ *and finite variance* σ^2. *Then*

$$\lim_{n \to \infty} P\left\{ \frac{X_1 + \cdots + X_n - n\mu}{\sigma \sqrt{n}} < x \right\} = \phi(x)$$

EXPONENTIAL RANDOM VARIABLES

A continuous random variable having probability density function

$$f(x) = \lambda e^{-\lambda x}, \qquad 0 < x < \infty$$

for some $\lambda > 0$ is said to be an exponential random variable with parameter λ. Its cumulative distribution is given by

$$F(x) = \int_0^x \lambda e^{-\lambda x} \, dx = 1 - e^{-\lambda x}, \qquad 0 < x < \infty$$

It is easy to verify that the expected value and variance of such a random variable are as follows:

$$E[X] = \frac{1}{\lambda} \qquad \text{and} \qquad \text{Var}(X) = \frac{1}{\lambda^2}$$

The key property of exponential random variables is that they possess the "memoryless property," where we say that the nonnegative random variable X is memoryless if

$$P\{X > s + t | X > s\} = P\{X > t\} \qquad \text{for all } s, t \geq 0 \qquad (2.10)$$

To understand why the above is called the memoryless property, imagine that X represents the lifetime of some unit, and consider the probability that a unit of age s will survive an additional time t. Since this will occur if the lifetime of the unit exceeds $t + s$ given that it is still alive at time s, we see that

$$P\{\text{additional life of an item of age } s \text{ exceeds } t\} = P\{X > s + t | X > s\}$$

Thus, Equation (2.10) is a statement of fact that the distribution of the remaining life of an item of age s does not depend on s. That is, it is not necessary to remember the age of the unit to know its distribution of remaining life.

Equation (2.10) is equivalent to

$$P\{X > s + t\} = P\{X > s\} P\{X > t\}$$

As the above equation is satisfied whenever X is an exponential random variable—since, in this case, $P\{X > x\} = e^{-\lambda x}$—we see that exponential random variables are memoryless (and indeed it is not difficult to show that they are the only memoryless random variables).

Another useful property of exponential random variables is that they remain exponential when multiplied by a positive constant. To see this suppose that X is exponential with parameter λ, and let c be a positive number. Then

$$P\{cX \leq x\} = P\left\{X \leq \frac{x}{c}\right\} = 1 - e^{-\lambda x/c}$$

which shows that cX is exponential with parameter λ/c.

THE POISSON PROCESS AND GAMMA RANDOM VARIABLES

Suppose that "events" are occurring at random time points and let $N(t)$ denote the number of events that occur in the time interval $[0, t]$. These events are said to constitute a *Poisson process having rate* λ, $\lambda > 0$, if

(a) $N(0) = 0$.

(b) The numbers of events occurring in disjoint time intervals are independent.

(c) The distribution of the number of events that occur in a given interval depends only on the length of the interval and not on its location.

(d) $\lim_{h \to 0} \dfrac{P\{N(h) = 1\}}{h} = \lambda.$

(e) $\lim_{h \to 0} \dfrac{P\{N(h) \geq 2\}}{h} = 0.$

Thus Condition (a) states that the process begins at time 0. Condition (b), the *independent increment* assumption, states that the number of events by time t [i.e., $N(t)$] is independent of the number of events that occur between t and $t + s$ [i.e., $N(t + s) - N(t)$]. Condition (c), the *stationary increment* assumption, states that the probability distribution of $N(t + s) - N(t)$ is the same for all values of t. Conditions (d) and (e) state that in a small interval of length h, the probability of one event occurring is approximately λh, whereas the probability of two or more is approximately 0.

We now argue that these assumptions imply that the number of events occurring in an interval of length t is a Poisson random variable with mean λt. To do so, consider the interval $[0, t]$, and break it up into n nonoverlapping subintervals of length t/n (Figure 2.3). Consider first the number of these subintervals that contain an event. As each subinterval independently [by Condition (b)] contains an event with the same probability [by Condition (c)], which is approximately equal to $\lambda t/n$, it follows that the number of such intervals is a binomial random variable with parameters n and $p \approx \lambda t/n$. Hence, by the argument yielding the convergence of the binomial to the Poisson, we see by letting $n \to \infty$ that the number of such subintervals converges to a Poisson random variable with mean λt. As it can be shown that Condition (e) implies that the probability that any of these subintervals contains two or more events goes to 0 as $n \to \infty$, it follows that $N(t)$, the number of events that occur in $[0, t]$, is a Poisson random variable with mean λt.

For a Poisson process let us denote by X_1 the time of the first event. Furthermore, for $n > 1$, let X_n denote the elapsed time between the $(n - 1)$st and the nth event. The sequence $\{X_n, n = 1, 2, \ldots\}$ is called the *sequence of interarrival times*. For instance, if $X_1 = 5$ and $X_2 = 10$, then the first event of the Poisson process will occur at time 5 and the second at time 15.

Figure 2.3

We now determine the distribution of the X_n. To do so, we first note that the event $\{X_1 > t\}$ takes place if and only if no events of the Poisson process occur in the interval $[0, t]$, and thus

$$P\{X_1 > t\} = P\{N(t) = 0\} = e^{-\lambda t}$$

Hence, X_1 has an exponential distribution with mean $1/\lambda$. To obtain the distribution of X_2, note that

$$\begin{aligned}
P\{X_2 > t | X_1 = s\} &= P\{0 \text{ events in } (s, s+t] | X_1 = s\} \\
&= P\{0 \text{ events in } (s, s+t]\} \\
&= e^{-\lambda t}
\end{aligned}$$

where the last two equations followed from independent and stationary increments. Therefore, from the foregoing, we conclude that X_2 is also an exponential random variable with mean $1/\lambda$ and, furthermore, that X_2 is independent of X_1. Repeating the same argument yields:

Proposition   *The interarrival times $X_1, X_2, \ldots$ are independent and identically distributed exponential random variables with parameter λ.*

Let $S_n = \Sigma_{i=1}^n X_i$ denote the time of the nth event. Since S_n will be less than or equal to t if and only if there have been at least n events by time t, we see that

$$P\{S_n \leq t\} = P\{N(t) \geq n\}$$
$$= \sum_{j=n}^{\infty} e^{-\lambda t} \frac{(\lambda t)^j}{j!}$$

Since the left-hand side is the cumulative distribution function of S_n, we obtain, upon differentiation, that the density function of S_n—call it $f_n(t)$—is given by

$$\begin{aligned}
f_n(t) &= \sum_{j=n}^{\infty} \lambda e^{-\lambda t} \frac{j(\lambda t)^{j-1}}{j!} - \sum_{j=n}^{\infty} \lambda e^{-\lambda t} \frac{(\lambda t)^j}{j!} \\
&= \sum_{j=n}^{\infty} \lambda e^{-\lambda t} \frac{(\lambda t)^{j-1}}{(j-1)!} - \sum_{j=n}^{\infty} \lambda e^{-\lambda t} \frac{(\lambda t)^j}{j!} \\
&= \lambda e^{-\lambda t} \frac{(\lambda t)^{n-1}}{(n-1)!}
\end{aligned}$$

Definition   *A random variable having probability density function*

$$f(t) = \lambda e^{-\lambda t} \frac{(\lambda t)^{n-1}}{(n-1)!}, \qquad t > 0$$

is said to be a gamma random variable with parameters (n, λ).

Thus we see that S_n, the time of the nth event of a Poisson process having rate λ, is a gamma random variable with parameters (n, λ). In addition, we obtain from the representation $S_n = \sum_{i=1}^{n} X_i$ and the previous proposition, which stated that these X_i are independent exponentials with rate λ, the following corollary.

Corollary *The sum of n independent exponential random variables, each having parameter λ, is a gamma random variable with parameters (n, λ).*

THE NONHOMOGENEOUS POISSON PROCESS

From a modeling point of view the major weakness of the Poisson process is its assumption that events are just as likely to occur in all intervals of equal size. A generalization, which relaxes this assumption, leads to the so-called nonhomogeneous or nonstationary process.

If "events" are occurring randomly in time, and $N(t)$ denotes the number of events that occur by time t, then we say that $\{N(t), t \geq 0\}$ constitutes a nonhomogeneous Poisson process with intensity function $\lambda(t), t \geq 0$, if

   (a) $N(0) = 0$.
   (b) The numbers of events that occur in disjoint time intervals are independent.
   (c) $\lim_{h \to 0} P\{\text{exactly 1 event between } t \text{ and } t + h\}/h = \lambda(t)$.
   (d) $\lim_{h \to 0} P\{2 \text{ or more events between } t \text{ and } t + h\}/h = 0$.

The function $m(t)$, defined by

$$m(t) = \int_0^t \lambda(s) \, ds, \qquad t \geq 0$$

is called the mean-value function. The following result can be established.

Proposition $N(t + s) - N(t)$ *is a Poisson random variable with mean* $m(t + s) - m(t)$.

The quantity $\lambda(t)$, called the intensity at time t, indicates how likely it is that an event will occur around the time t. [Note that when $\lambda(t) \equiv \lambda$ the nonhomogeneous reverts to the usual Poisson process.] The following proposition gives a useful way of interpreting a nonhomogeneous Poisson process.

Proposition *Suppose that events are occurring according to a Poisson process having rate λ, and suppose that, independently of anything that came before, an event that occurs at time t is counted with probability $p(t)$. Then the process of counted events constitutes a nonhomogeneous Poisson process with intensity function $\lambda(t) = \lambda p(t)$.*

Proof   This proposition is proved by noting that the previously given conditions are all satisfied. Conditions (a), (b), and (d) follow since the corresponding result is true for all (not just the counted) events. Conditions (c) follows since

$$P\{1 \text{ counted event between } t \text{ and } t + h\}$$
$$= P\{1 \text{ event and it is counted}\}$$
$$+ P\{2 \text{ or more events and exactly 1 is counted}\}$$
$$\approx \lambda h p(t) \qquad \blacksquare$$

2.10   Conditional Expectation and Conditional Variance

If X and Y are jointly discrete random variables, we define $E[X|Y = y]$, the conditional expectation of X given that $Y = y$, by

$$E[X|Y = y] = \sum_x xP\{X = x|Y = y\}$$

$$= \frac{\sum_x xP\{X = x, Y = y\}}{P\{Y = y\}}$$

In other words, the conditional expectation of X, given that $Y = y$, is defined as before as a weighted average of all the possible values of X but now with the weight given to the value x being equal to the conditional probability that X equals x given that Y equals y.

Similarly, if X and Y are jointly continuous with joint density function $f(x, y)$, we define the conditional expectation of X, given that $Y = y$, by

$$E[X|Y = y] = \frac{\int xf(x, y) \, dx}{\int f(x, y) \, dx}$$

Let $E[X|Y]$ denote that function of the random variable Y whose value at $Y = y$ is $E[X|Y = y]$; and note that $E[X|Y]$ is itself a random variable. The following proposition is quite useful.

Proposition

$$E[E[X|Y]] = E[X] \qquad (2.11)$$

If Y is a discrete random variable, then Equation (2.11) states that

$$E[X] = \sum_y E[X|Y = y]P\{Y = y\}$$

whereas if Y is continuous with density g, then (2.11) states

$$E[X] = \int E[X|Y = y]g(y) \, dy$$

We now give a proof of the preceding proposition when X and Y are discrete:

$$\sum_y E[X|Y = y]P\{Y = y\} = \sum_y \sum_x xP\{X = x|Y = y\}P\{Y = y\}$$

$$= \sum_y \sum_x xP\{X = x, Y = y\}$$

$$= \sum_x x \sum_y P\{X = x, Y = y\}$$

$$= \sum_x xP\{X = x\}$$

$$= E[X]$$

We can also define the conditional variance of X, given the value of Y, as follows:

$$\text{Var}(X|Y) = E[(X - E[X|Y])^2|Y]$$

That is, $\text{Var}(X|Y)$ is a function of Y, which at $Y = y$ is equal to the variance of X given that $Y = y$. By the same reasoning that yields the identity $\text{Var}(X) = E[X^2] - (E[X])^2$ we have that

$$\text{Var}(X|Y) = E[X^2|Y] - (E[X|Y])^2$$

Taking expectations of both sides of the above equation gives

$$E[\text{Var}(X|Y)] = E[E[X^2|Y]] - E[(E[X|Y])^2]$$

$$= E[X^2] - E[(E[X|Y])^2] \tag{2.12}$$

Also, because $E[E[X|Y]] = E[X]$, we have that

$$\text{Var}(E[X|Y]) = E[(E[X|Y])^2] - (E[X])^2 \tag{2.13}$$

Upon adding Equations (2.12) and (2.13) we obtain the following identity, known as the conditional variance formula.

The Conditional Variance Formula

$$\text{Var}(X) = E[\text{Var}(X|Y)] + \text{Var}(E[X|Y])$$

Exercises

1. (a) For any events A and B show that

$$A \cup B = A \cup A^c B$$

$$B = AB \cup A^c B$$

(b) Show that

$$P(A \cup B) = P(A) + P(B) - P(AB)$$

2. Consider an experiment that consists of six horses, numbered 1 through 6, running a race, and suppose that the sample space is given by

$$S = \{\text{all orderings of } (1, 2, 3, 4, 5, 6)\}$$

Let A denote the event that the number 1 horse is among the top three finishers, let B denote the event that the number 2 horse comes in second, and let C denote the event that the number 3 horse comes in third.

(a) Describe the event $A \cup B$. How many outcomes are contained in this event?

(b) How many outcomes are contained in the event AB?

(c) How many outcomes are contained in the event ABC?

(d) How many outcomes are contained in the event $A \cup BC$?

3. A couple has two children. What is the probability that both are girls given that the eldest is a girl? Assume that all four possibilities are equally likely.

4. The king comes from a family of two children. What is the probability that the other child is his brother?

5. The random variable X takes on one of the values 1, 2, 3, 4 with probabilities

$$P\{X = i\} = ic, \qquad i = 1, 2, 3, 4$$

for some value c. Find $P\{2 \le X \le 3\}$.

6. The continuous random variable X has a probability density function given by

$$f(x) = cx, \qquad 0 < x < 1$$

Find $P\{X > \frac{1}{2}\}$.

7. If X and Y have a joint probability density function specified by

$$f(x, y) = 2e^{-(x+2y)}, \qquad 0 < x < \infty, 0 < y < \infty$$

find $P\{X < Y\}$.

8. Find the expected value of the random variable specified in Exercise 5.

9. Find $E[X]$ for the random variable of Exercise 6.

10. There are 10 different types of coupon and each time one obtains a coupon it is equally likely to be any of the 10 types. Let X denote the number of

distinct types contained in a collection of N coupons, and find $E[X]$. [Hint: For $i = 1, \ldots, 10$ let

$$X_t = \begin{cases} 1 & \text{if a type } i \text{ coupon is among the } N \\ 0 & \text{otherwise} \end{cases}$$

and make use of the representation $X = \Sigma_{i=1}^{10} X_i$.

11. A die having six sides is rolled. If each of the six possible outcomes is equally likely, determine the variance of the number that appears.

12. Suppose that X has probability density function

$$f(x) = ce^x, \qquad 0 < x < 1$$

Determine Var(X).

13. Show that Var$(aX + b) = a^2$Var(X).

14. Suppose that X, the amount of liquid apple contained in a container of commercial apple juice, is a random variable having mean 4 grams.

(a) What can be said about the probability that a given container contains more than 6 grams of liquid apple?

(b) If Var$(X) = 4$(grams)^2, what can be said about the probability that a given container will contain between 3 and 5 grams of liquid apple?

15. An airplane needs at least half of its engines to safely complete its mission. If each engine independently functions with probability p, for what values of p is a three-engine plane safer than a five-engine plane?

16. For a binomial random variable X with parameters (n, p), show that $P\{X = i\}$ first increases and then decreases, reaching its maximum value when i is the largest integer less than or equal to $(n + 1)p$.

17. If X and Y are independent binomial random variables with respective parameters (n, p) and (m, p), argue, without any calculations, that $X + Y$ is binomial with parameters $(n + m, p)$.

18. Explain why the following random variables all have approximately a Poisson distribution:

(a) The number of misprints in a given chapter of this book.

(b) The number of wrong telephone numbers dialed daily.

(c) The number of customers that enter a given post office on a given day.

19. If X is a Poisson random variable with parameter λ, show that

(a) $E[X] = \lambda$.

(b) Var$(X) = \lambda$.

20. Let X and Y be independent Poisson random variables with respective parameters λ_1 and λ_2. Use the result of Exercise 17 to heuristically argue that $X + Y$ is Poisson with parameter $\lambda_1 + \lambda_2$. Then give an analytic proof of this. [Hint:

$$P\{X + Y = k\} = \sum_{i=0}^{k} P\{X = i, Y = k - i\} = \sum_{i=0}^{k} P\{X = i\}P\{Y = k - i\}]$$

21. Explain how to make use of the relationship

$$p_{i+1} = \frac{\lambda}{i + 1} p_i$$

to compute efficiently the Poisson probabilities.

22. Find $P\{X > n\}$ when X is a geometric random variable with parameter p.

23. Two players play a certain game until one has won a total of five games. If player A wins each individual game with probability 0.6, what is the probability she will win the match?

24. Consider the hypergeometric model of Section 2.8, and suppose that the white balls are all numbered. For $i = 1, \ldots, N$ let

$$Y_i = \begin{cases} 1 & \text{if white ball numbered } i \text{ is selected} \\ 0 & \text{otherwise} \end{cases}$$

Argue that $X = \sum_{i=1}^{N} Y_i$, and then use this representation to determine $E[X]$. Verify that it checks with the result given in Section 2.8.

25. The bus will arrive at a time that is uniformly distributed between 8 and 8:30 A.M. If we arrive at 8 A.M., what is the probability that we will wait between 5 and 15 minutes?

26. For a normal random variable with parameters μ and σ^2 show that

(a) $E[X] = \mu$.
(b) $\text{Var}(X) = \sigma^2$.

27. Let X be a binomial random variable with parameters (n, p). Explain why

$$P\left\{\frac{X - np}{\sqrt{np(1 - p)}} \leq x\right\} \approx \frac{1}{\sqrt{2\pi}} \int_{-\infty}^{x} e^{-x^2/2} \, dx$$

when n is large.

28. If X is an exponential random variable with parameter λ, show that

(a) $E[X] = 1/\lambda$.
(b) $\text{Var}(X) = 1/\lambda^2$.

29. Persons A, B, and C are waiting at a bank having two tellers when it opens in the morning. Persons A and B each go to a teller and C waits on line. If the time it takes to serve a customer is an exponential random variable with parameter λ, what is the probability that C is the last to leave the bank? [Hint: No computations are necessary.]

30. Let X and Y be independent exponential random variables with respective rates λ and μ. Show that

$$P\{X < Y\} = \frac{\lambda}{\lambda + \mu}$$

31. Consider a Poisson process in which events occur at a rate 0.3 per hour. What is the probability that no events occur between 10 A.M. and 2 P.M.?

32. For a Poisson process with rate λ, find $P\{N(s) = k|N(t) = n\}$ when $s < t$.

33. Repeat Exercise 32 for $s > t$.

34. If X is a gamma random variable with parameters (n, λ), find
    (a) $E[X]$.
    (b) $\text{Var}(X)$.

35. An urn contains four white and six black balls. A random sample of size 4 is chosen. Let X denote the number of white balls in the sample. An additional ball is now selected from the remaining six balls in the urn. Let Y equal 1 if this ball is white and 0 if it is black. Find
    (a) $E[Y|X = 2]$.
    (b) $E[X|Y = 1]$.
    (c) $\text{Var}(Y|X = 0)$.
    (d) $\text{Var}(X|Y = 1)$.

36. If X and Y are independent and identically distributed exponential random variables, show that the conditional distribution of X, given that $X + Y = t$, is the uniform distribution on $(0, t)$.

References

Feller, W., *An Introduction to Probability Theory and Its Applications,* Third Ed., Wiley, New York, 1968.

Ross, S. M., *A First Course in Probability,* Fourth Ed., Macmillan, New York, 1993.

Ross, S. M., *Introduction to Probability Models,* Fifth Ed., Academic Press, New York, 1993.

Chapter 3 | Random Numbers

Introduction

The building block of a simulation study is the ability to generate random numbers, where a random number represents the value of a random variable uniformly distributed on (0, 1). In this chapter we explain how such numbers are computer generated and also begin to illustrate their uses.

3.1 Pseudorandom Number Generation

Whereas random numbers were originally either manually or mechanically generated, by using such techniques as spinning wheels, or dice rolling, or card shuffling, the modern approach is to use a computer to successively generate pseudorandom numbers. These pseudorandom numbers constitute a sequence of values, which, although they are deterministically generated, have all the appearances of being independent uniform (0, 1) random variables.

One of the most common approaches to generating pseudorandom numbers starts with an initial value x_0, called the seed, and then recursively computes successive values x_n, $n \geq 1$, by letting

$$x_n = ax_{n-1} \quad \text{modulo } m \tag{3.1}$$

where a and m are given positive integers, and where the above means that ax_{n-1} is divided by m and the remainder is taken as the value of x_n. Thus, each x_n is either 0, 1, . . . , $m - 1$ and the quantity x_n/m—called a pseudorandom number—is taken as an approximation to the value of a uniform $(0, 1)$ random variable.

The approach specified by Equation (3.1) to generate random numbers is called the multiplicative congruential method. Since each of the numbers x_n assumes one of the values $0, 1, \ldots, m - 1$, it follows that after some finite number (of at most m) of generated values a value must repeat itself; and once this happens the whole sequence will begin to repeat. Thus, we want to choose the constants a and m so that, for any initial seed x_0, the number of variables that can be generated before this repetition occurs is large.

In general the constants a and m should be chosen to satisfy three criteria:

1. For any initial seed, the resultant sequence has the "appearance" of being a sequence of independent uniform $(0, 1)$ random variables.

2. For any initial seed, the number of variables that can be generated before repetition begins is large.

3. The values can be computed efficiently on a digital computer.

A guideline that appears to be of help in satisfying the above three conditions is that m should be chosen to be a large prime number that can be fitted to the computer word size. For a 32-bit word machine (where the first bit is a sign bit) it has been shown that the choices of $m = 2^{31} - 1$ and $a = 7^5 = 16,807$ result in desirable properties. (For a 36-bit word machine the choices of $m = 2^{35} - 31$ and $a = 5^5$ appear to work well.)

Another generator of pseudorandom numbers uses recursions of the type

$$x_n = (ax_{n-1} + c) \text{ modulo } m$$

Such generators are called mixed congruential generators (as they involve both an additive and a multiplicative term). When using generators of this type, one often chooses m to equal the computer's word length, since this makes the computation of $(ax_{n-1} + c)$ modulo m—that is, the division of $ax_{n-1} + c$ by m—quite efficient.

Most computer languages already have a built-in random number generator which can be called to generate random numbers. For instance, BASIC utilizes two commands:

```
1  RANDOMIZE
2  U = RND
```

The result of the RANDOMIZE instruction is the request for the user to input the seed x_0. Once this is done, the quantity RND will represent the next pseudorandom number. For instance, the following program prints out the values of 10 pseudorandom numbers.

```
10  RANDOMIZE
20  FOR I = 1 TO 10
30  U = RND
40  PRINT U
50  NEXT
```

As our starting point in the computer simulation of systems we suppose that we can generate a sequence of pseudorandom numbers which can be taken as an approximation to the values of a sequence of independent uniform (0, 1) random variables. That is, we do not explore the interesting theoretical questions, which involve material outside the scope of this text, relating to the construction of "good" pseudorandom number generators. Rather, we assume that we have a "black box" that gives a random number on request.

3.2   Using Random Numbers to Evaluate Integrals

One of the earliest applications of random numbers was in the computation of integrals. Let $g(x)$ be a function and suppose we wanted to compute θ where

$$\theta = \int_0^1 g(x)\, dx$$

To compute the value of θ, note that if U is uniformly distributed over (0, 1), then we can express θ as

$$\theta = E[g(U)]$$

If $U_1, \ldots, U_k$ are independent uniform (0, 1) random variables, it thus follows that the random variables $g(U_1), \ldots, g(U_k)$ are independent and identically distributed random variables having mean θ. Therefore, by the strong law of large numbers, it follows that, with probability 1,

$$\sum_{i=1}^{k} \frac{g(U_i)}{k} \rightarrow E[g(U)] = \theta \qquad \text{as } k \rightarrow \infty$$

Hence we can approximate θ by generating a large number of random numbers u_i and taking as our approximation the average value of $g(u_i)$. This approach to approximating integrals is called the *Monte Carlo* approach.

The following BASIC algorithm can be used to approximate θ.

```
10  RANDOMIZE
20  INPUT K
30  S = 0
40  FOR I = 1 TO K
50  U = RND
60  S = S + g(U)
70  NEXT
80  PRINT S/K
```

The value printed is the approximation to $\theta = \int_0^1 g(x)\,dx$.

If we wanted to compute

$$\theta = \int_a^b g(x)\,dx$$

then, by making the substitution $y = (x - a)/(b - a)$, $dy = dx/(b - a)$, we see that

$$\theta = \int_0^1 g(a + [b - a]y)\,(b - a)\,dy$$

$$= \int_0^1 h(y)\,dy$$

where $h(y) = (b - a)g(a + [b - a]y)$. Thus, we can approximate θ by continually generating random numbers and then taking the average value of h evaluated at these random numbers.

Similarly, if we wanted

$$\theta = \int_0^\infty g(x)\,dx$$

we could apply the substitution $y = 1/(x + 1)$, $dy = -dx/(x + 1)^2 = -y^2\,dx$, to obtain the identity

$$\theta = \int_0^1 h(y)\,dy$$

where

$$h(y) = \frac{g\left(\dfrac{1}{y} - 1\right)}{y^2}$$

The utility of using random numbers to approximate integrals becomes more apparent in the case of multidimensional integrals. Suppose that g is a function with an n-dimensional argument and that we are interested in computing

$$\theta = \int_0^1 \int_0^1 \cdots \int_0^1 g(x_1, \ldots, x_n) \, dx_1 \, dx_2 \cdots dx_n$$

The key to the Monte Carlo approach to estimate θ lies in the fact that θ can be expressed as the following expectation:

$$\theta = E[g(U_1, \ldots, U_n)]$$

where $U_1, \ldots, U_n$ are independent uniform $(0, 1)$ random variables. Hence, if we generate k independent sets, each consisting of n independent uniform $(0, 1)$ random variables

$$U_1^1, \ldots, U_n^1$$
$$U_1^2, \ldots, U_n^2$$
$$\vdots$$
$$U_1^k, \ldots, U_n^k$$

then, since the random variables $g(U_1^i, \ldots, U_n^i), i = 1, \ldots, k$, are all independent and identically distributed random variables with mean θ, we can estimate θ by $\sum_{i=1}^k g(U_1^i, \ldots, U_n^i)/k$.

For an application of the above, consider the following approach to estimating π.

Example 3a   The Estimation of π. Suppose that the random vector (X, Y) is uniformly distributed in the square of area 4 centered at the origin. That is, it is a random point in the following region specified in Figure 3.1. Let us consider now the probability that this random point in the square is contained within the inscribed circle of radius 1 (see Figure 3.2). Note that since (X, Y) is uniformly distributed in the square it follows that

$$P\{(X, Y) \text{ is in the circle}\} = P\{X^2 + Y^2 \le 1\}$$
$$= \frac{\text{Area of the circle}}{\text{Area of the square}} = \frac{\pi}{4}$$

Hence, if we generate a large number of random points in the square, the proportion of points that fall within the circle will be approximately $\pi/4$. Now if X and

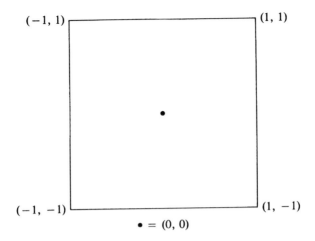

Figure 3.1

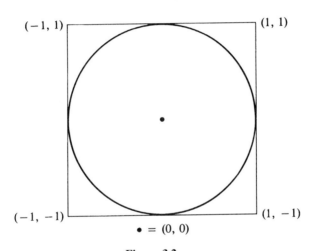

Figure 3.2

Y were independent and both were uniformly distributed over $(-1, 1)$, their joint density would be

$$f(x, y) = f(x)f(y)$$
$$= \frac{1}{2} \cdot \frac{1}{2}$$
$$= \frac{1}{4}, \qquad -1 \leq x \leq 1, \quad -1 \leq y \leq 1$$

Since the density function of (X, Y) is constant in the square, it thus follows (by definition) that (X, Y) is uniformly distributed in the square. Now if U is uniform on $(0, 1)$ then $2U$ is uniform on $(0, 2)$, and so $2U - 1$ is uniform on $(-1, 1)$. Therefore, if we generate random numbers U_1 and U_2, set $X = 2U_1 - 1$ and $Y = 2U_2 - 1$, and define

$$I = \begin{cases} 1 & \text{if } X^2 + Y^2 \le 1 \\ 0 & \text{otherwise} \end{cases}$$

then

$$E[I] = P\{X^2 + Y^2 \le 1\} = \frac{\pi}{4}$$

Hence we can estimate $\pi/4$ by generating a large number of pairs of random numbers u_1, u_2 and estimating $\pi/4$ by the fraction of pairs for which $(2u_1 - 1)^2 + (2u_2 - 1)^2 \le 1$. ■

Thus, random number generators can be used to generate the values of uniform $(0, 1)$ random variables. Starting with these random numbers we show in Chapters 4 and 5 how we can generate the values of random variables from arbitrary distributions. With this ability to generate arbitrary random variables we will be able to simulate a probability system—that is, we will be able to generate, according to the specified probability laws of the system, all the random quantities of this system as it evolves over time.

Exercises

1. If $x_0 = 5$ and

$$x_n = 3x_{n-1} \bmod 150$$

find $x_1, \ldots, x_{10}$.

2. If $x_0 = 3$ and

$$x_n = 5x_{n-1} + 7 \bmod 200$$

find $x_1, \ldots, x_{10}$.

In Exercises 3–9 use simulation to approximate the following integrals. Compare your estimate with the exact answer if known.

3. $\int_0^1 \exp\{e^x\}dx$

4. $\int_0^1 (1 - x^2)^{3/2} \, dx$

5. $\int_{-2}^2 e^{x+x^2} \, dx$

6. $\int_0^\infty x(1 + x^2)^{-2} \, dx$

7. $\int_{-\infty}^\infty e^{-x^2} \, dx$

8. $\int_0^1 \int_0^1 e^{(x+y)^2} \, dy \, dx$

9. $\int_0^\infty \int_0^x e^{-(x+y)} \, dy \, dx$

[*Hint:* Let $I_y(x) = \begin{cases} 1 & \text{if } y < x \\ 0 & \text{if } y \geq x \end{cases}$ and use this function

to equate the integral to one in which both terms go from 0 to ∞.]

10. Use simulation to approximate $\text{Cov}(U, e^U)$, where U is uniform on $(0, 1)$. Compare your approximation with the exact answer.

11. Let U be uniform on $(0, 1)$. Use simulation to approximate the following:

    (a) $\text{Cov}(U, \sqrt{1 - U^2})$.
    (b) $\text{Cov}(U^2, \sqrt{1 - U^2})$.

12. For uniform $(0, 1)$ random variables $U_1, U_2, \ldots$ define

$$N = \text{Minimum} \left\{ n: \sum_{i=1}^n U_i > 1 \right\}$$

That is, N is equal to the number of random numbers that must be summed to exceed 1.

    (a) Estimate $E[N]$ by generating 100 values of N.
    (b) Estimate $E[N]$ by generating 1000 values of N.
    (c) Estimate $E[N]$ by generating 10,000 values of N.
    (d) What do you think is the value of $E[N]$?

13. Let U_i, $i \geq 1$, be random numbers. Define N by

$$N = \text{Maximum} \left\{ n: \prod_{i=1}^{n} U_i \geq e^{-3} \right\}$$

where $\prod_{i=1}^{0} U_i \equiv 1$.

(a) Find $E[N]$ by simulation.

(b) Find $P\{N = i\}$, for $i = 0, 1, 2, 3, 4, 5, 6$, by simulation.

References

Knuth, D., *The Art of Computer Programming,* Vol. 2, *Seminumerical Algorithms,* Addison-Wesley, Reading, MA, 1981.

L'Ecuyer, P., "Random Numbers for Simulation," *Commun. Assoc. Comput. Mach.,* **33,** 1990.

Marsaglia, G., "Random Numbers Fall Mainly in the Planes," *Proc. Natl. Acad. Sci.,* **61,** 25–28, 1962.

Marsaglia, G., "The Structure of Linear Congruential Sequences," *Applications of Number Theory to Numerical Analysis,* S. K. Zaremba, ed., Academic Press, London, pp. 249–255, 1972.

Naylor, T., *Computer Simulation Techniques,* Wiley, New York, 1966.

Ripley, B., *Stochastic Simulation,* Wiley, New York, 1986.

von Neumann, J., "Various Techniques Used in Connection with Random Digits, 'Monte Carlo Method,' " *U.S. National Bureau of Standards Applied Mathematics Series,* No. 12, 36–38, 1951.

Chapter 4 | Generating Discrete Random Variables

4.1 The Inverse Transform Method

Suppose we want to generate the value of a discrete random variable X having probability mass function

$$P\{X = x_j\} = p_j, \qquad j = 0, 1, \ldots, \sum_j p_j = 1$$

To accomplish this, we generate a random number U—that is, U is uniformly distributed over $(0, 1)$—and set

$$X = \begin{cases} x_0 & \text{if} & U < p_0 \\ x_1 & \text{if} & p_0 \le U < p_0 + p_1 \\ \vdots & \\ x_j & \text{if} & \sum_{i=1}^{j-1} p_i \le U < \sum_{i=1}^{j} p_i \\ \vdots & \end{cases}$$

Since, for $0 < a < b < 1$, $P\{a \le U < b\} = b - a$, we have that

$$P\{X = x_j\} = P\left\{ \sum_{i=1}^{j-1} p_i \le U < \sum_{i=1}^{j} p_i \right\} = p_j$$

and so X has the desired distribution.

45

Remarks

1. The preceding can be written algorithmically as

> Generate a random number U
> If $U < p_0$ set $X = x_0$ and stop
> If $U < p_0 + p_1$ set $X = x_1$ and stop
> If $U < p_0 + p_1 + p_2$ set $X = x_2$ and stop
> $\vdots$

2. If the x_i, $i \geq 0$, are ordered so that $x_0 < x_1 < x_2 < \cdots$ and if we let F denote the distribution function of X, then $F(x_k) = \sum_{i=0}^{k} p_i$ and so

$$X \text{ will equal } x_j \quad \text{if} \quad F(x_{j-1}) \leq U < F(x_j)$$

In other words, after generating a random number U we determine the value of X by finding the interval $(F(x_{j-1}), F(x_j))$ in which U lies [or, equivalently, by finding the inverse of $F(U)$]. It is for this reason that the above is called the discrete inverse transform method for generating X. ∎

The amount of time it takes to generate a discrete random variable by the above method is proportional to the number of intervals one must search. For this reason it is sometimes worthwhile to consider the possible values x_j of X in decreasing order of the p_j.

Example 4a   If we wanted to simulate a random variable X such that

$$p_1 = 0.20, \quad p_2 = 0.15, \quad p_3 = 0.25, \quad p_4 = 0.40 \quad \text{where } p_j = P\{X = j\}$$

then we could generate U and do the following:

> If $U < 0.20$ set $X = 1$ and stop
> If $U < 0.35$ set $X = 2$ and stop
> If $U < 0.60$ set $X = 3$ and stop
> Otherwise set $X = 4$

However, a more efficient procedure is the following:

> If $U < 0.40$ set $X = 4$ and stop
> If $U < 0.65$ set $X = 3$ and stop
> If $U < 0.85$ set $X = 1$ and stop
> Otherwise set $X = 2$ ∎

One case where it is not necessary to search for the appropriate interval in which the random number lies is when the desired random variable is the discrete uniform random variable. That is, suppose we want to generate the value of X which is equally likely to take on any of the values $1, \ldots, n$. That is, $P\{X = j\} = 1/n, j = 1, \ldots, n$. Using the above results it follows that we can accomplish this by generating U and then setting

$$X = j \quad \text{if} \quad \frac{j-1}{n} \leq U < \frac{j}{n}$$

Therefore, X will equal j if $j - 1 \leq nU < j$; or, in other words,

$$X = \text{Int}(nU) + 1$$

where $\text{Int}(x)$— sometimes written as $[x]$— is the integer part of x (i.e., the largest integer less than or equal to x).

Discrete uniform random variables are quite important in simulation, as is indicated in the following two examples.

Example 4b Generating a Random Permutation. Suppose we are interested in generating a permutation of the numbers $1, 2, \ldots, n$ which is such that all $n!$ possible orderings are equally likely. The following algorithm will accomplish this by first choosing one of the numbers $1, \ldots, n$ at random and then putting that number in position n; it then chooses at random one of the remaining $n - 1$ numbers and puts that number in position $n - 1$; it then chooses at random one of the remaining $n - 2$ numbers and puts it in position $n - 2$; and so on (where choosing a number at random means that each of the remaining numbers is equally likely to be chosen). However, so that we do not have to consider exactly which of the numbers remain to be positioned, it is convenient and efficient to keep the numbers in an ordered list and then randomly choose the position of the number rather than the number itself. That is, starting with any initial ordering $P_1, P_2, \ldots, P_n$ we pick one of the positions $1, \ldots, n$ at random and then interchange the number in that position with the one in position n. Now we randomly choose one of the positions $1, \ldots, n - 1$ and interchange the number in this position with the one in position $n - 1$, and so on.

Recalling that $\text{Int}(kU) + 1$ will be equally likely to take on any of the values $1, 2, \ldots, k$, we see that the above algorithm for generating a random permutation can be written as follows:

STEP 1:   Let $P_1, P_2, \ldots, P_n$ be any permutation of $1, 2, \ldots, n$ (e.g., we can choose $P_j = j, j = 1, \ldots, n$).

STEP 2:   Set $k = n$.

STEP 3:   Generate a random number U and let $I = \text{Int}(kU) + 1$.

STEP 4:   Interchange the values of P_I and P_k.

STEP 5:   Let $k = k - 1$ and if $k > 1$ go to Step 3.

STEP 6: $P_1, \ldots, P_n$ is the desired random permutation.

For instance, suppose $n = 4$ and the initial permutation is 1, 2, 3, 4. If the first value of I (which is equally likely to be either 1, 2, 3, or 4) is $I = 3$, then the elements in positions 3 and 4 are interchanged and so the new permutation is 1, 2, 4, 3. If the next value of I is $I = 2$, then the elements in positions 2 and 3 are interchanged and so the new permutation is 1, 4, 2, 3. If the final value of I is $I = 2$, then the final permutation is 1, 4, 2, 3, and this is the value of the random permutation.

One very important property of the above algorithm is that it can also be used to generate a random subset, say of size r, of the integers 1, . . . , n. Namely, just follow the algorithm until the positions $n, n - 1, \ldots, n - r + 1$ are filled. The elements in these positions constitute the random subset. (In doing this we can always suppose that $r \leq n/2$; for if $r > n/2$ then we could choose a random subset of size $n - r$ and let the elements not in this subset be the random subset of size r.)

It should be noted that the ability to generate a random subset is particularly important in medical trials. For instance, suppose that a medical center is planning to test a new drug designed to reduce its user's blood cholesterol level. To test its effectiveness, the medical center has recruited 1000 volunteers to be subjects in the test. To take into account the possibility that the subjects' blood cholesterol levels may be affected by factors external to the test (such as changing weather conditions), it has been decided to split the volunteers into two groups of size 500—a *treatment* group that will be given the drug and a *control* that will be given a placebo. Both the volunteers and the administrators of the drug will not be told who is in each group (such a test is called *double-blind*). It remains to determine which of the volunteers should be chosen to constitute the treatment group. Clearly, one would want the treatment group and the control group to be as similar as possible in all respects with the exception that members in the first group are to receive the drug while those in the other group receive a placebo; for then it would be possible to conclude that any difference in response between the groups is indeed due to the drug. There is general agreement that the best way to accomplish this is to choose the 500 volunteers to be in the treatment group in a completely random fashion. That is, the choice should be made so that each of the $\binom{1000}{500}$ subsets of 500 volunteers is equally likely to constitute the set of volunteers. ■

Example 4c Calculating Averages. Suppose we want to approximate $\bar{a} = \sum_{i=1}^{n} a(i)/n$, where n is large and the values $a(i)$, $i = 1, \ldots, n$, are complicated and not easily calculated. One way to accomplish this is to note that if X is a discrete uniform random variable over the integers $1, \ldots, n$, then the random variable $a(X)$ has a mean given by

$$E[a(X)] = \sum_{i=1}^{n} a(i)P\{X = i\} = \sum_{i=1}^{n} \frac{a(i)}{n} = \bar{a}$$

Hence, if we generate k discrete uniform random variables X_i, $i = 1, \ldots, k$—by generating k random numbers U_i and setting $X_i = \text{Int}(nU_i) + 1$—then each of the k random variables $a(X_i)$ will have mean $\bar{a}$, and so by the strong law of large numbers it follows that when k is large (though much smaller than n) the average of these values should approximately equal $\bar{a}$. Hence, we can approximate $\bar{a}$ by using

$$\bar{a} \approx \sum_{i=1}^{k} \frac{a(X_i)}{k}$$

∎

Another random variable that can be generated without needing to search for the relevant interval in which the random number falls is the geometric.

Example 4d Recall that X is said to be a geometric random variable with parameter p if

$$P\{X = i\} = pq^{i-1}, \qquad i \geq 1, \text{ where } q = 1 - p$$

X can be thought of as representing the time of the first success when independent trials, each of which is a success with probability p, are performed. Since

$$\sum_{i=1}^{j-1} P\{X = i\} = 1 - P\{X > j - 1\}$$

$$= 1 - P\{\text{first } j - 1 \text{ trials are all failures}\}$$

$$= 1 - q^{j-1}, \qquad j \geq 1$$

we can generate the value of X by generating a random number U and setting X equal to that value j for which

$$1 - q^{j-1} \leq U < 1 - q^{j}$$

or, equivalently, for which

$$q^{j} < 1 - U \leq q^{j-1}$$

That is, we can define X by

$$X = \text{Min}\{j: q^j < 1 - U\}$$

Hence, using the fact that the logarithm is a monotone function, and so $a < b$ is equivalent to $\log(a) < \log(b)$, we obtain that X can be expressed as

$$X = \text{Min}\{j: j \log(q) < \log(1 - U)\}$$

$$= \text{Min}\left\{j: j > \frac{\log(1 - U)}{\log(q)}\right\}$$

where the last inequality changed sign since $\log(q)$ is negative since $0 < q < 1$. Hence, using Int( ) notation we can express X as

$$X = \text{Int}\left(\frac{\log(1 - U)}{\log(q)}\right) + 1$$

Finally, by noting that $1 - U$ is also uniformly distributed on $(0, 1)$, it follows that

$$X \equiv \text{Int}\left(\frac{\log(U)}{\log(q)}\right) + 1$$

is also geometric with parameter p. ∎

4.2   Generating a Poisson Random Variable

The random variable X is Poisson with mean λ if

$$p_i = P\{X = i\} = e^{-\lambda} \frac{\lambda^i}{i!} \qquad i = 0, 1, \ldots$$

The key to using the inverse transform method to generate such a random variable is the following identity (proved in Section 2.4 of Chapter 2):

$$p_{i+1} = \frac{\lambda}{i + 1} p_i, \qquad i \geq 0 \tag{4.1}$$

Upon using the above recursion to compute the Poisson probabilities as they become needed, the inverse transform algorithm for generating a Poisson random variable with mean λ can be expressed as follows. (The quantity i refers to the value presently under consideration; $p = p_i$ is the probability that X equals i, and $F = F(i)$ is the probability that X is less than or equal to i.)

STEP 1: Generate a random number U.

STEP 2: $i = 0, p = e^{-\lambda}, F = p$.

STEP 3: If $U < F$, set $X = i$ and stop.

STEP 4: $p = \lambda p/(i + 1), F = F + p, i = i + 1$.

STEP 5: Go to Step 3.

(In the above it should be noted that when we write, for example, $i = i + 1$, we do not mean that i is equal to $i + 1$ but rather that the value of i should be increased by 1.) To see that the above algorithm does indeed generate a Poisson random variable with mean λ, note that it first generates a random number U and then checks whether or not $U < e^{-\lambda} = p_0$. If so, it sets $X = 0$. If not, then it computes (in Step 4) p_1 by using the recursion (4.1). It now checks whether $U < p_0 + p_1$ (where the right-hand side is the new value of F), and if so it sets $X = 1$; and so on.

The above algorithm successively checks whether the Poisson value is 0, then whether it is 1, then 2, and so on. Thus, the number of comparisons needed will be 1 greater than the generated value of the Poisson. Hence, on average, the above will need to make $1 + \lambda$ searches. Whereas this is fine when λ is small, it can be greatly improved upon when λ is large. Indeed, since a Poisson random variable with mean λ is most likely to take on one of the two integral values closest to λ, a more efficient algorithm would first check one of these values, rather than starting at 0 and working upward. Algorithm 4-1, written in BASIC and presented in the Appendix of Programs, lets $I = \text{Int}(\lambda)$ and computes p_I (by first taking logarithms and then by raising the result to the power e). It then uses Equation (4.1) to recursively determine $F(I)$. It now generates a Poisson random variable with mean λ by generating a random number U, and then noting whether or not $X \leq I$ by seeing whether or not $U \leq F(I)$. It then searches downward starting from $X = I$ in the case where $X \leq I$ and upward starting from $X = I + 1$ otherwise. (Algorithm 4-1 also avoids the potential difficulty that, due to round-off error, when λ is large the computer might take $e^{-\lambda}$ to equal 0.)

Remark The number of searches needed by Algorithm 4-1 is roughly 1 more than the absolute difference between the random variable X and its mean λ. Since for λ large a Poisson is (by the central limit theorem) approximately normal with mean and variance both equal to λ, it follows that

Average number of searches $\simeq 1 + E[|X - \lambda|]$ where $X \sim N(\lambda, \lambda)^\dagger$

$$= 1 + \sqrt{\lambda} E\left[\frac{|X - \lambda|}{\sqrt{\lambda}}\right]$$

$$= 1 + \sqrt{\lambda} E[|Z|]   \text{where } Z \sim N(0, 1)$$

$$1 + 0.798\sqrt{\lambda}   \text{(see Exercise 12)}$$

That is, using Algorithm 4-1, the average number of searches grows with the square root of λ rather than with λ as λ becomes larger and larger. ■

4.3 Generating Binomial Random Variables

Suppose we want to generate the value of a binomial (n, p) random variable X—that is, X is such that

$$P\{X = i\} = \frac{n!}{i!(n - i)!} p^i(1 - p)^{n-i},   i = 0, 1, \ldots, n$$

To do so, we employ the inverse transform method by making use of the recursive identity

$$P\{X = i + 1\} = \frac{n - i}{i + 1} \frac{p}{1 - p} P\{X = i\}$$

With i denoting the value currently under consideration, pr $= P\{X = i\}$ the probability that X is equal to i, and $F = F(i)$ the probability that X is less than or equal to i, the algorithm can be expressed as follows:

Inverse Transform Algorithm for Generating a Binomial (n, p) Random Variable

STEP 1: Generate a random number U.

STEP 2: $c = p/(1 - p)$, $i = 0$, pr $= (1 - p)^n$, $F = $ pr.

STEP 3: If $U < F$, set $X = i$ and stop.

STEP 4: pr $= [c(n - i)/(i + 1)]$pr, $F = F + $ pr, $i = i + 1$.

STEP 5: Go to Step 3.

---

† We use the notation $X \sim F$ to mean that X has distribution function F. The symbol $N(\mu, \sigma^2)$ stands for a normal distribution with mean μ and variance σ^2.

The preceding algorithm first checks whether $X = 0$, then whether $X = 1$, and so on. Hence, the number of searches it makes is 1 more than the value of X. Therefore, on average, it will take $1 + np$ searches to generate X. Since a binomial (n, p) random variable represents the number of successes in n independent trials when each is a success with probability p, it follows that such a random variable can also be generated by subtracting from n the value of a binomial $(n, 1 - p)$ random variable (why is that?). Hence, when $p > 1/2$, we can generate a binomial $(n, 1 - p)$ random variable by the above method and subtract its value from n to obtain the desired generation.

Remarks

1. Another way of generating a binomial (n, p) random variable is by utilizing its interpretation as the number of successes in n independent trials by generating n random numbers $U_1, \ldots, U_n$ and then setting X equal to the number of the U_i that are less than or equal to p. By regarding the ith trial as a success if $U_1 < p$ and noting that the probability of this event is equal to p, it is easy to see that this results in a binomial (n, p) random variable. However, this approach requires n random numbers and makes n comparisons, whereas the inverse transform algorithm only requires one random number and makes, on average, $1 + np$ comparisons (along with an equal number of divisions).

2. As in the Poisson case, when the mean np is large it is better to first determine if the generated value is less than or equal to $I \equiv \text{Int}(np)$ or whether it is greater than I. In the former case one should then start the search with $X = I$, then $X = I - 1, \ldots$, and so on, whereas in the latter case one should start searching with $I + 1$ and go upward. ∎

4.4 The Acceptance–Rejection Technique

Suppose we have an efficient method for simulating a random variable having probability mass function $\{q_j, j \geq 0\}$. We can use this as the basis for simulating from the distribution having mass function $\{p_j, j \geq 0\}$ by first simulating a random variable Y having mass function $\{q_j\}$ and then accepting this simulated value with a probability proportional to p_Y/q_Y.

Specifically, let c be a constant such that

$$\frac{p_j}{q_j} \leq c \qquad \text{for all } j \text{ such that } p_j > 0 \tag{4.2}$$

We now have the following technique, called the rejection method or the acceptance rejection method, for simulating a random variable X having mass function $p_j = P\{X = j\}$.

Rejection Method

STEP 1: Simulate the value of Y, having probability mass function q_j.

STEP 2: Generate a random number U.

STEP 3: If $U < p_Y/cq_Y$, set $X = Y$ and stop. Otherwise, return to Step 1.

The rejection method is pictorially represented in Figure 4.1.

We now prove that the rejection method works.

Theorem   *The acceptance–rejection algorithm generates a random variable X such that*

$$P\{X = j\} = p_j, \qquad j = 0, \ldots$$

In addition, the number of iterations of the algorithm needed to obtain X is a geometric random variable with mean c.

Proof   To begin, let us determine the probability that a single iteration produces the accepted value j.

$$P\{Y = j, \text{ it is accepted}\} = P\{Y = j\}P\{accept|Y = j\}$$

$$= q_j \frac{p_j}{cq_j}$$

$$= \frac{p_j}{c}$$

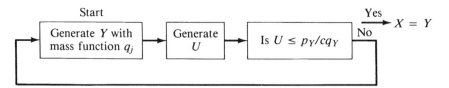

Figure 4.1   Acceptance–rejection

Summing over j yields the probability that a generated random variable is accepted:

$$P\{accepted\} = \sum_j \frac{p_j}{c} = \frac{1}{c}$$

As each iteration independently results in an accepted value with probability $1/c$, we see that the number of iterations needed is geometric with mean c. Also,

$$P\{X = j\} = \sum_n P\{j \text{ accepted on iteration } n\}$$

$$= \sum_n (1 - 1/c)^{n-1} \frac{p_j}{c}$$

$$= p_j \qquad \blacksquare$$

Remarks

1. The reader should note that the way in which we "accept the value Y with probability p_Y/cq_Y" is by generating a random number U and then accepting Y if $U \leq p_Y/cq_Y$.

2. Since each iteration of the algorithm will, independently, result in an accepted value with probability $P\{Acceptance\} = K = 1/c$, it follows that the number of iterations needed will have a geometric distribution with parameter $1/c$ and will thus have mean c. Therefore the closer c is to 1—and it can never be less than 1 [which can be seen by writing the inequality (4.2) as $p_i \leq cq_i$ and then summing both sides]—the more efficient is this approach; this is intuitively clear since the closer c is to 1 the more alike are the two mass functions $\{p_j\}$ and $\{q_j\}$. $\blacksquare$

Example 4e   Suppose we wanted to simulate the value of a random variable X that takes one of the values 1, 2, . . . , 10 with respective probabilities 0.11, 0.12, 0.09, 0.08, 0.12, 0.10, 0.09, 0.09, 0.10, 0.10. Whereas one possibility is to use the inverse transform algorithm, a better approach is to use the rejection method with q being the discrete uniform density on 1, . . . , 10. That is, $q_j = 1/10$, $j =, 1 . . . , 10$. For this choice of $\{q_j\}$ we can choose c by

$$c = \text{Max} \frac{p_j}{q_j} = 1.2$$

and so the algorithm would be as follows:

STEP 1:   Generate a random number U_1 and set $Y = \text{Int}(10U_1) + 1$.

STEP 2:   Generate a second random number U_2.

STEP 3:   If $U_2 \leq p_Y/.12$, set $X = Y$ and stop. Otherwise return to Step 1.

The constant 0.12 in Step 3 arises since $cq_Y = 1.2/10 = 0.12$. On average, this algorithm requires only 1.2 iterations of the above to obtain the generated value of X. ■

The power of the rejection method, a version of which was initially proposed by the famous mathematician John von Neumann, will become even more readily apparent when we consider its analogue when generating continuous random variables.

4.5   The Composition Approach

Suppose that we had an efficient method to simulate the value of a random variable having either of the two probability mass functions $\{p_j^1, j \geq 0\}$ or $\{p_j^2, j \geq 0\}$, and that we wanted to simulate the value of the random variable X having mass function

$$P\{X = j\} = \alpha p_j^1 + (1 - \alpha)p_j^2, \qquad j \geq 0 \qquad (4.3)$$

where $0 < \alpha < 1$. One way to simulate such a random variable X is to note that if X_1 and X_2 are random variables having respective mass functions $\{p_j^1\}$ *and* $\{p_j^2\}$, then the random variable X defined by

$$X = \begin{cases} X_1 & \text{with probability } \alpha \\ X_2 & \text{with probability } 1 - \alpha \end{cases}$$

will have its mass function given by (4.3). From this it follows that we can generate the value of such a random variable by first generating a random number U and then generating a value of X_1 if $U < \alpha$ and of X_2 if $U > \alpha$.

Example 4f   Suppose we want to generate the value of a random variable X such that

$$p_j = P\{X = j\} = \begin{cases} 0.05 & \text{for } j = 1, 2, 3, 4, 5 \\ 0.15 & \text{for } j = 6, 7, 8, 9, 10 \end{cases}$$

By noting that $p_j = 0.5p_j^1 + 0.5p_j^2$, where

$$p_j^1 = 0.1, \ j = 1, \ldots, 10 \quad \text{and} \quad p_j^2 = \begin{cases} 0 & \text{for } j = 1, 2, 3, 4, 5 \\ 0.2 & \text{for } j = 6, 7, 8, 9, 10 \end{cases}$$

we can accomplish this by first generating a random number U and then generating from the discrete uniform over 1, . . . , 10 if $U < 0.5$ and from the discrete uniform over 6, 7, 8, 9, 10 otherwise. That is, we can simulate X as follows:

STEP 1: Generate a random number U_1.

STEP 2: Generate a random number U_2.

STEP 3: If $U_1 < 0.5$, set $X = \text{Int}(10U_2) + 1$. Otherwise, set $X = \text{Int}(5U_2) + 6$. ■

If F_i, $i = 1, . . . , n$ are distribution functions and α_i, $i = 1, . . . , n$, are nonnegative numbers summing to 1, then the distribution function F given by

$$F(x) = \sum_{i=1}^{n} \alpha_i F_i(x)$$

is said to be a *mixture*, or a *composition*, of the distribution functions F_i, $i = 1, . . . , n$ One way to simulate from F is first to simulate a random variable I, equal to i with probability α_i, $i = 1, . . . , n$, and then to simulate from the distribution F_I. (That is, if the simulated value of I is $I = j$, then the second simulation is from F_j.) This approach to simulating from F is often referred to as the *composition method*.

Exercises

1. Write a program to generate n values from the probability mass function $p_1 = \frac{1}{3}$, $p_2 = \frac{2}{3}$.
   (a) Let $n = 100$, run the program, and determine the proportion of values that are equal to 1.
   (b) Repeat (a) with $n = 1000$.
   (c) Repeat (a) with $n = 10,000$.

2. Write a computer program that, when given a probability mass function $\{p_j, j = 1, . . . , n\}$ as an input, gives as an output the value of a random variable having this mass function.

3. Give an efficient algorithm to simulate the value of a random variable X such that
   $$P\{X = 1\} = 0.3, \quad P\{X = 2\} = 0.2, \quad P\{X = 3\} = 0.35, \quad P\{X = 4\} = 0.15$$

4. A deck of 100 cards—numbered 1, 2, . . . , 100—are shuffled and then turned over one at a time. Say that a "hit" occurs whenever card i is the

*i*th card to be turned over, $i = 1, \ldots, 100$. Write a simulation program to estimate the expectation and variance of the total number of hits. Run the program. Find the exact answers and compare them with your estimates.

5. Another method of generating a random permutation, different from the one presented in Example 4b, is to successively generate a random permutation of the elements $1, 2, \ldots, n$ starting with $n = 1$, then $n = 2$, and so on. (Of course, the random permutation when $n = 1$ is 1.) Once one has a random permutation of the first $n - 1$ elements—call it $P_1, \ldots, P_{n-1}$—the random permutation of the n elements $1, \ldots, n$ is obtained by putting n in the final position—to obtain the permutation $P_1, \ldots, P_{n-1}, n$—and then interchanging the element in position n (namely, n) with the element in a randomly chosen position which is equally likely to be either position 1, position 2, $\ldots$, or position n.

   (a) Write an algorithm that accomplishes the above.
   (b) Prove by mathematical induction on n that the algorithm works, in that the permutation obtained is equally likely to be any of the $n!$ permutations of $1, 2, \ldots, n$.

6. (a) Using 100 random numbers explain how you could find an approximation for $\sum_{i=1}^{N} e^{i/N}$, where $N = 10,000$.
   (b) Obtain the approximation.
   (c) Is your approximation a good one?

7. A pair of fair dice are to be continually rolled until all the possible outcomes $2, 3, \ldots, 12$ have occurred at least once. Develop a simulation study to estimate the expected number of dice rolls that are needed.

8. Suppose that each item on a list of n items has a value attached to it, and let $v(i)$ denote the value attached to the ith item on the list. Suppose that n is very large, and also that each item may appear at many different places on the list. Explain how random numbers can be used to estimate the sum of the values of the different items on the list (where the value of each item is to be counted once no matter how many times the item appears on the list).

9. Consider the n events $A_1, \ldots, A_n$ where the A_i, $i = 1, \ldots, n$, consists of the following n_i outcomes: $A_i = \{a_{i,1}, a_{i,2}, \ldots, a_{i,n_i}\}$. Suppose that for any given outcome a, $P\{a\}$, the probability that the experiment results in outcome a, is known. Explain how one can use the results of Exercise 8 to estimate $P\{\cup_{i=1}^{n} A_i\}$, the probability that at least one of the events A_i occurs. Note that the events A_i, $i = 1, \ldots, n$, are not assumed to be mutually exclusive.

10. The negative binomial probability mass function with parameters (r, p), where r is a positive integer and $0 < p < 1$, is given by

$$P_j = \frac{(j - 1)!}{(j - r)!(r - 1)!} p^r (1 - p)^{j-r}, \qquad j = r, r + 1, \cdots$$

(a) Use the relationship between negative binomial and geometric random variables and the results of Example 4d to obtain an algorithm for simulating from this distribution.

(b) Verify the relation

$$P_{j+1} = \frac{j(1 - p)}{j + 1 - r} P_j$$

(c) Use the relation in part (b) to give a second algorithm for generating negative binomial random variables.

(d) Use the interpretation of the negative binomial distribution as the number of trials it takes to amass a total of r successes when each trial independently results in a success with probability p, to obtain still another approach for generating such a random variable.

11. If Z is a standard normal random variable, show that

$$E[|Z|] = \left(\frac{2}{\pi}\right)^{1/2} \approx 0.798$$

12. Give two methods for generating a random variable X such that

$$P\{X = i\} = \frac{e^{-\lambda} \lambda^i / i!}{\sum_{j=0}^{k} e^{-\lambda} \lambda^j / j!}, \qquad i = 0, \ldots, k$$

13. Let X be a binomial random variable with parameters n and p. Suppose that we want to generate a random variable Y whose probability mass function is the same as the conditional mass function of X given that $X \geq k$, for some $k \leq n$. Let $\alpha = P\{X \geq k\}$ and suppose that the value of α has been computed.

(a) Give the inverse transform method for generating Y.

(b) Give a second method for generating Y.

(c) For what values of α, small or large, would the algorithm in (b) be inefficient?

14. Give a method for simulating from the probability mass function p_j, $j = 5, 6, \ldots, 14$, where

$$p_j = \begin{cases} 0.11 & \text{when } j \text{ is odd and } 5 \leq j \leq 13 \\ 0.09 & \text{when } j \text{ is even and } 6 \leq j \leq 14 \end{cases}$$

15. Suppose that the random variable X can take on any of the values $1, \ldots ,$ 10 with respective probabilities 0.06, 0.06, 0.06, 0.06, 0.06, 0.15, 0.13, 0.14, 0.15, 0.13. Use the composition approach to give an algorithm that generates the value of X.

16. Present a method to generate the value of X, where

$$P\{X = j\} = \left(\frac{1}{2}\right)^{j+1} + \frac{\left(\frac{1}{2}\right)2^{j-1}}{3^j}, \qquad j = 1, 2, \ldots$$

17. Let X have mass function $p_j = P\{X = j\}$, $\sum_{j=1}^{\infty} p_j = 1$. Let

$$\lambda_n = P\{X = n | X > n - 1\} = \frac{p_n}{1 - \sum_{j=1}^{n-1} p_j}, \qquad n = 1, \ldots$$

(a) Show that $p_1 = \lambda_1$ and

$$p_n = (1 - \lambda_1)(1 - \lambda_2) \cdots (1 - \lambda_{n-1})\lambda_n$$

The quantities λ_n, $n \geq 1$, are called the discrete hazard rates since if we think of X as the lifetime of some item then λ_n represents the probability that an item that has reached the age n will die during that time period. The following approach to simulating discrete random variables, called the discrete hazard rate method, generates a succession of random numbers, stopping when the nth random number is less than λ_n. The algorithm can be written as follows:

STEP 1: $X = 1$.

STEP 2:   Generate a random number U.

STEP 3:   If $U < \lambda_X$, stop.

STEP 4: $X = X + 1$.

STEP 5:   Go to Step 2.

(b) Show that the value of X when the above stops has the desired mass function.

(c) Suppose that X is a geometric random variable with parameter p. Determine the values λ_n, $n \geq 1$. Explain what the above algorithm is doing in this case and why its validity is clear.

18. Suppose that $0 \leq \lambda_n \leq \lambda$, for all $n \geq 1$. Consider the following algorithm to generate a random variable having discrete hazard rates $\{\lambda_n\}$.

STEP 1: $S = 0$.

STEP 2:   Generate U and set $Y = \text{Int}\left(\dfrac{\log(U)}{\log(1 - \lambda)}\right) + 1$.

STEP 3: $S = S + Y$.

STEP 4:   Generate U.

STEP 5:   If $U \leq \lambda_S/\lambda$, set $X = S$ and stop. Otherwise, go to 2.

(a) What is the distribution of Y in Step 2?

(b) Explain what the algorithm is doing.

(c) Argue that X is a random variable with discrete hazard rates $\{\lambda_n\}$.

Chapter 5 | Generating Continuous Random Variables

Introduction

Each of the techniques for generating a discrete random variable has its analog in the continuous case. In Sections 5.1 and 5.2 we present the inverse transform approach and the rejection approach for generating continuous random variables. In Section 5.3 we consider a powerful approach for generating normal random variables, known as the polar method. Finally, in Sections 5.4 and 5.5 we consider the problem of generating Poisson and nonhomogeneous Poisson processes.

5.1 The Inverse Transform Algorithm

Consider a continuous random variable having distribution function F. A general method for generating such a random variable —called the inverse transformation method—is based on the following proposition.

Proposition *Let U be a uniform $(0, 1)$ random variable. For any continuous distribution function F the random variable X defined by*

$$X = F^{-1}(U)$$

has distribution F. [$F^{-1}(u)$ is defined to be that value of x such that $F(x) = u$.]

Proof Let F_X denote the distribution function of $X = F^{-1}(U)$. Then

$$F_X(x) = P\{X \leq x\}$$

$$= P\{F^{-1}(U) \leq x\} \tag{5.1}$$

Now since F is a distribution function it follows that $F(x)$ is a monotone increasing function of x and so the inequality "$a \leq b$" is equivalent to the inequality "$F(a) \leq F(b)$." Hence, from Equation (5.1), we see that

$$F_X(x) = P\{F(F^{-1}(U) \leq F(x))\}$$
$$= P\{U \leq F(x)\} \quad \text{since } F(F^{-1}(U)) = U$$
$$= F(x) \quad \quad \text{since } U \text{ is uniform } (0, 1) \quad \blacksquare$$

The above proposition thus shows that we can generate a random variable X from the continuous distribution function F by generating a random number U and then setting $X = F^{-1}(U)$.

Example 5a Suppose we wanted to generate a random variable X having distribution function

$$F(x) = x^n, \quad 0 < x < 1$$

If we let $x = F^{-1}(u)$, then

$$u = F(x) = x^n \quad \text{or, equivalently,} \quad x = u^{1/n}$$

Hence we can generate such a random variable X by generating a random number U and then setting $X = U^{1/n}$. $\blacksquare$

The inverse transform method yields a powerful approach to generating exponential random variables, as is indicated in the next example.

Example 5b If X is an exponential random variable with rate 1, then its distribution function is given by

$$F(x) = 1 - e^{-x}$$

If we let $x = F^{-1}(u)$, then

$$u = F(x) = 1 - e^{-x}$$

or

$$1 - u = e^{-x}$$

or, taking logarithms,

$$x = -\log(1 - u)$$

Hence we can generate an exponential with parameter 1 by generating a random number U and then setting

$$X = F^{-1}(U) = -\log(1 - U)$$

A small savings in time can be obtained by noting that $1 - U$ is also uniform on $(0, 1)$ and thus $-\log(1 - U)$ has the same distribution as $-\log U$. That is, the negative logarithm of a random number is exponentially distributed with rate 1.

In addition, note that if X is exponential with mean 1 then, for any positive c, cX is exponential with mean c. Hence, an exponential random variable X with rate λ (mean $1/\lambda$) can be generated by generating a random number U and setting

$$X = -\frac{1}{\lambda} \log U$$

∎

Remark   The above also provides us with another algorithm for generating a Poisson random variable. To begin, recall that a Poisson process with rate λ results when the times between successive events are independent exponentials with rate λ. (See Section 2.5 of Chapter 2.) For such a process $N(1)$, the number of events by time 1, is Poisson distributed with mean λ. However, if we let X_1, $i = 1, \ldots$, denote the successive interarrival times, then the nth event will occur at time $\sum_{i=1}^{n} X_i$, and so the number of events by time 1 can be expressed as

$$N(1) = \text{Max}\left\{ n: \sum_{i=1}^{n} X_i \leq 1 \right\}$$

That is, the number of events by time 1 is equal to the largest n for which the nth event has occurred by time 1. (For example, if the fourth event occurred by time 1 but the fifth event did not, then clearly there would have been a total of four events by time 1.) Hence, using the results of Example 5b, we can generate $N = N(1)$, a Poisson random variable with mean λ, by generating random numbers $U_1, \ldots, U_n, \ldots$ and setting

$$N = \text{Max}\left\{ n: \sum_{i=1}^{n} -\frac{1}{\lambda} \log U_i \leq 1 \right\}$$
$$= \text{Max}\left\{ n: \sum_{i=1}^{n} \log U_i \geq -\lambda \right\}$$
$$= \text{Max}\{ n: \log(U_1 \cdots U_n) \geq -\lambda \}$$
$$= \text{Max}\{ n: U_1 \cdots U_n \geq e^{-\lambda} \}$$

Hence, a Poisson random variable N with mean λ can be generated by successively generating random numbers until their product falls below $e^{-\lambda}$, and then setting N equal to 1 less than the number of random numbers required. That is,

$$N = \text{Min}\{ n: U_1 \cdots U_n < e^{-\lambda} \} - 1$$

∎

The results of Example 5b along with the relationship between the gamma and the exponential distribution can be used to efficiently generate a gamma (n, λ) random variable.

Example 5c Suppose we wanted to generate the value of a gamma (n, λ) random variable. Since the distribution function F of such a random variable is given by

$$F(x) = \int_0^x \frac{\lambda e^{-\lambda y}(\lambda y)^{n-1}}{(n-1)!} \, dy$$

it is not possible to give a closed form expression for its inverse. However, by using the result that a gamma (n, λ) random variable X can be regarded as being the sum of n independent exponentials, each with rate λ (see Section 2.3 of Chapter 2), we can make use of Example 5b to generate X. Specifically, we can generate a gamma (n, λ) random variable by generating n random numbers $U_1, \ldots, U_n$ and then setting

$$X = -\frac{1}{\lambda} \log U_1 - \cdots - \frac{1}{\lambda} \log U_n$$

$$= -\frac{1}{\lambda} \log(U_1 \cdots U_n)$$

where the use of the identity $\sum_{i=1}^n \log x_i = \log(x_1 \cdots x_n)$ is computationally time saving in that it requires only one rather than n logarithm computations. ■

The results of Example 5c can be used to provide an efficient way of generating a set of exponential random variables by first generating their sum and then, conditional on the value of that sum, generating the individual values. For example, we could generate X and Y, a pair of independent and identically distributed exponentials having mean 1, by first generating $X + Y$ and then using the result (Exercise 36 of Chapter 2) that, given that $X + Y = t$, the conditional distribution of X is uniform on $(0, t)$. The following algorithm can thus be used to generate a pair of exponentials with mean 1.

STEP 1:   Generate random numbers U_1 and U_2.
STEP 2:   Set $t = -\log(U_1 U_2)$.
STEP 3:   Generate a random number U_3.
STEP 4: $X = tU_3$, $Y = t - X$.

Comparing the above with the more direct approach of generating two random numbers U_1 and U_2 and then setting $X = -\log U_1$, $Y = -\log U_2$ shows that the above algorithm saves a logarithmic computation at the cost of two multiplications and the generation of a random number.

We can also generate k independent exponentials with mean 1 by first generating their sum, say by $-\log(U_1 \cdots U_k)$, and then generating $k - 1$ additional random numbers $U_1, \ldots, U_{k-1}$, which should then be ordered. If $U_{(1)} < U_{(2)} < \cdots < U_{(k-1)}$ are their ordered values, and if $-\log(U_1 \cdots U_k) = t$, then the k exponentials are

$$t[U_{(i)} - U_{(i-1)}], \qquad i = 1, 2, \ldots, k, \text{ where } U_{(0)} \equiv 0, \ U_{(k)} \equiv t$$

5.2 The Rejection Method

Suppose we have a method for generating a random variable having density function $g(x)$. We can use this as the basis for generating from the continuous distribution having density function of $f(x)$ by generating Y from g and then accepting this generated value with a probability proportional to $f(Y)/g(Y)$.

Specifically, let c be a constant such that

$$\frac{f(y)}{g(y)} \le c \qquad \text{for all } y$$

We then have the following technique (illustrated in Figure 5.1) for generating a random variable having density f.

The Rejection Method

STEP 1:   Generate Y having density g.

STEP 2:   Generate a random number U.

STEP 3:   If $U \le \dfrac{f(Y)}{cg(Y)}$, set $X = Y$. Otherwise, return to Step 1.

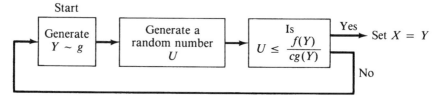

Figure 5.1   The rejection method for simulating a random variable X having density function f

The reader should note that the rejection method is exactly the same as in the case of discrete random variables with the only difference being that densities replace mass functions. In exactly the same way as we did in the discrete case we can prove the following result.

Theorem

(i) *The random variable generated by the rejection method has density f.*

(ii) *The number of iterations of the algorithm that are needed is a geometric random variable with mean c.*

As in the discrete case it should be noted that the way in which one accepts the value Y with probability $f(Y)/cg(Y)$ is by generating a random number U and then accepting Y if $U \le f(Y)/cg(Y)$.

Example 5d Let us use the rejection method to generate a random variable having density function

$$f(x) = 20x(1 - x)^3, \qquad 0 < x < 1$$

Since this random variable (which is beta with parameters 2, 4) is concentrated in the interval $(0, 1)$, let us consider the rejection method with

$$g(x) = 1, \qquad 0 < x < 1$$

To determine the constant c such that $f(x)/g(x) \le c$, we use calculus to determine the maximum value of

$$\frac{f(x)}{g(x)} = 20x(1 - x)^3$$

Differentiation of this quantity yields

$$\frac{d}{dx}\left(\frac{f(x)}{g(x)}\right) = 20\,[(1 - x)^3 - 3x(1 - x)^2]$$

Setting this equal to 0 shows that the maximal value is attained when $x = \frac{1}{4}$ and thus

$$\frac{f(x)}{g(x)} \le 20\left(\frac{1}{4}\right)\left(\frac{3}{4}\right)^3 = \frac{135}{64} \equiv c$$

Hence,

$$\frac{f(x)}{cg(x)} = \frac{256}{27}\,x(1 - x)^3$$

and thus the rejection procedure is as follows:

STEP 1:   Generate random numbers U_1 and U_2.

STEP 2:   If $U_2 \leq \dfrac{256}{27} U_1 (1 - U_1)^3$, stop and set $X = U_1$. Otherwise, return to Step 1.

The average number of times that Step 1 will be performed is $c = \dfrac{135}{64} \approx 2.11.$ ∎

Example 5e   Suppose we wanted to generate a random variable having the gamma $(\frac{3}{2}, 1)$ density

$$f(x) = Kx^{1/2}e^{-x}, \qquad x > 0$$

where $K = 1/\Gamma\left(\frac{3}{2}\right) = 2/\sqrt{\pi}$. Because such a random variable is concentrated on the positive axis and has mean $\frac{3}{2}$, it is natural to try the rejection technique with an exponential random variable with the same mean. Hence, let

$$g(x) = \frac{2}{3} e^{-2x/3}, \qquad x > 0$$

Now

$$\frac{f(x)}{g(x)} = \frac{3K}{2} x^{1/2} e^{-x/3}$$

By differentiating and setting the resultant derivative equal to 0, we obtain that the maximal value of this ratio is obtained when

$$\frac{1}{2} x^{-1/2} e^{-x/3} = \frac{1}{3} x^{1/2} e^{-x/3}$$

that is, when $x = \frac{3}{2}$. Hence

$$c = \text{Max} \frac{f(x)}{g(x)} = \frac{3K}{2} \left(\frac{3}{2}\right)^{1/2} e^{-1/2}$$

$$= \frac{3^{3/2}}{(2\pi e)^{1/2}} \qquad \text{since } K = 2/\sqrt{\pi}$$

Since

$$\frac{f(x)}{cg(x)} = (2e/3)^{1/2} x^{1/2} e^{-x/3}$$

we see that a gamma $(\frac{3}{2}, 1)$ random variable can be generated as follows:

STEP 1:   Generate a random number U_1 and set $Y = -\frac{3}{2} \log U_1$.

STEP 2:   Generate a random number U_2.

STEP 3:   If $U_2 < (2eY/3)^{1/2} e^{-Y/3}$, set $X = Y$. Otherwise, return to Step 1.

The average number of iterations that will be needed is

$$c = 3 \left(\frac{3}{2\pi e} \right)^{1/2} \approx 1.257. \qquad \blacksquare$$

Remark   Even though the gamma $(\frac{3}{2}, 1)$ random variable has mean $\frac{3}{2}$, it is not immediately apparent that we should use the rejection with an exponential with the same mean. Indeed, suppose that we let

$$g(x) = \lambda e^{-\lambda x}$$

Then

$$\frac{f(x)}{g(x)} = \frac{Kx^{1/2} e^{-(1-\lambda)x}}{\lambda}$$

The maximal value of this ratio is obtained when

$$\frac{1}{2} x^{-1/2} = (1 - \lambda)x^{1/2}$$

or when $x = [2(1 - \lambda)]^{-1}$ [provided $\lambda < 1$; if $\lambda \geq 1$, it is easy to see that the ratio $f(x)/g(x)$ assumes arbitrarily large values]. Hence, if we use the exponential with mean $1/\lambda$, then the average number of iterations of the algorithm that will be needed is

$$c = \text{Max} \frac{f(x)}{g(x)} = \frac{K}{\lambda} [2(1 - \lambda)]^{-1/2} e^{-1/2}$$

Thus, the best choice of λ is the one that minimizes the above or, equivalently, that maximizes $\lambda(1 - \lambda)^{1/2}$. Calculus now shows that this value is such that

$$(1 - \lambda)^{1/2} = \frac{\lambda(1 - \lambda)^{-1/2}}{2}$$

or, equivalently,

$$1 - \lambda = \lambda/2 \qquad \text{or} \qquad \lambda = \frac{2}{3}$$

Hence, the best exponential to use in the rejection method to generate a gamma $(\frac{3}{2}, 1)$ random variable is indeed the exponential with mean $\frac{3}{2}$. $\blacksquare$

Our next example shows how the rejection technique can be used to generate normal random variables.

Example 5f Generating a Normal Random Variable. To generate a standard normal random variable Z (i.e., one with mean 0 and variance 1), note first that the absolute value of Z has probability density function

$$f(x) = \frac{2}{\sqrt{2\pi}} e^{-x^2/2} \qquad 0 < x < \infty \tag{5.2}$$

We start by generating from the preceding density function by using the rejection method with g being the exponential density function with mean 1—that is,

$$g(x) = e^{-x} \qquad 0 < x < \infty$$

Now

$$\frac{f(x)}{g(x)} = \sqrt{2/\pi} \; e^{x - x^2/2}$$

and so the maximum value of $f(x)/g(x)$ occurs at the value of x that maximizes $x - x^2/2$. Calculus shows that this occurs when $x = 1$, and so we can take

$$c = \text{Max} \frac{f(x)}{g(x)} = \frac{f(1)}{g(1)} = \sqrt{2e/\pi}$$

Because

$$\frac{f(x)}{cg(x)} = \exp\left\{ x - \frac{x^2}{2} - \frac{1}{2} \right\}$$

$$= \exp\left\{ -\frac{(x - 1)^2}{2} \right\}$$

it follows that we can generate the absolute value of a unit normal random variable as follows:

STEP 1: Generate Y, an exponential random variable with rate 1.

STEP 2: Generate a random number U.

STEP 3: If $U \le \exp\{-(Y - 1)^2/2\}$, set $X = Y$. Otherwise, return to Step 1.

Once we have simulated a random variable X having density function as in Equation (5.2)—and such a random variable is thus distributed as the absolute value of a unit normal—we can then obtain a unit normal Z by letting Z be equally likely to be either X or $-X$.

In Step 3, the value Y is accepted if $U \leq \exp\{-(Y-1)^2/2\}$, which is equivalent to $-\log U \geq (Y-1)^2/2$. However, in Example 5b it was shown that $-\log U$ is exponential with rate 1, and so the above is equivalent to the following:

STEP 1: Generate independent exponentials with rate 1, Y_1 and Y_2.

STEP 2: If $Y_2 \geq (Y_1 - 1)^2/2$, set $X = Y_1$. Otherwise, return to Step 1.

Suppose now that the foregoing results in Y_1 being accepted—and so we know that Y_2 is larger than $(Y_1 - 1)^2/2$. By how much does the one exceed the other? To answer this, recall that Y_2 is exponential with rate 1, and so, given that it exceeds some value, the amount by which Y_2 exceeds $(Y_1 - 1)^2/2$ [i.e., its "additional life" beyond the time $(Y_1 - 1)^2/2$] is (by the memoryless property) also exponentially distributed with rate 1. That is, when we accept in Step 2 we obtain not only X (the absolute value of a unit normal) but by computing $Y_2 - (Y_1 - 1)^2/2$ we can also generate an exponential random variable (independent of X) having rate 1.

Hence, summing up, we have the following algorithm that generates an exponential with rate 1 and an independent standard normal random variable.

STEP 1: Generate Y_1, an exponential random variable with rate 1.

STEP 2: Generate Y_2, an exponential random variable with rate 1.

STEP 3: If $Y_2 - (Y_1 - 1)^2/2 > 0$, set $Y = Y_2 - (Y_1 - 1)^2/2$ and go to Step 4. Otherwise, go to Step 1.

STEP 4: Generate a random number U and set

$$
Z = \begin{cases} Y_1 & \text{if } U \leq \dfrac{1}{2} \\ -Y_1 & \text{if } U > \dfrac{1}{2} \end{cases}
$$

The random variables Z and Y generated by the foregoing are independent with Z being normal with mean 0 and variance 1 and Y being exponential with rate 1. (If you want the normal random variable to have mean μ and variance σ^2, just take $\mu + \sigma Z$.) ∎

Remarks

1. Since $c = \sqrt{2e/\pi} \approx 1.32$, the foregoing requires a geometric distributed number of iterations of Step 2 with mean 1.32.

2. If we want to generate a sequence of standard normal random variables, we can use the exponential random variable Y obtained in Step 3 as

the initial exponential needed in Step 1 for the next normal to be generated. Hence, on the average, we can simulate a standard normal by generating 1.64 (= 2 × 1.32 − 1) exponentials and computing 1.32 squares. ■

5.3 The Polar Method for Generating Normal Random Variables

Let X and Y be independent unit normal random variables and let R and θ denote the polar coordinates of the vector (X, Y). That is (see Figure 5.2),

$$R^2 = X^2 + Y^2$$

$$\tan \theta = \frac{Y}{X}$$

Since X and Y are independent, their joint density is the product of their individual densities and is thus given by

$$
\begin{aligned}
f(x, y) &= \frac{1}{\sqrt{2\pi}} e^{-x^2/2} \frac{1}{\sqrt{2\pi}} e^{-y^2/2} \\
&= \frac{1}{2\pi} e^{-(x^2 + y^2)/2}
\end{aligned}
$$

(5.3)

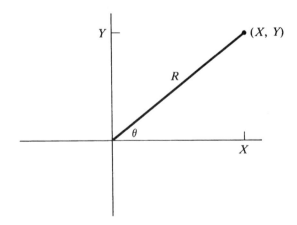

Figure 5.2

To determine the joint density of R^2 and Θ—call it $f(d, \theta)$—we make the change of variables

$$d = x^2 + y^2, \qquad \theta = \tan^{-1}\left(\frac{y}{x}\right)$$

As the Jacobian of this transformation—that is, the determinant of partial derivatives of d and θ with respect to x and y—is easily shown to equal 2, it follows from Equation (5.3) that the joint density function of R^2 and Θ is given by

$$f(d, \theta) = \frac{1}{2}\frac{1}{2\pi} e^{-d/2}, \qquad 0 < d < \infty, \qquad 0 < \theta < 2\pi$$

However, as this is equal to the product of an exponential density having mean 2 (namely, $\frac{1}{2} e^{-d/2}$) and the uniform density on $(0, 2\pi)$ (namely, $1/2\pi$), it follows that

$$R^2 \text{ and } \Theta \text{ are independent, with } R^2 \text{ being exponential with mean 2} \atop \text{and } \Theta \text{ being uniformly distributed over } (0, 2\pi) \qquad (5.4)$$

We can now generate a pair of independent standard normal random variables X and Y by using (5.4) to first generate their polar coordinates and then transforming back to rectangular coordinates. This is accomplished as follows:

STEP 1:   Generate random numbers U_1 and U_2.

STEP 2: $R^2 = -2 \log U_1$ (and thus R^2 is exponential with mean 2). Set $\Theta = 2\pi U_2$ (and thus Θ is uniform between 0 and 2π).

STEP 3:   Now let

$$X = R \cos \Theta = \sqrt{-2 \log U_1} \, \cos(2\pi U_2)$$
$$(5.5)$$
$$Y = R \sin \Theta = \sqrt{-2 \log U_1} \, \sin(2\pi U_2)$$

The transformations given by Equations (5.5) are known as the Box–Muller transformations.

Unfortunately, the use of the Box–Muller transformations (5.5) to generate a pair of independent unit normals is computationally not very efficient: The reason for this is the need to compute the sine and cosine trigonometric functions. There is, however, fortuitously a way to get around this time-consuming difficulty by an indirect computation of the sine and cosine of a random angle (as opposed to a direct computation which generates U and then computes the sine and cosine of $2\pi U$). To begin, note that if U is uniform on $(0, 1)$ then $2U$ is uniform on

(0, 2) and so $2U - 1$ is uniform on $(-1, 1)$. Thus, if we generate random numbers U_1 and U_2 and set

$$V_1 = 2U_1 - 1$$

$$V_2 = 2U_2 - 1$$

then (V_1, V_2) is uniformly distributed in the square of area 4 centered at $(0, 0)$—see Figure 5.3.

Suppose now that we continually generate such pairs (V_1, V_2) until we obtain one that is contained in the circle of radius 1 centered at $(0, 0)$—that is, until (V_1, V_2) is such that $V_1^2 + V_2^2 \leq 1$. It now follows that such a pair (V_1, V_2) is uniformly distributed in the circle. If we let R and Θ denote the polar coordinates of this pair, then it is not difficult to verify that R and Θ are independent, with R^2 being uniformly distributed on $(0, 1)$ (see Exercise 19) and with Θ being uniformly distributed over $(0, 2\pi)$. Since Θ is thus a random angle, it follows that we can generate the sine and cosine of a random angle Θ by generating a random point (V_1, V_2) in the circle and then setting

$$\sin \Theta = \frac{V_2}{R} = \frac{V_2}{(V_1^2 + V_2^2)^{1/2}}$$

$$\cos \Theta = \frac{V_1}{R} = \frac{V_1}{(V_1^2 + V_2^2)^{1/2}}$$

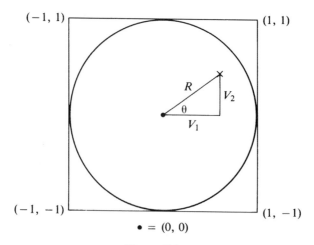

$\bullet = (0, 0)$

Figure 5.3

It now follows from the Box–Muller transformation (5.5) that we can generate independent unit normals by generating a random number U and setting

$$X = (-2 \log U)^{1/2} \frac{V_1}{(V_1^2 + V_2^2)^{1/2}}$$

$$Y = (-2 \log U)^{1/2} \frac{V_2}{(V_1^2 + V_2^2)^{1/2}}$$

(5.6)

In fact, since $R^2 = V_1^2 + V_2^2$ is itself uniformly distributed over $(0, 1)$ and is independent of the random angle Θ, we can use it as the random number U needed in Equations (5.6). Therefore, letting $S = R^2$, we obtain that

$$X = (-2 \log S)^{1/2} \frac{V_1}{S^{1/2}} = V_1 \left(\frac{-2 \log S}{S} \right)^{1/2}$$

$$Y = (-2 \log S)^{1/2} \frac{V_2}{S^{1/2}} = V_2 \left(\frac{-2 \log S}{S} \right)^{1/2}$$

are independent unit normals when (V_1, V_2) is a randomly chosen point in the circle of radius 1 centered at the origin, and $S = V_1^2 + V_2^2$.

Summing up, we thus have the following approach to generating a pair of independent unit normals:

STEP 1: Generate random numbers, U_1 and U_2.

STEP 2: Set $V_1 = 2U_1 - 1$, $V_2 = 2U_2 - 1$, $S = V_1^2 + V_2^2$.

STEP 3: If $S > 1$ return to Step 1.

STEP 4: Return the independent unit normals

$$X = \sqrt{\frac{-2 \log S}{S}} V_1, \qquad Y = \sqrt{\frac{-2 \log S}{S}} V_2$$

The above is called the polar method. Since the probability that a random point in the square will fall within the circle is equal to $\pi/4$ (the area of the circle divided by the area of the square), it follows that, on average, the polar method will require $4/\pi = 1.273$ iterations of Step 1. Hence it will, on average, require 2.546 random numbers, 1 logarithm, 1 square root, 1 division, and 4.546 multiplications to generate two independent unit normals.

5.4 Generating a Poisson Process

Suppose we wanted to generate the first n event times of a Poisson process with rate λ. To do so we make use of the result that the times between successive events for such a process are independent exponential random variables each with rate λ. Thus, one way to generate the process is to generate these interarrival times. So if we generate n random numbers U_1, $U_2, \ldots, U_n$ and set $X_1 = -1/\lambda \log U_i$, then X_i can be regarded as the time between the $(i - 1)$st and the ith event of the Poisson process. Since the actual time of the jth event will equal the sum of the first j interarrival times, it thus follows that the generated values of the first n event times are $\Sigma_{i=1}^{j} X_i, j = 1, \ldots, n$.

If we wanted to generate the first T time units of the Poisson process, we can follow the above procedure of successively generating the interarrival times, stopping when their sum exceeds T. That is, the following algorithm can be used to generate all the event times occurring in $(0, T)$ of a Poisson process having rate λ. In the algorithm t refers to time, I is the number of events that have occurred by time t, and $S(I)$ is the most recent event time.

Generating the First T Time Units of a Poisson Process with Rate λ

STEP 1: $t = 0, I = 0$.

STEP 2: Generate a random number U.

STEP 3: $t = t - \frac{1}{\lambda} \log U$. If $t < T$, stop.

STEP 4: $I = I + 1, S(I) = t$.

STEP 5: Go to Step 2.

The final value of I in the above algorithm will represent the number of events that occur by time T, and the values $S(1), \ldots, S(I)$ will be the I event times in increasing order.

There is another approach for simulating the first T time units of a Poisson process that is also quite efficient. It starts by simulating $N(T)$—the total number of events that occur by time T—and then makes use of a result which states that, given $N(T)$, the times at which these events occur are distributed independently and uniformly over $(0, T)$. [This is quite intuitive since by the stationary increment axiom it is intuitive that an arbitrary event time is uniformly distributed over the interval, and by the independent increment axiom it is intuitive that, given $N(T)$, these $N(T)$ event times would be independent.] Hence we can start by generating the value of $N(T)$, a Poisson random variable with mean λT (by the approach presented in Section 4.3 of Chapter 4 if λ is large or either by that approach or by the method outlined in Section 5.2 of this chapter if λ is not large). If the generated value of $N(T)$ is n, we then generate n random numbers—call them

$U_1, \ldots, U_n$—and, as TU_i will be uniformly distributed over $(0, T)$, the set of event times will thus be $\{TU_1, \ldots, TU_n\}$. If we were to stop here, this approach would certainly be more efficient than simulating the exponentially distributed interarrival times. However, we usually desire the event times in increasing order [e.g., so as to be able to know $N(s)$ for all $s < T$]; thus, we would also need to order the values TU_i, $i = 1, \ldots, n$.

5.5 Generating a Nonhomogeneous Poisson Process

An extremely important counting process for modeling purposes is the nonhomogeneous Poisson process, which relaxes the Poisson process assumption of stationary increments. Thus, it allows for the possibility that the arrival rate need not be constant but can vary with time. It is usually very difficult to obtain analytical results for a mathematical model that assumes a nonhomogeneous Poisson arrival process, and as a result such processes are not applied as often as they should be. However, since the use of simulation helps one to analyze such models, we expect that such mathematical models will become more common.

Suppose that we wanted to simulate the first T time units of a nonhomogeneous Poisson process with intensity function $\lambda(t)$. The first method we present, called the *thinning* or *random sampling* approach, starts by choosing a value λ which is such that

$$\lambda(t) \leq \lambda \qquad \text{for all } t \leq T$$

Now, as shown in Chapter 2, such a nonhomogeneous Poisson process can be generated by a random selection of the event times of a Poisson process having rate λ. That is, if an event of a Poisson process with rate λ that occurs at time t is counted (independently of what has transpired previously) with probability $\lambda(t)/\lambda$, then the process of counted events is a nonhomogeneous Poisson process with intensity function $\lambda(t)$, $0 \leq t \leq T$. Hence, by simulating a Poisson process and then randomly counting its events, we can generate the desired nonhomogeneous Poisson process. This can be written algorithmically as follows.

Generating the First T Time Units of a Nonhomogeneous Poisson Process

STEP 1: $t = 0, I = 0$.
STEP 2: Generate a random number U.
STEP 3: $t = t - \frac{1}{\lambda} \log U$. If $t > T$, stop.
STEP 4: Generate a random number U.

STEP 5:   If $U \leq \lambda(t)/\lambda$, set $I = I + 1$, $S(I) = t$.

STEP 6:   Go to Step 2.

In the above $\lambda(t)$ is the intensity function and λ is such that $\lambda(t) \leq \lambda$. The final value of I represents the number of events time T, and $S(1), \ldots, S(I)$ are the event times.

The above procedure, referred to as the thinning algorithm (because it "thins" the homogeneous Poisson points), is clearly most efficient, in the sense of having the fewest number of rejected events times, when $\lambda(t)$ is near λ throughout the interval. Thus, an obvious improvement is to break up the interval into subintervals and then use the procedure over each subinterval. That is, determine appropriate values k, $0 = t_0 < t_1 < t_2 < \cdots < t_k < t_{k+1} = T$, $\lambda_1, \ldots, \lambda_{k+1}$ such that

$$\lambda(s) \leq \lambda_i, \qquad \text{if } t_{i-1} \leq s < t_i, \qquad i = 1, \ldots, k + 1 \qquad (5.7)$$

Now generate the nonhomogeneous Poisson process over the interval (t_{i-1}, t_i) by generating exponential random variables with rate λ_i, and accepting the generated event occurring at time s, $s \in (t_{i-1}, t_i)$, with probability $\lambda(s)/\lambda_i$. Because of the memoryless property of the exponential and the fact that the rate of an exponential can be changed upon multiplication by a constant, it follows that there is no loss of efficiency in going from one subinterval to the next. That is, if we are at $t \in (t_{i-1}, t_i)$ and generate X, an exponential with rate λ_i, which is such that $t + X > t_i$, then we can use $\lambda_i[X - (t_i - t)]/\lambda_{i+1}$ as the next exponential with rate λ_{i+1}.

We thus have the following algorithm for generating the first T time units of a nonhomogeneous Poisson process with intensity function $\lambda(s)$ when the relations (5.7) are satisfied. In the algorithm t represents the present time, J the present interval (i.e., $J = j$ when $t_{j-1} \leq t < t_j$), I the number of events so far, and $S(1), \ldots, S(I)$ the event times.

Generating the First T Time Units of a Nonhomogeneous Poisson Process

STEP 1: $t = 0$, $J = 1$, $I = 0$.

STEP 2:   Generate a random number U and set $X = \frac{-1}{\lambda_J} \log U$.

STEP 3:   If $t + X > t_J$, go to Step 8.

STEP 4: $t = t + X$.

STEP 5: Generate a random number U.

STEP 6: If $U \leq \lambda(t)/\lambda_J$, set $I = I + 1$, $S(I) = t$.

STEP 7: Go to Step 2.

STEP 8: If $J = k + 1$, stop.

STEP 9: $X = (X - t_J + t)\lambda_J\lambda_{J+1}$, $t = t_J$, $J = J + 1$.

STEP 10: Go to Step 3.

Suppose now that over some subinterval (t_{i-1}, t_i) it follows that $\lambda, > 0$, where

$$\lambda_i \equiv \text{Infimum}\{\lambda(s): t_{i-1} \leq s < t_i\}$$

In such a situation we should not use the thinning algorithm directly but rather should first simulate a Poisson process with rate λ_i over the desired interval and then simulate a nonhomogeneous Poisson process with the intensity function $\lambda(s) = \lambda(s) - \lambda_i$ when $s \in (t_{i-1}, t_i)$. (The final exponential generated for the Poisson process, which carries one beyond the desired boundary, need not be wasted but can be suitably transformed so as to be reusable.) The superposition (or merging) of the two processes yields the desired process over the interval. The reason for doing it this way is that it saves the need to generate uniform random variables for a Poisson distributed number, with mean $\lambda_i(t_i - t_{i-1})$, of the event times. For example, consider the case where

$$\lambda(s) = 10 + s, \qquad 0 < s < 1$$

Using the thinning method with $\lambda = 11$ would generate an expected number of 11 events, each of which would require a random number to determine whether or not to accept it. On the other hand, to generate a Poisson process with rate 10 and then merge it with a nonhomogeneous Poisson process with rate $\lambda(s) = s$, $0 < s < 1$ (generated by the thinning algorithm with $\lambda = 1$), would yield an equally distributed number of event times but with the expected number needing to be checked to determine acceptance being equal to 1.

A second method for simulating a nonhomogeneous Poisson process having intensity function $\lambda(t)$, $t > 0$, is to directly generate the successive event times. So let $S_1, S_2, \ldots$ denote the successive event times of such a process. As these random variables are clearly dependent, we generate them in sequence—starting with S_1, and then using the generated value of S_1 to generate S_2, and so on.

To start, note that if an event occurs at time s, then, independent of what has occurred prior to s, the additional time until the next event has the distribution F_s, given by

$$F_s(x) = P\{\text{time from } s \text{ until next event is less than } x|\text{ event at } s\}$$

$$= P\{\text{next event is before } x + s|\text{ event at } s\}$$

$$= P\{\text{event between } s \text{ and } s + x|\text{ event at } s\}$$

$$= P\{\text{event between } s \text{ and } s + x\} \qquad \text{by independent increments}$$

$$= 1 - P\{0 \text{ events in } (s, s + x)\}$$

$$= 1 - \exp\left(-\int_{s}^{s+x} \lambda(y)\, dy\right)$$

$$= 1 - \exp\left(-\int_{0}^{x} \lambda(s + y)\, dy\right) \tag{5.8}$$

We can now simulate the event times $S_1, S_2, \ldots$ by generating S_1 from the distribution F_0; then if the simulated value of S_1 is s_1, we generate S_2 by adding s_1 to a generated value from the distribution F_{s_1}, and if this sum is s_2 we generate S_3 by adding s_2 to a generated value from the distribution F_{s_2} and so on. The method used to simulate from these distributions should of course depend on their form. In the following example the distributions F_s are easily inverted and so the inverse transform method can be applied.

Example 5g Suppose that $\lambda(t) = 1/(t + a)$, $t \geq 0$, for some positive constant a. Then

$$\int_{0}^{x} \lambda(s + y)\, dy = \int_{0}^{x} \frac{1}{s + y + a}\, dy = \log\left(\frac{x + s + a}{s + a}\right)$$

Hence, from Equation (5.8),

$$F_s(x) = 1 - \frac{s + a}{x + s + a} = \frac{x}{x + s + a}$$

To invert this, suppose that $x = F_s^{-1}(u)$, and so

$$u = F_s(x) = \frac{x}{x + s + a}$$

or, equivalently,

$$x = \frac{u(s + a)}{1 - u}$$

That is,

$$F_s^{-1}(u) = (s + a)\frac{u}{1 - u}$$

We can therefore generate the successive event times $S_1, S_2, \ldots$ by generating random numbers $U_1, U_2, \ldots$ and then recursively setting

$$S_1 = \frac{aU_1}{1 - U_1}$$

$$S_2 = S_1 + (S_1 + a)\frac{U_2}{1 - U_2} = \frac{S_1 + aU_2}{1 - U_2}$$

and, in general,

$$S_j = S_{j-1} + (S_{j-1} + a)\frac{U_j}{1 - U_j} = \frac{S_{j-1} + aU_j}{1 - U_j}, \qquad j \geq 2 \qquad \blacksquare$$

Exercises

1. Give a method for generating a random variable having density function
$$f(x) = e^x/(e - 1), \qquad 0 \leq x \leq 1$$

2. Give a method to generate a random variable having density function

$$f(x) = \begin{cases} \dfrac{x - 2}{2} & \text{if } 2 \leq x \leq 3 \\ \dfrac{2 - x/3}{2} & \text{if } 3 \leq x \leq 6 \end{cases}$$

3. Use the inverse transform method to generate a random variable having distribution function
$$F(x) = \frac{x^2 + x}{2}, \qquad 0 \leq x \leq 1$$

4. Give a method for generating a random variable having distribution function
$$F(x) = 1 - \exp(-\alpha x^\beta), \qquad 0 < x < \infty$$

A random variable having such a distribution is said to be a Weibull random variable.

5. Give a method for generating a random variable having density function

$$f(x) = \begin{cases} e^{2x}, & -\infty < x < 0 \\ e^{-2x}, & 0 < x < \infty \end{cases}$$

6. Let X be an exponential random variable with mean 1. Give an efficient algorithm for simulating a random variable whose distribution is the conditional distribution of X given that $X < 0.05$. That is, its density function is

$$f(x) = \frac{e^{-x}}{1 - e^{-0.05}}, \qquad 0 < x < 0.05$$

Generate 1000 such variables and use them to estimate of $E[X|X < 0.05]$. Then determine the exact value of $E[X|X < 0.05]$.

7. (The Composition Method) Suppose it is relatively easy to generate random variables from any of the distributions F_i, $i = 1, \ldots, n$. How could we generate a random variable having the distribution function

$$F(x) = \sum_{i=1}^{n} p_i F_i(x)$$

where p_i, $i = 1, \ldots, n$, are nonnegative numbers whose sum is 1?

8. Using the result of Exercise 7, give algorithms for generating random variables from the following distributions.

(a) $F(x) = \dfrac{x + x^3 + x^5}{3}, \qquad 0 \le x \le 1$

(b) $F(x) = \begin{cases} \dfrac{1 - e^{-2x} + 2x}{3} & \text{if } 0 < x < 1 \\[2mm] \dfrac{3 - e^{-2x}}{3} & \text{if } 1 < x < \infty \end{cases}$

(c) $F(x) = \displaystyle\sum_{i=1}^{n} \alpha_i x^i, \qquad 0 \le x \le 1, \qquad \text{where } \alpha_i \ge 0, \qquad \sum_{i=1}^{n} \alpha_i = 1$

9. Give a method to generate a random variable having distribution function

$$F(x) = \int_{0}^{\infty} x^y e^{-y} \, dy, \qquad 0 \le x \le 1$$

Hint: Think in terms of the composition method of Exercise 7. In particular, let F denote the distribution function of X, and suppose that the conditional distribution of X given that $Y = y$ is

$$P\{X \le x | Y = y\} = x^y, \qquad 0 \le x \le 1$$

10. Write an algorithm that can be used to generate exponential random variables in sets of 3. Compare the computational requirements of this method with the one presented after Example 5c which generates them in pairs.

11. Suppose it is easy to generate a random variable from any of the distributions F_i, $i = 1, \ldots, n$. How can we generate from the following distributions?

(a) $F(x) = \prod_{i=1}^{n} F_i(x)$

(b) $F(x) = 1 - \prod_{i=1}^{n} [1 - F_i(x)]$

Hint: If X_i, $i = 1, \ldots, n$, are independent random variables, with X_i having distribution F_i, which random variable has distribution function F?

12. Using the rejection method and the results of Exercise 11, give two other methods, aside from the inverse transform method, that can be used to generate a random variable having distribution function

$$F(x) = x^n, \qquad 0 \le x \le 1$$

Discuss the efficiency of the three approaches to generating from F.

13. Let G be a distribution function with density g and suppose, for constants $a < b$, we want to generate a random variable from the distribution function

$$F(x) = \frac{G(x) - G(a)}{G(b) - G(a)}, \qquad a \le x \le b$$

(a) If X has distribution G, then F is the conditional distribution of X given what information?
(b) Show that the rejection method reduces in this case to generating a random variable X having distribution G and then accepting it if it lies between a and b.

14. Give two methods for generating a random variable having density function

$$f(x) = xe^{-x}, \qquad 0 \le x < \infty$$

and compare their efficiency.

15. Give an algorithm that generates a random variable having density

$$f(x) = 30(x^2 - 2x^3 + x^4), \qquad 0 \le x \le 1$$

Discuss the efficiency of this approach.

16. In Example 5f we simulated a normal random variable by using the rejection technique with an exponential distribution with rate 1. Show that among all exponential density functions $g(x) = \lambda e^{-\lambda x}$ the number of iterations needed is minimized when $\lambda = 1$.

17. Write a program that generates normal random variables by the method of Example 5f.

18. Write a program that generates normal random variables by the polar method.

19. Let (X, Y) be uniformly distributed in a circle of radius 1. Show that if R is the distance from the center of the circle to (X, Y) then R^2 is uniform on $(0, 1)$.

20. Write a program that generates the first T time units of a Poisson process having rate λ.

21. To complete a job a worker must go through k stages in sequence. The time to complete stage i is an exponential random variable with rate λ_i, $i = 1, \ldots, k$. However, after completing stage i the worker will only go to the next stage with probability $\alpha_i = 1, \ldots, k - 1$. That is, after completing stage i the worker will stop working with probability $1 - \alpha_i$. If we let X denote the amount of time that the worker spends on the job, then X is called a *Coxian* random variable. Write an algorithm for generating such a random variable.

22. Buses arrive at a sporting event according to a Poisson process with rate 5 per hour. Each bus is equally likely to contain either 20, 21, $\ldots$, 40 fans, with the numbers in the different buses being independent. Write an algorithm to simulate the arrival of fans to the event by time $t = 1$.

23. (a) Write a program that uses the thinning algorithm to generate the first 10 time units of a nonhomogeneous Poisson process with intensity function

$$\lambda(t) = 3 + \frac{4}{t + 1}$$

(b) Give a way to improve upon the thinning algorithm for this example.

24. Give an efficient algorithm to generate the first 10 times units of nonhomogeneous Poisson process having intensity function

$$\lambda(t) = \begin{cases} \dfrac{t}{5}, & 0 < t < 5 \\ 1 + 5(t - 5), & 5 < t < 10 \end{cases}$$

References

Dagpunar, T., *Principles of Random Variate Generation,* Clarendon Press, Oxford, 1988.

Devroye, L., *Nonuniform Random Variate Generation,* Springer-Verlag, New York, 1986.

Fishman, G. S., *Principles of Discrete Event Simulation,* Wiley, New York, 1978.

Knuth, D., *The Art of Computer Programming,* Vol. 2, *Seminumerical Algorithms,* Addison-Wesley, Reading, MA, 1981

Law, A. M., and W. D. Kelton, *Simulation Modelling and Analysis,* Second Ed., McGraw-Hill, New York, 1991.

Lewis, P. A. W., and G. S. Shedler, "Simulation of Nonhomogeneous Poisson Processes by Thinning," *Nav. Res. Log. Quart.,* **26,** 403–413, 1979.

Marsaglia, G., "Generating Discrete Random Variables in a Computer," *Commun. Assoc. Comput. Mach.,* **6,** 37–38, 1963.

Morgan, B. J. T., *Elements of Simulation,* Chapman and Hall, London, 1983.

Ripley, B. D., "Computer Generation of Random Variables: A Tutorial," *Inst. Statist. Rev.,* **51,** 301–319, 1983.

Ripley, B. D., *Stochastic Simulation,* Wiley, New York, 1986.

Rubenstein, R. Y., *Simulation and the Monte Carlo Method,* Wiley, New York, 1981.

Schmeiser, B. W., "Random Variate Generation, a Survey," *Proc. 1980 Winter Simulation Conf.,* Orlando, FL; pp. 79–104, 1980.

Chapter 6 | The Discrete Event Simulation Approach

Introduction

Simulating a probabilistic model involves generating the stochastic mechanisms of the model and then observing the resultant flow of the model over time. Depending on the reasons for the simulation, there will be certain quantities of interest that we will want to determine. However, because the model's evolution over time often involves a complex logical structure of its elements, it is not always apparent how to keep track of this evolution so as to determine these quantities of interest. A general framework, built around the idea of "discrete events," has been developed to help one follow a model over time and determine the relevant quantities of interest. The approach to simulation based on this framework is often referred to as the *discrete event simulation approach*.

6.1 Simulation via Discrete Events

The key elements in a discrete event simulation are variables and events. To do the simulation we continually keep track of certain variables. In general, there are three types of variables that are often utilized—the time variable, counter variables, and the system state variable.

Variables

1. Time variable t Refers to the amount of (simulated) time that has elapsed

2. Counter variables   These variables keep a count of the number of times that certain events have occurred by time t

3. System state (**SS**) variable   This describes the "state of the system" at the time t

Whenever an "event" occurs the values of the above variables are changed, or updated, and we collect, as output, any relevant data of interest. In order to determine when the next event will occur, an "event list," which lists the nearest future events and when they are scheduled to occur, is maintained. Whenever an event "occurs" we then reset the time and all state and counter variables and collect the relevant data. In this way we are able to "follow" the system as it evolves over time.

As the preceding is only meant to give a very rough idea of the elements of a discrete event simulation, it is useful to look at some examples. In Section 6.2 we consider the simulation of a single-server waiting line, or queueing, system. In Sections 6.3 and 6.4 we consider multiple-server queueing systems. The model of Section 6.3 supposes that the servers are arranged in a series fashion, and the one of 6.4 that they are arranged in a parallel fashion. In Section 6.5 we consider an inventory stocking model and in 6.6 a multimachine repair problem. In Section 6.7 we consider a model concerning stock options.

In all the queueing models, we suppose that the customers arrive in accordance with a nonhomogeneous Poisson process with a bounded intensity function $\lambda(t)$, $t > 0$. In simulating these models we will make use of the following subroutine to generate the value of a random variable T_s, defined to equal the time of the first arrival after time s.

Let λ be such that $\lambda(t) \leq \lambda$ for all t. Assuming that $\lambda(t)$, $t > 0$, and λ are specified, the following subroutine generates the value of T_s.

A Subroutine for Generating T_s

STEP 1: Let $t = s$.
STEP 2: Generate U.
STEP 3: Let $t = t - \frac{1}{\lambda} \log U$.
STEP 4: Generate U.
STEP 5: If $U \leq \lambda(t)/\lambda$, set $T_s = t$ and stop.
STEP 6: Go to Step 2.

6.2   A Single-Server Queueing System

Consider a service station in which customers arrive in accordance with a nonhomogeneous Poisson process with intensity function $\lambda(t)$, $t \geq 0$. There is a single server, and upon arrival a customer either enters service if this server is free at that moment or else joins the waiting queue if the server is busy. When the server completes serving a customer it then either begins serving the customer that had been waiting the longest (the so-called "first come first served" discipline) if there are any waiting customers, or, if there are no waiting customers, it remains free until the next customer's arrival. The amount of time it takes to service a customer is a random variable (independent of all other service times and of the arrival process), having probability distribution G. In addition, there is a fixed time T after which no additional arrivals are allowed to enter the system, although the server completes servicing all those that are already in the system at time T.

Suppose that we are interested in simulating the above system to determine such quantities as (a) the average time a customer spends in the system and (b) the average time past T that the last customer departs—that is, the average time at which the server can go home.

To do a simulation of the above system we use the following variables:

1. Time variable t
2. Counter variables N_A: the number of arrivals (by time t)
                        N_D: the number of departures (by time t)
3. System state variable n: the number of customers in the system (at time t)

Since the natural time to change the above quantities is when there is either an arrival or a departure, we take these as the "events." That is, there are two types of event: arrivals and departures. The event list contains the time of the next arrival and the time of the departure of the customer presently in service. That is, the event list is

$$\mathbf{EL} = t_A, t_D$$

where t_A is the time of the next arrival (after t) and t_D is the service completion time of the customer presently being served. If there is no customer presently being served, then t_D is set equal to ∞.

The output variables that will be collected are $A(i)$, the arrival time of customer i; $D(i)$, the departure time of customer i; and T_p, the time past T that the last customer departs.

To begin the simulation, we initialize the variables and the event times as follows:

Initialize

Set $t = N_A = N_D = 0$.

Set **SS** $= 0$.

Generate T_0, and set $t_A = T_0$, $t_D = \infty$.

To update the system, we move along the time axis until we encounter the next event. To see how this is accomplished, we must consider different cases, depending on which member of the event list is smaller. In the following, Y refers to a service time random variable having distribution G.

$$t = \text{time variable}, \qquad \mathbf{SS} = n, \qquad \mathbf{EL} = t_A, t_D$$

Case 1 $\quad t_A \leq t_D, t_A \leq T$

Reset: $t = t_A$ (we move along to time t_A).

Reset: $N_A = N_A + 1$ (since there is an additional arrival at time t_A).

Reset: $n = n + 1$ (because there is now one more customer).

Generate T_t, and reset $t_A = T_t$ (this is the time of the next arrival).

If $n = 1$, generate Y and reset $t_D = t + Y$ (because the system had been empty and so we need to generate the service time of the new customer).

Collect output data $A(N_A) = t$ (because customer N_A arrived at time t).

Case 2 $\quad t_D < t_A, t_D \leq T$

Reset: $t = t_D$.

Reset: $n = n - 1$.

Reset: $N_D = N_D + 1$ (since a departure occurred at time t).

If $n = 0$, reset $t_D = \infty$; otherwise, generate Y and reset $t_D = t + Y$.

Collect the output data $D(N_D) = t$ (since customer N_D just departed).

Case 3 $\quad \min (t_A, t_D) > T, n > 0$

Reset: $t = t_D$

Reset: $n = n - 1$

Reset: $N_D = N_D + 1$

If $n > 0$, generate Y and reset $t_D = t + Y$.

Collect the output data $D(N_D) = t$.

Case 4 $\min(t_A, t_D) > T, n = 0$

Collect output data $T_p = \max(t - T, 0)$.

The preceding is illustrated in the flow diagram presented in Figure 6.1. Each time we arrive at a "stop" box we would have collected the data N_A, the total number of arrivals, which will equal N_D, the total number of departures. For each $i, i = 1, \ldots , N_A$, we have $A(i)$ and $D(i)$, the respective arrival and departure times of customer i [and thus $D(i) - A(i)$ represents the amount of time that customer i spent in the system]. Finally, we will have T_p, the time past T at which the last customer departed. Each time we collect the above data we say that a simulation run has been completed. After each run we then reinitialize and generate another run until it has been decided that enough data have been collected. (In Chapter 7 we consider the question of when to end the simulation.) The average of all the values of T_p that have been generated will be our estimate of the mean time past T that the last customer departs; similarly, the average of all the observed values of $D - A$ (i.e., the average time, over all customers observed in all our simulation runs, that a customer spends in the system) will be our estimate of the average time that a customer spends in the system.

Remark   If we want to save output data giving the number of customers in the system at each point of time, all that is necessary is to output the system state and time variable pair (n, t) whenever an event occurs. For instance, if the data $(1, 4)$ and $(0, 6)$ were output then, with $n(t)$ being the number in the system at time t, we would know that

$$n(t) = 0, \quad \text{if} \quad 0 \leq t < 4$$
$$n(t) = 1, \quad \text{if} \quad 4 \leq t < 6$$
$$n(t) = 0, \quad \text{if} \quad t = 6$$

6.3   A Queueing System with Two Servers in Series

Consider a two-server system in which customers arrive in accordance with a nonhomogeneous Poisson process, and suppose that each arrival must first be served by server 1 and upon completion of service at 1 the customer goes over to server 2. Such a system is called a *tandem* or *sequential* queueing system.

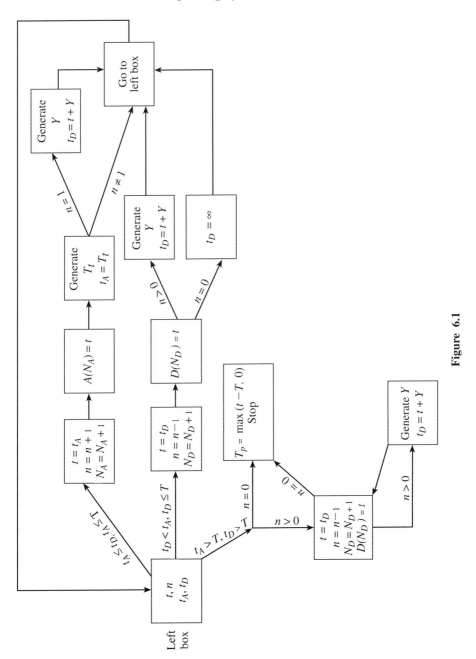

Figure 6.1

Upon arrival the customer will either enter service with server 1 if that server is free, or join the queue of server 1 otherwise. Similarly, when the customer completes service at server 1 it then either enters service with server 2 if that server is free, or else it joins its queue. After being served at server 2 the customer departs the system. The service times at server i have distribution G_i, $i = 1, 2$. (See Figure 6.2.)

Suppose that we are interested in using simulation to study the distribution of the amounts of time that a customer spends both at server 1 and at server 2. To do so, we will use the following variables.

Time Variable t

System State (SS) Variable

(n_1, n_2): if there are n_1 customers at server 1 (including both those in queue and in service) and n_2 at server 2

Counter Variables

N_A: the number of arrivals by time t
N_D: the number of departures by time t

Output Variables

$A_1(n)$: the arrival time of customer n, $n \geq 1$
$A_2(n)$: the arrival time of customer n at server 2, $n \geq 1$
$D(n)$: the departure time of customer n, $n \geq 1$

Event List t_A, t_1, t_2, where t_A is the time of the next arrival, and t_i is the service completion time of the customer presently being served by server i, $i = 1, 2$. If

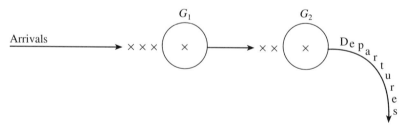

Figure 6.2

there is no customer presently with server i, then $t_i = \infty$, $i = 1, 2$. The event list always consists of the three variables t_A, t_1, t_2.

To begin the simulation, we initialize the variables and the event list as follows:

Initialize

Set $t = N_A = N_D = 0$.

Set **SS** $= (0, 0)$.

Generate T_0, and set $t_A = T_0$, $t_1 = t_2 = \infty$.

To update the system, we move along in time until we encounter the next event. We must consider different cases, depending on which member of the event list is smallest. In the following, Y_i refers to a random variable having distribution G_i, $i = 1, 2$.

$$\mathbf{SS} = (n_1, n_2) \qquad \mathbf{EL} = t_A, t_1, t_2$$

Case 1 $t_A = \min(t_A, t_1, t_2)$

Reset: $t = t_A$.

Reset: $N_A = N_A + 1$.

Reset: $n_1 = n_1 + 1$.

Generate T_t, and reset $t_A = T_t$.

If $n_1 = 1$, generate Y_1 and reset $t_1 = t + Y_1$.

Collect output data $A_1(N_A) = t$.

Case 2 $t_1 < t_A$, $t_1 \leq t_2$

Reset: $t = t_1$.

Reset: $n_1 = n_1 - 1$, $n_2 = n_2 + 1$.

If $n_1 = 0$, reset $t_1 = \infty$; otherwise, generate Y_1 and reset $t_1 = t + Y_1$.

If $n_2 = 1$, generate Y_2 and reset $t_2 = t + Y_2$.

Collect the output data $A_2(N_A - n_1) = t$.

Case 3 $t_2 < t_A$, $t_2 < t_1$

Reset: $t = t_2$.

Reset: $N_D = N_D + 1$.

Reset: $n_2 = n_2 - 1$.

If $n_2 = 0$, reset $t_2 = \infty$.

If $n_2 > 0$, generate Y_2, and reset $t_2 = t + Y_2$.

Collect the output data $D(N_D) = t$.

Using the preceding updating scheme it is now an easy matter to simulate the system and collect the relevant data.

6.4   A Queueing System with Two Parallel Servers

Consider a model in which customers arrive at a system having two servers. Upon arrival the customer will join the queue if both servers are busy, enter service with server 1 if that server is free, or enter service with server 2 otherwise. When the customer completes service with a server (no matter which one), that customer then departs the system and the customer that has been in queue the longest (if there are any customers in queue) enters service. The service distribution at server i is G_i, $i = 1, 2$. (See Figure 6.3.)

Suppose that we want to simulate the preceding model, keeping track of the amounts of time spent in the system by each customer, and the number of services performed by each server. Because there are multiple servers, it follows that customers will not necessarily depart in the order in which they arrive. Hence, to know which customer is departing the system upon a service completion we will have to keep track of which customers are in the system. So let us number the customers as they arrive, with the first arrival being customer number 1, the next being number 2, and so on. We will then make use of the following variables:

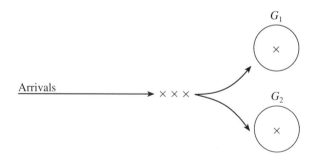

Figure 6.3

Time Variable t

System State Variable (SS)

$(n, i_1, i_2, \ldots, i_n)$ if there are n customers in the system, i_1 is with server 1, i_2 is with server 2, i_3 is first in line, i_4 is next, and so on.

Note that **SS** $= (0)$ when the system is empty, and **SS** $= (1, j, 0)$ or $(1, 0, j)$ when the only customer is j and he is being served by server 1 or server 2, respectively.

Counter Variables

N_A: the number of arrivals by time t

C_j: the number of customers served by j, $j = 1, 2$, by time t

Output Variables

$A(n)$: the arrival time of customer n, $n \geq 1$

$D(n)$: the departure time of customer n, $n \geq 1$

Event list $\quad t_A, t_1, t_2$

where t_A is the time of the next arrival, and t_i is the service completion time of the customer presently being served by server i, $i = 1, 2$. If there is no customer presently with server i, then we set $t_i = \infty$, $i = 1, 2$. In the following, the event list will always consist of the three variables t_A, t_1, t_2.

To begin the simulation, we initialize the variables and event list as follows:

Initialize

Set $t = N_A = C_1 = C_2 = 0$.

Set **SS** $= (0)$.

Generate T_0, and set $t_A = T_0$, $t_1 = t_2 = \infty$.

To update the system, we move along in time until we encounter the next event. In the following cases, Y_i always refers to a random variable having distribution G_i, $i = 1, 2$.

Case 1 $SS = (n, i_1, i_2, \ldots, i_n)$ and $t_A = \min(t_A, t_1, t_2)$

Reset: $t = t_A$.
Reset: $N_A = N_A + 1$.
Generate T_t and reset $t_A = T_t$.
Collect the output data $A(N_A) = t$.

If $SS = (0)$:

Reset: $SS = (1, N_A, 0)$.
Generate Y_1 and reset $t_1 = t + Y_1$.

If $SS = (1, j, 0)$:

Reset: $SS = (2, j, N_A)$.
Generate Y_2 and reset $t_2 = t + Y_2$.

If $SS = (1, 0, j)$:

Reset $SS = (2, N_A, j)$.
Generate Y_1 and reset $t_1 = t + Y_1$.

If $n > 1$:

Reset: $SS = (n + 1, i_1, \ldots, i_n, N_A)$.

Case 2 $SS = (n, i_1, i_2, \ldots, i_n)$ and $t_1 < t_A, t_1 \leq t_2$

Reset: $t = t_1$.
Reset: $C_1 = C_1 + 1$.
Collect the output data $D(i_1) = t$.

If $n_1 = 1$:

Reset: $SS = (0)$.
Reset: $t_1 = \infty$.

If $n_1 = 2$:

Reset: $SS = (1, 0, i_2)$.
Reset: $t_1 = \infty$.

If $n_1 > 2$:

Reset $\mathbf{SS} = (n - 1, i_3, i_2, \ldots, i_n)$.

Generate Y_1 and reset $t_1 = t + Y_1$.

Case 3 $\mathbf{SS} = (n, i_1, i_2, \ldots, i_n)$ and $t_2 < t_A$, $t_2 < t_1$

The updatings in Case 3 are left as an exercise.

If we simulate the system according to the preceding, stopping the simulation at some predetermined termination point, then by using the output variables as well as the final values of the counting variables C_1 and C_2, we obtain data on the arrival and departure times of the various customers as well as on the number of services performed by each server.

6.5   An Inventory Model

Consider a shop that stocks a particular type of product that it sells for a price of r per unit. Customers demanding this product appear in accordance with a Poisson process with rate λ, and the amount demanded by each one is a random variable having distribution G. In order to meet demands, the shopkeeper must keep an amount of the product on hand and whenever the on-hand inventory becomes low, additional units are ordered from the distributor. The shopkeeper uses a so-called (s,S) ordering policy; namely, whenever the on hand inventory is less than s and there is no presently outstanding order, then an amount is ordered to bring it up to S, where $s < S$. That is, if the present inventory level is x and no order is outstanding, then if $x < s$ the amount $S - x$ is ordered. The cost of ordering y units of the product is a specified function $c(y)$, and it takes L units of time until the order is delivered, with the payment being made upon delivery. In addition, the shop pays an inventory holding cost of h per unit item per unit time. Suppose further that whenever a customer demands more of the product than is presently available, then the amount on hand is sold and the remainder of the order is lost to the shop.

Let us see how we can use simulation to estimate the shop's expected profit up to some fixed time T. To do so, we start by defining the variables and events as follows.

Time Variable t

System State Variable (x, y)

where x is the amount of inventory on hand, and y is the amount on order.

Counter Variables

C, the total amount of ordering costs by t

H, the total amount of inventory holding costs by t

R, the total amount of revenue earned by time t

Events will consist of either a customer or an order arriving. The event times are

t_0, the arrival time of the next customer

t_1, the time at which the order being filled will be delivered. If there is no outstanding order then we take the value of t_1 to be ∞.

The updating is accomplished by considering which of the event times is smaller. If we are presently at time t and we have the values of the preceding variables, then we move along in time as follows.

Case 1 $t_0 < t_1$

Reset: $H = H + (t_0 - t)xh$ since between times t and t_0 we incur a holding cost of $(t_0 - t)h$ for each of the x units in inventory.

Reset: $t = t_0$.

Generate D, a random variable having distribution G. D is the demand of the customer that arrived at time t_0.

Let $w = \min(D, x)$ be the amount of the order that can be filled. The inventory after filling this order is $x - w$.

Reset: $R = R + wr$.

Reset: $x = x - w$.

If $x < s$ and $y = 0$ then reset $y = S - x$, $t_1 = t + L$.

Generate U and reset $t_0 = t - \dfrac{1}{\lambda} \log(U)$.

Case 2 $t_1 \leq t_0$

Reset: $H = H + (t_1 - t)xh$.

Reset: $t = t_1$.

Reset: $C = C + c(y)$.

Reset: $x = x + y$.

Reset: $y = 0$, $t_1 = \infty$.

By using the preceding updating schedule it is easy to write a simulation program to analyze the model. We could then run the simulation until the first event occurs after some large preassigned time T, and we could then use $(R - C - H)/T$ as an estimate of the shop's average profit per unit time. Doing this for varying values of s and S would then enable us to determine a good inventory ordering policy for the shop.

6.6   A Repair Problem

A system needs n working machines to be operational. To guard against machine breakdown, additional machines are kept available as spares. Whenever a machine breaks down it is immediately replaced by a spare and is itself sent to the repair facility, which consists of a single repairperson who repairs failed machines one at a time. Once a failed machine has been repaired it becomes available as a spare to be used when the need arises (see Figure 6.4). All repair times are independent random variables having the common distribution function G. Each time a machine is put into use the amount of time it functions before breaking down is a random variable, independent of the past, having distribution function F.

The system is said to "crash" when a machine fails and no spares are available. Assuming that there are initially $n + s$ functional machines of which n are put

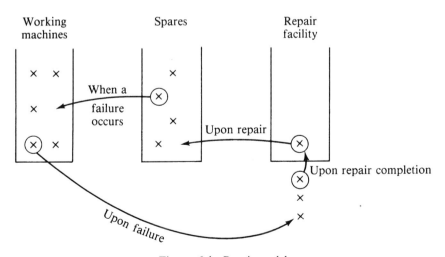

Figure 6.4   Repair model

in use and s are kept as spares, we are interested in simulating this system so as to approximate $E[T]$, where T is the time at which the system crashes.

To simulate the preceding we utilize the following variables.

1. Time variable t
2. System state variable r: the number of machines that are down at time t

Since the system state variable will change either when a working machine breaks down or when a repair is completed, we say that an "event" occurs whenever either of these occurs. In order to know when the next event will occur, we need to keep track of the times at which the machines presently in use will fail and the time at which the machine presently being repaired (if there is a machine in repair) will complete its repair. Because we will always need to determine the smallest of the n failure times, it is convenient to store these n times in an ordered list. Thus it is convenient to let the event list be as follows:

$$\text{Event List: } t_1 \le t_2 \le t_3 \le \cdots \le t_n, t^*$$

where $t_1, \ldots, t_n$ are the times (in order) at which the n machines presently in use will fail, and t^* is the time at which the machine presently in repair will become operational, or if there is no machine presently being repaired then $t^* = \infty$.

To begin the simulation, we initialize these quantities as follows.

Initialize

Set $t = r = 0$, $t^* = \infty$.

Generate $X_1, \ldots, X_n$, independent random variables each having distribution F. Order these values and let t_i be the ith smallest one, $i = 1, \ldots, n$.

Set Event list: $t_1, \ldots, t_n, t^*$.

Updating of the system proceeds according to the following two cases.

Case 1 $t_1 < t^*$

Reset: $t = t_1$.

Reset: $r = r + 1$ (because another machine has failed).

If $r = s + 1$, stop this run and collect the data $T = t$ (since, as there are now $s + 1$ machines down, no spares are available).

If $r < s + 1$, generate a random variable X having distribution F. This random variable will represent the working time of the spare which will now be put into use. Now reorder the values $t_2, t_3, \ldots, t_n, t + X$ and let t_i be the ith smallest of these values, $i = 1, \ldots, n$.

If $r = 1$, generate a random variable Y having distribution function G and reset $t^* = t + Y$. (This is necessary because in this case the machine that has just failed is the only failed machine and thus repair will immediately begin on it; Y will be its repair time and so its repair will be completed at time $t + Y$.)

Case 2 $t^* \leq t_1$

Reset: $t = t^*$.

Reset: $r = r - 1$.

If $r > 0$, generate a random variable Y having distribution function G, and representing the repair time of the machine just entering service, and reset $t^* = t + Y$.

If $r = 0$, set $t^* = \infty$.

The above rules for updating are illustrated in Figure 6.5.

Each time we stop (which occurs when $r = s + 1$) we say that a run is completed. The output for the run is the value of the crash time T. We then reinitialize and simulate another run. In all, we do a total of, say, k runs with the successive output variables being $T_1, \ldots, T_k$. Since these k random variables are independent and each represents a crash time, their average—that is, $\sum_{i=1}^{k} T_i / k$, is the estimate of $E[T]$, the mean crash time. The question of determining when to stop the simulation—that is, determining the value of k—is considered in Chapter 7, which presents the methods to statistically analyze the output from simulation runs.

6.7   Exercising a Stock Option

Let $S_n, n \geq 0$ denote the price of a specified stock at the end of day n. A common model is to suppose that

$$S_n = S_0 \exp\{X_1 + \cdots + X_n\}, \qquad n \geq 0$$

where $X_1, X_2, \ldots$ is a sequence of independent normal random variables, each with mean μ and variance σ^2. This model, which supposes that the each day's percentage increase in price over the previous day has a common distribution,

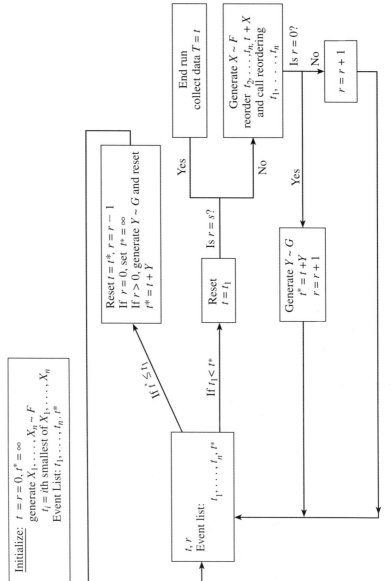

Figure 6.5

is called the *lognormal random walk model*. Let $\alpha = \mu + \sigma^2/2$. Suppose now that you own an option to purchase one unit of this stock at a fixed price K, called the *striking price*, at the end of any of the next N days. If you exercise this option when the stock's price is S then, because you only pay the amount K, we will call this a gain of $S - K$ (since you could theoretically immediately turn around and sell the stock at the price S). The expected gain in owning the option (which clearly would never be exercised if the stock's price does not exceed K during the time period of interest) depends on the option exercising policy you employ. Now, it can be shown that if $\alpha \geq 0$ then the optimal policy is to wait until the last possible moment and then exercise the option if the price exceeds K and not exercise otherwise. Since $X_1 + \cdots + X_N$ is a normal random variable with mean $N\mu$ and variance $N\sigma^2$, it is not difficult to explicitly compute the return from this policy. However, it is not at all easy to characterize an optimal, or even a near optimal, policy when $\alpha < 0$, and for any reasonably good policy it is not possible to explicitly evaluate the expected gain. We will now give a policy that can be employed when $\alpha < 0$. This policy, although far from being an optimal policy, appears to be reasonably good. It calls for exercising the option when there are m days to go whenever, for each $i = 1, \ldots, m$, that action leads to a higher expected payoff than letting exactly i days go by and then either exercising (if the price at that point is greater than K) or giving up on ever exercising.

Let $P_m = S_{N-m}$ denote the price of the stock when there are m days to go before the option expires. The policy we suggest is as follows:

Policy If there are m days to go, then exercise the option at this time if

$$P_m > K$$

and, if for each $i = 1, \ldots, m$

$$P_m > K + P_m e^{i\alpha} \Phi(\sigma\sqrt{i} + b_i) - K\Phi(b_i)$$

where

$$b_i = \frac{i\mu - \log(K/P_m)}{\sigma\sqrt{i}}$$

and where $\Phi(x)$ is the standard normal distribution function and can be accurately approximated by the following formula: For $x \geq 0$

$$\Phi(x) \approx 1 - \frac{1}{\sqrt{2\pi}}(a_1 y + a_2 y^2 + a_3 y^3)e^{-x^2/2}$$

For $x < 0$, $\Phi(x) \approx 1 - \Phi(-x)$; where

$$y = \frac{1}{1 + 0.33267x}$$
$$a_1 = 0.4361836$$
$$a_2 = -0.1201676$$
$$a_3 = 0.9372980$$ ■

Let SP denote the price of the stock when the option is exercised, if it is exercised, and let SP be K if the option is never exercised. To determine the expected worth of the preceding policy—that is, to determine $E[SP] - K$—it is necessary to resort to simulation. For given parameters μ, σ, N, K, S_0 it is easy enough to simulate the price of the stock on separate days by generating X, a normal random variable with mean μ and standard deviation σ, and then using the relation

$$P_{m-1} = P_m e^X$$

Thus, if P_m is the price with m days to go and the policy does not call for exercising the option at this time, then we would generate X and determine the new price P_{m-1} and have the computer check whether the policy calls for exercising at this point. If so, then for that simulation run $SP = P_{m-1}$; if not, then we would determine the price at the end of the next day, and so on. The average value, over a large number of simulation runs, of $SP - K$ would then be our estimate of the expected value of owning the option when you are using the preceding policy.

6.8   Verification of the Simulation Model

The end product of the discrete event approach to simulation is a computer program which one hopes is free of error. To verify that there are indeed no bugs in the program, one should, of course, use all the "standard" techniques of debugging computer programs. However, there are several techniques that are particularly applicable in debugging simulation models, and we now discuss some of them.

As with all large programs one should attempt to debug in "modules" or subroutines. That is, one should attempt to break down the program into small and manageable entities that are logical wholes and then attempt to debug these entities. For example, in simulation models the generation of random variables constitutes one such module, and these modules should be checked separately.

The simulation should always be written broadly with a large number of input variables. Oftentimes by choosing suitable values we can reduce the simulation model to one that can be evaluated analytically or that has been previously extensively studied, so as to compare our simulated results with known answers.

In the testing stage, the program should be written to give as output all the random quantities it generates. By suitably choosing simple special cases, we can then compare the simulated output with the answer worked out by hand (and verified by others). For example, suppose we are simulating the first T time units of a k server queueing system. After inputting the values $T = 8$ (meant to be a small number) and $k = 2$, suppose the simulation program generates the following data:

Customer number:	1	2	3	4	5	6
Arrival time:	1.5	3.6	3.9	5.2	6.4	7.7
Service time:	3.4	2.2	5.1	2.4	3.3	6.2

and suppose that the program gives as output that the average time spent in the system by these six customers is 5.12.

However, by going through the calculations by hand (and having them verified by others), we see that the first customer spent 3.4 time units in the system; the second spent 2.2 (recall there are two servers); the third arrived at time 3.9, entered service at time 4.9 (when the first customer left), and spent 5.1 time units in service—thus, customer 3 spent a time 6.1 in the system; customer 4 arrived at time 5.2, entered service at time 5.8 (when number 2 departed), and departed after an additional time 2.4—thus, customer 4 spent a time 3.0 in the system; and so on. These calculations are presented below:

Arrival time:	1.5	3.6	3.9	5.2	6.4	7.7
Time when service began:	1.5	3.6	4.9	5.8	8.2	10.0
Departure time:	4.9	5.8	10.0	8.2	11.5	16.2
Time in system:	3.4	2.2	6.1	3.0	5.1	8.5

Hence, the output for the average time spent in the system by all arrivals up to time $T = 8$ should have been

$$\frac{3.4 + 2.2 + 6.1 + 3.0 + 5.1 + 8.5}{6} = 4.71666 \ldots$$

thus showing that there is an error in the computer program which gave the output value 5.12.

A useful technique when searching for errors in the computer program is to utilize a *trace*. In a trace, the state variable, the event list, and the counter variables are all printed out after each event occurs. This allows one to follow the simulated system over time so as to determine when it is not performing as intended. (If no errors are apparent when following such a trace, one should then check the calculations relating to the output variables.)

Exercises

1. Write a program to generate the desired output for the model of Section 6.2. Use it to estimate the average time that a customer spends in the system and the average amount of overtime put in by the server, in the case where the arrival process is a Poisson process with rate 10, the service time density is

$$g(x) = 20e^{-40x}(40x)^2, \qquad x > 0$$

and $T = 9$. First try 100 runs and then 1000.

2. Suppose in the model of Section 6.2 that we also wanted to obtain information about the amount of idle time a server would experience in a day. Explain how this could be accomplished.

3. Suppose that jobs arrive at a single server queueing system according to a nonhomogeneous Poisson process, whose rate is initially 4 per hour and increases steadily until it hits 19 per hour after 5 hours and then decreases steadily until it hits 4 per hour after an additional 5 hours. The rate then repeats indefinitely in this fashion—that is, $\lambda(t + 10) = \lambda(t)$. Suppose that the service distribution is exponential with rate 25 per hour. Suppose also that whenever the server completes a service and finds no jobs waiting he goes on break for a time that is uniformly distributed on $(0, 0.3)$. If upon returning from his break there are no jobs waiting, then he goes on another break. Use simulation to estimate the expected amount of time that the server is on break in the first 100 hours of operation. Do 500 simulation runs.

4. Fill in the updating scheme for Case 3 in the model of Section 6.4.

5. Consider a single-server queueing model in which customers arrive according to a nonhomogeneous Poisson process. Upon arriving they either enter service if the server is free or else they join the queue. Suppose, however, that each customer will only wait a random amount of time, having distribution F, in queue before leaving the system. Let G denote the service distribution. Define variables and events so as to analyze this model, and give the updating procedures. Suppose we are interested in

estimating the average number of lost customers by time T, where a customer that departs before entering service is considered lost.

6. Suppose in Exercise 5 that the arrival process is a Poisson process with rate 5; F is the uniform distribution on $(0, 5)$; and G is an exponential random variable with rate 4. Do 500 simulation runs to estimate the expected number of lost customers by time 100. Assume that customers are served in their order of arrival.

7. Repeat Exercise 6, this time supposing that each time the server completes a service, the next customer to be served is the one who has the earliest queue departure time. That is, if two customers are waiting and one would depart the queue if his service has not yet begun by time t_1 and the other if her service had not yet begun by time t_2, then the former would enter service if $t_1 < t_2$ and the latter otherwise. Do you think this will increase or decrease the average number that depart before entering service?

8. In the model of Section 6.4, suppose that G_1 is the exponential distribution with rate 4 and G_2 is exponential with rate 3. Suppose that the arrivals are according to a Poisson process with rate 6. Write a simulation program to generate data corresponding to the first 1000 arrivals. Use it to estimate

   (a) the average time spent in the system by these customers.
   (b) the proportion of services performed by server 1.
   (c) Do a second simulation of the first 1000 arrivals and use it to answer parts (a) and (b). Compare your answers to the ones previously obtained.

9. Suppose in the two-server parallel model of Section 6.4 that each server has its own queue, and that upon arrival a customer joins the shortest one. An arrival finding both queues at the same size (or finding both servers empty) goes to server 1.

   (a) Determine appropriate variables and events to analyze this model and give the updating procedure.

   Using the same distributions and parameters as in Exercise 8, find

   (b) the average time spent in the system by the first 1000 customers.
   (c) the proportion of the first 1000 services performed by server 1.

   Before running your program, do you expect your answers in parts (b) and (c) to be larger or smaller than the corresponding answers in Exercise 8?

10. Suppose in Exercise 9 that each arrival is sent to server 1 with probability p, independent of anything else.

    (a) Determine appropriate variables and events to analyze this model and give the updating procedure.

(b) Using the parameters of Exercise 9, and taking p equal to your estimate of part (c) of that problem, simulate the system to estimate the quantities defined in parts (b) and (c) of Exercise 9. Do you expect your answers to these problems to be larger or smaller than that obtained in Exercise 9?

11. For the repair model presented in Section 6.6:

(a) Write a computer program for this model.

(b) Use your program to estimate the mean crash time in the case where $n = 4$, $s = 3$, $F(x) = 1 - e^{-x}$, and $G(x)$ $1 - e^{-2x}$.

12. In the model of Section 6.6, suppose that the repair facility consists of two servers, each of whom takes a random amount of time having distribution G to service a failed machine. Draw a flow diagram for this system.

13. A system experiences shocks that occur in accordance with a Poisson process having a rate of 1/hour. Each shock has a certain amount of damage associated with it. These damages are assumed to be independent random variables (which are also independent of the times at which the shocks occur), having the common density function

$$f(x) = xe^{-x}, \qquad x > 0$$

Damages dissipate in time at an exponential rate α—that is, a shock whose initial damage is x will have remaining damage value $xe^{-\alpha s}$ at time s after it occurs. In addition, the damage values are cumulative. (Thus, for example, if by time t there have been a total of two shocks, which originated at times t_1 and t_2 and had initial damages x_1 and x_2, then the total damage at time t is $\sum_{i=1}^{2} x_i e^{-\alpha(t-t_i)}$.) The system fails when the total damage exceeds some fixed constant C.

(a) Suppose we are interested in utilizing a simulation study to estimate the mean time that the system fails. Define the "events" and "variables" of this model and draw a flow diagram indicating how the simulation is to be run.

(b) Write a program that would generate k runs.

(c) Verify your program by comparing output with a by-hand calculation.

(d) With $\alpha = 0.5$, $C = 5$, and $k = 1000$, run your program and use the output to estimate the expected time until the system fails.

14. Messages arrive at a communications facility in accordance with a Poisson process having a rate of 2/hour. The facility consists of three channels, and an arriving message will either go to a free channel if any of them are free or else will be lost if all channels are busy. The amount of time that a message ties up a channel is a random variable that depends on

the weather condition at the time the message arrives. Specifically, if the message arrives when the condition is "good," then its processing time is a random variable having distribution function

$$F(x) = x, \qquad 0 < x < 1$$

whereas if the condition is "bad" when a message arrives, then its processing time has distribution function

$$F(x) = x^3, \qquad 0 < x < 1$$

Initially, the condition is good, and it alternates between good and bad periods—with the good periods having fixed lengths of 2 hours and the bad periods having fixed lengths of 1 hour. (Thus, for example, at time 5 the condition changes from good to bad.)

Suppose we are interested in the distribution of the number of lost messages by time $T = 100$.

(a) Define the events and variables that enable us to use the discrete event approach.

(b) Write a flow diagram of the above.

(c) Write a program for the above.

(d) Verify your program by comparing an output with a hand calculation.

(e) Run your program to estimate the mean number of lost messages in the first 100 hours of operation.

15. Estimate, by a simulation study, the expected worth of owning an option to purchase a stock anytime in the next 20 days for a price of 100 if the present price of the stock is 100. Assume the model of Section 6.8, with $\mu = -0.05$, $\sigma = 0.3$, and employ the strategy presented there.

References

Banks, J., and J. Carson, *Discrete-Event System Simulation,* Prentice-Hall, New Jersey, 1984.

Clymer, J., *Systems Analysis using Simulation and Markov Models,* Prentice-Hall, New Jersey, 1990.

Gottfried, B., *Elements of Stochastic Process Simulation,* Prentice-Hall, New Jersey, 1984.

Law, A. M., and W. D. Kelton, *Simulation Modelling and Analysis,* Second Ed., McGraw-Hill, New York, 1991.

Mitrani, I., *Simulation Techniques for Discrete Event Systems,* Cambridge University Press, Cambridge, U.K., 1982.

Peterson, R., and E. Silver, *Decision Systems for Inventory Management and Production Planning,* Wiley, New York, 1979.

Pritsker, A., and C. Pedgen, *Introduction to Simulation and SLAM,* Halsted Press, New York, 1979.

Shannon, R. E., *Systems Simulation: The Art and Science,* Prentice-Hall, New Jersey, 1975.

Solomon, S. L., *Simulation of Waiting Line Systems,* Prentice-Hall, New Jersey, 1983.

Chapter 7 | Statistical Analysis of Simulated Data

Introduction

A simulation study is usually undertaken to determine the value of some quantity θ connected with a particular stochastic model. A simulation of the relevant system results in the output data X, a random variable whose expected value is the quantity of interest θ. A second independent simulation—that is, a second simulation run—provides a new and independent random variable having mean θ. This continues until we have amassed a total of k runs—and the k independent random variables $X_1, \ldots, X_k$—all of which are identically distributed with mean θ. The average of these k values, $\bar{X} = \sum_{i=1}^{k} X_i/k$, is then used as an estimator, or approximator, of θ.

In this chapter we consider the problem of deciding when to stop the simulation study—that is, deciding on the appropriate value of k. To help us decide when to stop, we will find it useful to consider the quality of our estimator of θ. In addition, we will also show how to obtain an interval in which we can assert that θ lies, with a certain degree of confidence.

The final two sections of this chapter show how we can estimate the quality of more complicated estimators than the sample mean—by using an important statistical technique known as "bootstrap estimators." The application of the bootstrap approach to simulation studies is given in the final section of this chapter.

7.1   The Sample Mean and Sample Variance

Suppose that $X_1, \ldots, X_n$ are independent random variables having the same distribution function. Let θ and σ^2 denote, respectively, their mean and variance—that is, $\theta = E[X_i]$ and $\sigma^2 = \text{Var}(X_i)$. The quantity

$$\bar{X} \equiv \sum_{i=1}^{n} \frac{X_i}{n}$$

which is the arithmetic average of the n data values, is called the *sample mean*. When the population mean θ is unknown, the sample mean is often used to estimate it.

Because

$$E[\bar{X}] = E\left[\sum_{i=1}^{n} \frac{X_i}{n}\right]$$

$$= \sum_{i=1}^{n} \frac{E[X_i]}{n} \tag{7.1}$$

$$= \frac{n\theta}{n} = \theta$$

it follows that $\bar{X}$ is an unbiased estimator of θ, where we say that an estimator of a parameter is an unbiased estimator of that parameter if its expected value is equal to the parameter.

To determine the "worth" of $\bar{X}$ as an estimator of the population mean θ, we consider its mean square error—that is, the expected value of the squared difference between $\bar{X}$ and θ. Now

$$E[(\bar{X} - \theta)^2] = \text{Var}(\bar{X}) \qquad (\text{since } E[\bar{X}] = \theta)$$

$$= \text{Var}\left(\frac{1}{n} \sum_{1}^{n} X_i\right)$$

$$= \frac{1}{n^2} \sum_{i=1}^{n} \text{Var}(X_i) \qquad (\text{by independence}) \tag{7.2}$$

$$= \frac{\sigma^2}{n} \qquad (\text{since } \text{Var}(X_i) = \sigma^2)$$

Thus, $\bar{X}$, the sample mean of the n data values $X_1, \ldots, X_n$, is a random variable with mean θ and variance σ^2/n. Since a random variable is unlikely to be too many standard deviations—equal to the square root of its variance—from its mean, if follows that $\bar{X}$ is a good estimator of θ when $\sigma/\sqrt{n}$ is small.

Remark The justification for the above statement that a random variable is unlikely to be too many standard deviations away from its mean follows from both the Chebyshev inequality and, more importantly for simulation studies, from the central limit theorem. Indeed, for any $c > 0$, Chebyshev's inequality (see Section 2.7 of Chapter 2) yields the rather conservative bound

$$P\left\{|\bar{X} - \theta| > \frac{c\sigma}{\sqrt{n}}\right\} \leq \frac{1}{c^2}$$

However, when n is large, as will usually be the case in simulations, we can apply the central limit theorem to assert that $(\bar{X} - \theta)/(\sigma/\sqrt{n})$ is approximately distributed as a unit normal random variable; and thus

$$P\{|\bar{X} - \theta| > c\sigma/\sqrt{n}\} \approx P\{|Z| > c\}, \qquad \text{where } Z \text{ is a unit normal}$$
$$= 2[1 - \phi(c)] \tag{7.3}$$

where ϕ is the unit normal distribution function. For example, since $\phi(1.96) = 0.975$, Equation (7.3) states that the probability that the sample mean differs from θ by more than $1.96\sigma/\sqrt{n}$ is approximately 0.05, whereas the weaker Chebyshev inequality only yields that this probability is less than $1/(1.96)^2 = 0.2603$. ∎

The difficulty with directly using the value of σ^2/n as an indication of how well the sample mean of n data values estimates the population mean is that the population variance σ^2 is not usually known. Thus, we also need to estimate it. Since

$$\sigma^2 = E[(X - \theta)^2]$$

is the average of the square of the difference between a datum value and its (unknown) mean, it might seem upon using $\bar{X}$ as the estimator of the mean that a natural estimator of σ^2 would be $\Sigma_{i=1}^{n}(X_i - \bar{X})^2/n$, the average of the squared distances between the data values and the estimated mean. However, to make the estimator unbiased (and for other technical reasons) we prefer to divide the sum of squares by $n - 1$ rather than n.

Definition   *The quantity S^2, defined by*

$$S^2 = \frac{\sum_{i=1}^{n} (X_i - \bar{X})^2}{n - 1}$$

is called the sample variance.

Using the algebraic identity

$$\sum_{i=1}^{n} (X_i - \bar{X})^2 = \sum_{i=1}^{n} X_i^2 - n\bar{X}^2 \tag{7.4}$$

whose proof is left as an exercise, we now show that the sample variance is an unbiased estimator of σ^2.

Proposition

$$E[S^2] = \sigma^2$$

Proof   Using the identity (7.4) we see that

$$(n - 1)E[S^2] = E\left[\sum_{i=1}^{n} X_i^2\right] - nE[\bar{X}^2] \tag{7.5}$$

$$= nE[X_1^2] - nE[\bar{X}^2]$$

where the last equality follows since the X_i all have the same distribution. Recalling that for any random variable Y, $\text{Var}(Y) = E[Y^2] - (E[Y])^2$ or, equivalently,

$$E[Y^2] = \text{Var}(Y) + (E[Y])^2$$

we obtain that

$$E[X_1^2] = \text{Var}(X_1) + (E[X_1])^2$$

$$= \sigma^2 + \theta^2$$

and

$$E[\bar{X}^2] = \text{Var}(\bar{X}) + (E[\bar{X}])^2$$

$$= \frac{\sigma^2}{n} + \theta^2 \qquad \text{[from (7.2) and (7.1)]}$$

Thus, from Equation (7.5), we obtain that

$$(n - 1)E[S^2] = n(\sigma^2 + \theta^2) - n\left(\frac{\sigma^2}{n} + \theta^2\right) = (n - 1)\sigma^2$$

which proves the result. ∎

We use the sample variance S^2 as our estimator of the population variance σ^2, and we use $S = \sqrt{S^2}$, the so-called sample standard deviation, as our estimator of σ.

Suppose now that, as in a simulation, we have the option of continually generating additional data values X_i. If our objective is to estimate the value of $\theta = E[X_i]$, when should we stop generating new data values? The answer to this question is that we should first choose an acceptable value d for the standard deviation of our estimator—for if d is the standard deviation of the estimator $\overline{X}$, then we can, for example, be 95% certain that $\overline{X}$ will not differ from θ by more than $1.96d$. We should then continue to generate new data until we have generated n data values for which our estimate of $\sigma/\sqrt{n}$—namely, $S/\sqrt{n}$—is less than the acceptable value d. Since the sample standard deviation S may not be a particular good estimate of σ (nor may the normal approximation be valid) when the sample size is small, we thus recommend the following procedure to determine when to stop generating new data values.

A Method for Determining When to Stop Generating New Data

1. Choose an acceptable value d for the standard deviation of the estimator.
2. Generate at least 30 data values.
3. Continue to generate additional data values, stopping when you have generated k values and $S/\sqrt{k} < d$, where S is the sample standard deviation based on those k values.
4. The estimate of θ is given by $\overline{X} = \sum_{i=1}^{k} X_i / k$.

Example 7a Consider a service system in which no new customers are allowed to enter after 5 P.M. Suppose that each day follows the same probability law and that we are interested in estimating the expected time at which the last customer departs the system. Furthermore, suppose we want to be at least 95% certain that our estimated answer will not differ from the true value by more than 15 seconds.

To satisfy the above requirement it is necessary that we continually generate data values relating to the time at which the last customer departs (each time by doing a simulation run) until we have generated a total of k values, where k is at least 30 and is such that $1.96S/\sqrt{k} < 15$ —where S is the sample standard deviation (measured in seconds) of these k data values. Our estimate of the expected time at which the last customer departs will be the average of the k data values. ■

In order to use the above technique for determining when to stop generating new values, it would be valuable if we had a method for recursively computing the successive sample means and sample variances, rather than having to recompute from scratch each time a new datum value is generated. We now show how this can be done. Consider the sequence of data values $X_1, X_2, \ldots$, and let

$$\bar{X}_j = \sum_{i=1}^{j} \frac{X_i}{j}$$

and

$$S_j^2 = \sum_{i=1}^{j} \frac{(X_i - \bar{X}_j)^2}{j - 1}, \qquad j \geq 2$$

denote, respectively, the sample mean and sample variance of the first j data values. The following recursion should be used to successively compute the current value of the sample mean and sample variance.

With $S_1^2 = 0$, $\bar{X}_0 = 0$.

$$\bar{X}_{j+1} = \bar{X}_j + \frac{X_{j+1} - \bar{X}_j}{j + 1} \tag{7.6}$$

$$S_{j+1}^2 = \left(1 - \frac{1}{j}\right)S_j^2 + (j + 1)(\bar{X}_{j+1} - \bar{X}_j)^2 \tag{7.7}$$

Example 7b If the first three data values are $X_1 = 5$, $X_2 = 14$, $X_3 = 9$, then Equations (7.6) and (7.7) yield that

$$\bar{X}_1 = 5$$

$$\bar{X}_2 = 5 + \frac{9}{2} = \frac{19}{2}$$

$$S_2^2 = 2\left(\frac{19}{2} - 5\right)^2 = \frac{81}{2}$$

$$\bar{X}_3 = \frac{19}{2} + \frac{1}{3}\left(9 - \frac{19}{2}\right) = \frac{28}{3}$$

$$S_3^2 = \frac{81}{4} + 3\left(\frac{28}{3} - \frac{19}{2}\right)^2 = \frac{61}{3}$$

■

The analysis is somewhat modified when the data values are Bernoulli (or 0–1) random variables, as is the case when we are estimating a probability. That is, suppose we can generate random variables X, such that

$$X_i = \begin{cases} 1 & \text{with probability } p \\ 0 & \text{with probability } 1 - p \end{cases}$$

and suppose we are interested in estimating $E[X_1] = p$. Since, in this situation,

$$\text{Var}(X_i) = p(1 - p)$$

there is no need to utilize the sample variance to estimate $\text{Var}(X_i)$. Indeed, if we have generated n values $X_1, \ldots, X_n$, then as the estimate of p will be

$$\bar{X}_n = \sum_{i=1}^{n} \frac{X_i}{n}$$

a natural estimate of $\text{Var}(X_i)$ is $\bar{X}_n(1 - \bar{X}_n)$. Hence, in this case, we have the following method for deciding when to stop.

1. Choose an acceptable value d for the standard deviation of the estimator.
2. Generate at least 30 data values.
3. Continue to generate additional data values, stopping when you have generated k values and $[\bar{X}_k(1 - \bar{X}_k)/k]^{1/2} < d$.
4. The estimate of p is $\bar{X}_k$, the average of the k data values.

Example 7c Suppose, in Example 7a, we were interested in estimating the probability that there was still a customer in the store at 5:30. To do so, we would simulate successive days and let

$$X_i = \begin{cases} 1 & \text{if there is a customer present at 5:30 on day } i \\ 0 & \text{otherwise} \end{cases}$$

We would simulate at least 30 days and continue to simulate until the kth day, where k is such that $[p_k(1 - p_k)/k]^{1/2} < d$, where $p_k = \bar{X}_k$ is the proportion of these k days in which there is a customer present at 5:30 and where d is an acceptable value for the standard deviation of the estimator p_k. ∎

7.2 Interval Estimates of a Population Mean

Suppose again that $X_1, X_2, \ldots, X_n$ are independent random variables from a common distribution having mean θ and variance σ^2. Although the sample mean

$\bar{X} = \sum_{i=1}^{n} X_i / n$ is an effective estimator of θ, we do not really expect that $\bar{X}$ will be equal to θ but rather that it will be "close." As a result, it is sometimes more valuable to be able to specify an interval for which we have a certain degree of confidence that θ lies within.

To obtain such an interval we need the (approximate) distribution of the estimator $\bar{X}$. To determine this, first recall, from Equations (7.1) and (7.2), that

$$E[\bar{X}] = \theta, \qquad \text{Var}(\bar{X}) = \frac{\sigma^2}{n}$$

and thus, from the central limit theorem, it follows that for large n

$$\sqrt{n}\frac{(\bar{X} - \theta)}{\sigma} \sim N(0, 1)$$

where $\sim N(0, 1)$ means "is approximately distributed as a unit normal." In addition, if we replace the unknown standard deviation σ by its estimator S, the sample standard deviation, then it still remains the case (by a result known as Slutsky's theorem) that the resulting quantity is approximately a unit normal. That is, when n is large

$$\sqrt{n}(\bar{X} - \theta)/S \sim N(0, 1) \tag{7.8}$$

Now for any α, $0 < \alpha < 1$, let z_α be such that

$$P\{Z > z_\alpha\} = \alpha$$

where Z is a unit normal random variable. (For example, $z_{.025} = 1.96$.) It follows from the symmetry of the unit normal density function about the origin that $z_{1-\alpha}$, the point at which the area under the density to its right is equal to $1 - \alpha$, is such that (see Figure 7.1)

$$z_{1-\alpha} = -z_\alpha$$

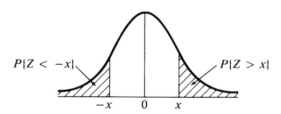

$$P\{Z < -x\} \qquad\qquad P\{Z > x\}$$

$$-x \qquad 0 \qquad x$$

Figure 7.1   Unit normal density

Therefore (see Figure 7.1)

$$P\{-z_{\alpha/2} < Z < z_{\alpha/2}\} = 1 - \alpha$$

It thus follows from (7.8) that

$$P\left\{-z_{\alpha/2} < \sqrt{n}\,\frac{(\bar{X} - \theta)}{S} < z_{\alpha/2}\right\} \approx 1 - \alpha$$

or, equivalently, upon multiplying by -1,

$$P\left\{-z_{\alpha/2} < \sqrt{n}\,\frac{(\theta - \bar{X})}{S} < z_{\alpha/2}\right\} \approx 1 - \alpha$$

which is equivalent to

$$P\left\{\bar{X} - z_{\alpha/2}\,\frac{S}{\sqrt{n}} < \theta < \bar{X} + z_{\alpha/2}\,\frac{S}{\sqrt{n}}\right\} \approx 1 - \alpha \qquad (7.9)$$

In other words, with probability $1 - \alpha$ the population mean θ will lie within the region $\bar{X} \pm z_{\alpha/2}S/\sqrt{n}$.

Definition *If the observed values of the sample mean and the sample standard deviation are $\bar{X} = \bar{x}$ and $S = s$, call the interval $\bar{x} \pm z_{\alpha/2}s/\sqrt{n}$ an (approximate) $100(1 - \alpha)$ percent confidence interval estimate of θ.*

Remarks

1. To clarify the meaning of a "$100(1 - \alpha)$ percent confidence interval," consider, for example, the case where $\alpha = 0.05$, and so $z_{\alpha/2} = 1.96$. Now before the data are observed, it will be true, with probability (approximately) equal to 0.95, that the sample mean $\bar{X}$ and the sample standard deviation S will be such that θ will lie between $\bar{X} \pm 1.96S/\sqrt{n}$. After $\bar{X}$ and S are observed to equal, respectively, $\bar{x}$ and s, there is no longer any probability concerning whether θ lies in the interval $\bar{x} \pm 1.96s/\sqrt{n}$, for either it does or it does not. However, we are "95% confident" that in this situation it does lie in this interval (since we know that over the long run such intervals will indeed contain the mean 95 percent of the time).

2. (A technical remark.) The above analysis is based on Equation (7.8), which states that $\sqrt{n}(\bar{X} - \theta)/S$ is approximately a unit normal random variable when n is large. Now if the original data values X_i were themselves normally distributed, then it is known that this quantity has (exactly) a t-distribution with $n - 1$ degrees of freedom. For this reason, many

authors have proposed using this approximate distribution in the general case where the original distribution need not be normal. However, since it is not clear that the

t-distribution with $n - 1$ degrees of freedom results in a better approximation than the normal in the general case, and because these two distributions are approximately equal for large n, we have used the normal approximation rather than introducing the t-random variable. ■

Consider now the case, as in a simulation study, where additional data values can be generated and the question is to determine when to stop generating new data values. One solution to this is to initially choose values α and l and to continue generating data until the approximate $100(1 - \alpha)$ percent confidence interval estimate of θ is less than l. Since the length of this interval will be $2z_{\alpha/2}S/\sqrt{n}$ we can accomplish this by the following technique.

1. Generate at least 30 data values.

2. Continue to generate additional data values, stopping when the number of values you have generated—call it k—is such that $2z_{\alpha/2}S/\sqrt{k} < l$, where S is the sample standard deviation based on those k values. [The value of S should be constantly updated, using the recursion given by (7.6) and (7.7), as new data are generated.]

3. If $\bar{x}$ and s are the observed values of $\bar{X}$ and S, then the $100(1 - \alpha)$ percent confidence interval estimate of θ, whose length is less than l, is
$\bar{x} \pm 2z_{\alpha/2}s/\sqrt{k}$.

A Technical Remark   The more statistically sophisticated reader might wonder about our use of an approximate confidence interval whose theory was based on the assumption that the sample size was fixed when in the above situation the sample size is clearly a random variable depending on the data values generated. This, however, can be justified when the sample size is large, and so from the viewpoint of simulation we can safely ignore this subtlety. ■

As noted in the previous section, the analysis is modified when $X_1, \ldots, X_n$ are Bernoulli random variables such that

$$X_i = \begin{cases} 1 & \text{with probability } p \\ 0 & \text{with probability } 1 - p \end{cases}$$

Since in this case $\text{Var}(X_i)$ can be estimated by $\bar{X}(1 - \bar{X})$, it follows that the equivalent statement to Equation (7.8) is that when n is large

$$\sqrt{n} \, \frac{(\bar{X} - p)}{\sqrt{\bar{X}(1 - \bar{X})}} \sim N(0, 1) \tag{7.10}$$

Hence, for any α,

$$P\left\{-z_{\alpha/2} < \sqrt{n}\,\frac{(\bar{X} - p)}{\sqrt{\bar{X}(1 - \bar{X})}} < z_{\alpha/2}\right\} = 1 - \alpha$$

or, equivalently,

$$P\{\bar{X} - z_{\alpha/2}\sqrt{\bar{X}(1 - \bar{X})/n} < p < \bar{X} + z_{\alpha/2}\sqrt{\bar{X}(1 - \bar{X})/n}\} = 1 - \alpha$$

Hence, if the observed value of $\bar{X}$ is p_n, we say that the "$100(1 - \alpha)$ percent confidence interval estimate" of p is

$$p_n \pm z_{\alpha/2}\sqrt{p_n(1 - p_n)/n}$$

7.3 The Bootstrapping Technique for Estimating Mean Square Errors

Suppose now that $X_1, \ldots, X_n$ are independent random variables having a common distribution function F, and suppose we are interested in using them to estimate some parameter $\theta(F)$ of the distribution F. For example, $\theta(F)$ could be (as in the previous sections of this chapter) the mean of F, or it could be the median or the variance of F, or any other parameter of F. Suppose further that an estimator of $\theta(F)$—call it $g(X_1, \ldots, X_n)$—has been proposed, and in order to judge its worth as an estimator of $\theta(F)$ we are interested in estimating its mean square error. That is, we are interested in estimating the value of

$$\text{MSE}(F) \equiv E_F[(g(X_1, \ldots, X_n) - \theta(F))^2]$$

[where our choice of notation $\text{MSE}(F)$ suppresses the dependence on the estimator g, and where we have used the notation E_F to indicate that the expectation is to be taken under the assumption that the random variables all have distribution F]. Now whereas there is an immediate estimator of the above MSE—namely, S^2/n—when $\theta(F) = E[X_i]$ and $g(X_1, \ldots, X_n) = \bar{X}$, it is not at all apparent how it can be estimated otherwise. We now present a useful technique, known as the bootstrap technique, for estimating this mean square error.

To begin, note that if the distribution function F were known then we could theoretically compute the expected square of the difference between θ and its estimator; that is, we could compute the mean square error. However, after we observe the values of the n data points, we have a pretty good idea what the underlying distribution looks like. Indeed, suppose that the observed values of the data are $X_i = x_i$, $i = 1, \ldots, n$. We can now estimate the underlying distribution function F by the so-called empirical distribution function F_e, where $F_e(x)$, the estimate of $F(x)$, the probability that a datum value is less than or equal to x, is just the proportion of the n data values that are less than or equal to x. That is,

$$F_e(x) = \frac{\text{number of } i:X_i \leq x}{n}$$

Another way of thinking about F_e is that it is the distribution function of a random variable X_e which is equally likely to take on any of the n values x_i, $i = 1, \ldots, n$. (If the values x_i are not all distinct, then the above is to be interpreted to mean that X_e will equal the value x_i with a probability equal to the number of j such that $x_j = x_i$ divided by n; that is, if $n = 3$ and $x_1 = x_2 = 1$, $x_3 = 2$, then X_e is a random variable that takes on the value 1 with probability $\frac{2}{3}$ and 2 with probability $\frac{1}{3}$.)

Now if F_e is "close" to F, as it should be when n is large [indeed, the strong law of large numbers implies that with probability 1, $F_e(x)$ converges to $F(x)$ as $n \to \infty$, and another result, known as the Glivenko–Cantelli theorem, states that this convergence will, with probability 1, be uniform in x], then $\theta(F_e)$ will probably be close to $\theta(F)$—assuming that θ is, in some sense, a continuous function of the distribution—and MSE(F) should approximately be equal to

$$\text{MSE}(F_e) = E_{F_e}[(g(X_1, \ldots, X_n) - \theta(F_e))^2]$$

In the above expression the X_i are to be regarded as being independent random variables having distribution function F_e. The quantity MSE(F_e) is called the *bootstrap approximation to the mean square error* MSE(F).

To obtain a feel for the effectiveness of the bootstrap approximation to the mean square error, let us consider the one case where its use is not necessary—namely, when estimating the mean of a distribution by the sample mean $\bar{X}$. (Its use is not necessary in this case because there already is an effective way of estimating the mean square error $E[(\bar{X} - \theta)^2] = \sigma^2/n$—namely, by using the observed value of S^2/n.)

Example 7d Suppose we are interested in estimating $\theta(F) = E[X]$ by using the sample mean $\bar{X} = \sum_{i=1}^{n} X_i/n$. If the observed data are x_i, $i = 1, \ldots, n$, then the empirical distribution F_e puts weight $1/n$ on each of the points $x_1, \ldots, x_n$ (combining weights if the x_i are not all distinct). Hence the mean of F_e is

$\theta(F_e) = \bar{x} = \sum_{i=1}^{n} x_i/n$, and thus the bootstrap estimate of the mean square error—call it $\text{MSE}(F_e)$—is given by

$$\text{MSE}(F_e) = E_{F_e}\left[\left(\sum_{i=1}^{n} \frac{X_i}{n} - \bar{x}\right)^2\right]$$

where $X_1, \ldots, X_n$ are independent random variables each distributed according to F_e. Since

$$E_{F_e}\left[\sum_{i=1}^{n} \frac{X_i}{n}\right] = E_{F_e}[X] = \bar{x}$$

it follows that

$$\text{MSE}(F_e) = \text{Var}_{F_e}\left(\sum_{i=1}^{n} \frac{X_i}{n}\right)$$

$$= \frac{\text{Var}_{F_e}(X)}{n}$$

Now

$$\text{Var}_{F_e}(X) = E_{F_e}[(X - E_{F_e}[X])^2]$$

$$= E_{F_e}[(X - \bar{x})^2]$$

$$= \frac{1}{n}\left[\sum_{i=1}^{n} (x_i - \bar{x})^2\right]$$

and so

$$\text{MSE}(F_e) = \frac{\sum_{i=1}^{n} (x_i - \bar{x})^2}{n^2}$$

which compares quite nicely with S^2/n, the usual estimate of the mean square error. Indeed, because the observed value of S^2/n is $\sum_{i=1}^{n} (x_i - \bar{x})^2/[n(n-1)]$, the bootstrap approximation is almost identical. ■

If the data values are $X_i = x_i$, $i = 1, \ldots, n$, then, as the empirical distribution function F_e puts weight $1/n$ on each of the points x_i, it is usually easy to compute the value of $\theta(F_e)$: for example, if the parameter of interest $\theta(F)$ was the variance of the distribution F, then $\theta(F_e) = \text{Var}_{F_e}(X) = \Sigma_{i=1}^n = (x_i - \bar{x})^2/n$. To determine the bootstrap approximation to the mean square error we then have to compute

$$\text{MSE}(F_e) = E_{F_e}[(g(X_1, \ldots, X_n) - \theta(F_e))^2]$$

However, since the above expectation is to be computed under the assumption that $X_1, \ldots, X_n$ are independent random variables distributed according to F_e, it follows that the vector $(X_1, \ldots, X_n)$ is equally likely to take on any of the n^n possible values $(x_{i_1}, x_{i_2}, \ldots, x_{i_n})$, $i_j \in \{1, 2, \ldots, n\}$, $j = 1, \ldots, n$. Therefore,

$$\text{MSE}(F_e) = \sum_{i_n} \cdots \sum_{i_1} \frac{[g(x_{i_1}, \ldots, x_{i_n}) - \theta(F_e)]^2}{n^n}$$

where each i_j goes from 1 to n, and so the computation of $\text{MSE}(F_e)$ requires, in general, summing n^n terms—an impossible task when n is large.

However, as we know, there is an effective way to approximate the average of a large number of terms, namely, by using simulation. Indeed, we could generate a set of n independent random variables $X_1^1, \ldots, X_n^1$ each having distribution function F_e and then set

$$Y_1 = [g(X_1^1, \ldots, X_n^1) - \theta(F_e)]^2$$

Next, we generate a second set $X_1^2, \ldots, X_n^2$ and compute

$$Y_2 = [g(X_1^2, \ldots, X_n^2) - \theta(F_e)]^2$$

and so on, until we have collected the variables $Y_1, Y_2, \ldots, Y_r$. Because these Y_i are independent random variables having mean $\text{MSE}(F_e)$, it follows that we can use their average $\Sigma_{i=1}^r Y_i/r$ as an estimate of $\text{MSE}(F_e)$.

Remarks

1. It is quite easy to generate a random variable X having distribution F_e. Because such a random variable should be equally likely to be $x_1, \ldots, x_n$, just generate a random number U and set $X = x_I$, where $I = \text{Int}(nU) + 1$. (It is easy to check that this will still work even when the x_i are not all distinct.)

2. The above simulation allows us to approximate $\text{MSE}(F_e)$, which is itself an approximation to the desired $\text{MSE}(F)$. As such, it has been reported that roughly 100 simulation runs—that is, choosing $r = 100$—is usually sufficient. ■

The following example illustrates the use of the bootstrap in analyzing the output of a queueing simulation.

Example 7e Suppose in Example 7a that we are interested in estimating the long-run average amount of time a customer spends in the system. That is, letting W_i be the amount of time the ith entering customer spends in the system, $i \geq 1$, we are interested in

$$\theta \equiv \lim_{n \to \infty} \frac{W_1 + W_2 + \cdots + W_n}{n}$$

To show that the above limit does indeed exist (note that the random variables W_i are neither independent nor identically distributed—why?), let N_i denote the number of customers that arrive on day i, and let

$$D_1 = W_1 + \cdots + W_{N_1}$$

$$D_2 = W_{N_1+1} + \cdots + W_{N_1+N_2}$$

and, in general, for $i > 2$,

$$D_i = W_{N_1+\cdots+N_{i-1}+1} + \cdots + W_{N_1+\cdots+N_1}$$

In words, D_i is the sum of the times in the system of all arrivals on day i. We can now express θ as

$$\theta = \lim_{m \to \infty} \frac{D_1 + D_2 + \cdots + D_m}{N_1 + N_2 + \cdots + N_m}$$

where the above follows because the ratio is just the average time in the system of all customers arriving in the first m days. Upon dividing numerator and denominator by m, we obtain

$$\theta = \lim_{m \to \infty} \frac{(D_1 + \cdots + D_m)/m}{(N_1 + \cdots + N_m)/m}$$

Now as each day follows the same probability law, it follows that the random variables $D_1, \ldots, D_m$ are all independent and identically distributed, as are the random variables $N_1, \ldots, N_m$. Hence, by the strong law of large numbers, it follows that the average of the first m of the D_i will, with probability 1, converge to their common expectation, with a similar statement being true for the N_i. Therefore, we see that

$$\theta = \frac{E[D]}{E[N]}$$

where $E[N]$ is the expected number of customers to arrive in a day, and $E[D]$ is the expected sum of the times those customers spend in the system.

To estimate θ we can thus simulate the system over k days, collecting on the ith run the data N_i, D_i, where N_i is the number of customers arriving on day i and D_i is the sum of the times they spend in the system, $i = 1, \ldots , k$. Because the quantity $E[D]$ can then be estimated by

$$\bar{D} = \frac{D_1 + D_2 + \cdots + D_k}{k}$$

and $E[N]$ by

$$\bar{N} = \frac{N_1 + N_2 + \cdots + N_k}{k}$$

it follows that $\theta = E[D]/E[N]$ can be estimated by

$$\text{Estimate of } \theta = \frac{\bar{D}}{\bar{N}} = \frac{D_1 + \cdots + D_k}{N_1 + \cdots + N_k}$$

which, it should be noted, is just the average time in the system of all arrivals during the first k days.

To estimate

$$\text{MSE} = E\left[\left(\frac{\sum\limits_{i=1}^{k} D_i}{\sum\limits_{i=1}^{k} N_i} - \theta\right)^2\right]$$

we employ the bootstrap approach. Suppose the observed value of D_i, N_i is d_i, n_i, $i = 1, \ldots , k$. That is, suppose that the simulation resulted in n_i arrivals on day i spending a total time d_i in the system. Thus the empirical joint distribution function of the random vector D, N puts equal weight on the k pairs d_i, n_i, $i = 1, \ldots , k$. That is, under the empirical distribution function we have

$$P_{F_e}\{D = d_i, N = n_i\} = \frac{1}{k}, \qquad i = 1, \ldots , k$$

Hence,

$$E_{F_e}[D] = \bar{d} = \frac{\sum\limits_{i=1}^{k} d_i}{k}, \qquad E_{F_e}[N] = \bar{n} = \frac{\sum\limits_{i=1}^{k} n_i}{k}$$

and thus,

$$\theta(F_e) = \frac{\bar{d}}{\bar{n}}$$

Hence,

$$\text{MSE}(F_e) = E_{F_e}\left[\left(\frac{\sum\limits_{i=1}^{k} D_i}{\sum\limits_{i=1}^{k} N_i} - \frac{\bar{d}}{\bar{n}}\right)^2\right]$$

where the above is to be computed under the assumption that the k pairs of random vectors D_i, N_i are independently distributed according to F_e.

Since an exact computation of $\text{MSE}(F_e)$ would require computing the sum of k^k terms, we now perform a simulation experiment to approximate it. We generate k independent pairs of random vectors D_i^1, N_i^1, $i = 1, \ldots, k$, according to the empirical distribution function F_e, and then compute

$$Y_1 = \left(\frac{\sum\limits_{i=1}^{k} D_i^1}{\sum\limits_{i=1}^{k} N_i^1} - \frac{\bar{d}}{\bar{n}}\right)^2$$

We then generate a second set D_i^2, N_i^2 and compute the corresponding Y_2. This continues until we have generated the r values $Y_1, \ldots, Y_r$ (where $r = 100$ should suffice). The average of these r values, $\sum_{i=1}^{r} Y_i/r$, is then used to estimate $\text{MSE}(F_e)$, which is itself our estimate of MSE, the mean square error of our estimate of the average amount of time a customer spends in the system. ∎

Remark: The Regenerative Approach The above analysis assumed that each day independently followed the same probability laws. In certain applications, the same probability laws describe the system not over days of fixed lengths but rather over cycles whose length is random. For example, consider a queueing system in which customers arrive in accordance with a Poisson process, and suppose that the first customer arrives at time 0. If the random time T represents the next time that an arrival finds the system empty, then we say that the time from 0 to T constitutes the first cycle. The second cycle would be the time from T until the first time point after T that an arrival finds the system empty, and so on. It is easy to see, in most models, that the movements of the process over each cycle are independent and identically distributed. Hence, if we regard a cycle as being a "day," then all of the preceding analysis remains valid. For example, θ, the average amount of time that a customer spends in the system, is given by $\theta = E[D]/E[N]$, where D is the sum of the times in the system of all arrivals in a cycle and N is the number of such arrivals. If we now generate k cycles, our estimate of θ is still $\sum_{i=1}^{k} D_i / \sum_{i=1}^{k} N_i$. In addition, the mean square error of this estimate can be approximated by using the bootstrap approach exactly as above.

The technique of analyzing a system by simulating "cycles," that is, random intervals during which the process follows the same probability law, is called the regenerative approach. ■

Exercises

1. For any set of numbers $x_1, \ldots, x_n$, prove algebraically that

$$\sum_{i=1}^{n} (x_i - \bar{x})^2 = \sum_{i=1}^{n} x_i^2 - n\bar{x}^2$$

where $\bar{x} = \sum_{i=1}^{n} x_i / n$.

2. Give a probabilistic proof of the result of Exercise 1, by letting X denote a random variable that is equally likely to take on any of the values $x_1, \ldots, x_n$, and then by applying the identity $\text{Var}(X) = E[X^2] - (E[X])^2$.

3. Write a program that uses the recursions given by Equations (7.6) and (7.7) to calculate the sample mean and sample variance of a data set.

4. Continue to generate unit normal random variables until you have generated n of them, where $n \geq 30$ is such that $S/\sqrt{n} < 0.1$, where S is the sample standard deviation of the n data values.

   (a) How many normals do you think will be generated?
   (b) How many normals did you generate?
   (c) What is the sample mean of all the normals generated?
   (d) What is the sample variance?
   (e) Comment on the results of (c) and (d). Were they surprising?

5. Repeat Exercise 4 with the exception that you now continue generating unit normals until $S/\sqrt{n} < 0.01$.

6. Estimate $\int_0^1 \exp(x^2)\,dx$ by generating random numbers. Generate at least 100 values and stop when the standard deviation of your estimator is less than 0.01.

7. To estimate $E[X]$, $X_1, \ldots, X_{16}$ have been simulated with the following values resulting: 10, 11, 10.5, 11.5, 14, 8, 13, 6, 15, 10, 11.5, 10.5, 12, 8, 16, 5. Based on these data, if we want the standard deviation of the estimator of $E[X]$ to be less than 0.1, roughly how many additional simulation runs will be needed?

Exercises 8 and 9 are concerned with estimating e.

8. It can be shown that if we add random numbers until their sum exceeds 1, then the expected number added is equal to e. That is, if

$$N = \min\left\{n: \sum_{i=1}^{n} U_i > 1\right\}$$

then $E[N] = e$.
   (a) Use this preceding to estimate e, using 1000 simulation runs.
   (b) Estimate the variance of the estimator in (a) and give a 95 percent confidence interval estimate of e.

9. Consider a sequence of random numbers and let M denote the first one that is less than its predecessor. That is,

$$M = \min\{n: U_1 \le U_2 \le \cdots \le U_{n-1} > U_n\}$$

   (a) Argue that $P\{M > n\} = \frac{1}{n!}$, $n \ge 0$.
   (b) Use the identity $E[M] = \sum_{n=0}^{\infty} P\{M > n\}$ to show that $E[M] = e$.
   (c) Use part (b) to estimate e, using 1000 simulation runs.
   (d) Estimate the variance of the estimator in (c) and give a 95 percent confidence interval estimate of e.

10. Use the approach that is presented in Example 3a of Chapter 3 to obtain an interval of size less than 0.1, which we can assert, with 95 percent confidence, contains π. How many runs were necessary?

11. Repeat Exercise 10 when we want the interval to be no greater than 0.01.

12. To estimate θ, we generated 20 independent values having mean θ. If the successive values obtained were

   102, 112, 131, 107, 114, 95, 133, 145, 139, 117
   93, 111, 124, 122, 136, 141, 119, 122, 151, 143

how many additional random variables do you think we will have to generate if we want to be 99 percent certain that our final estimate of θ is correct to within ± 0.5?

13. Let $X_1, \ldots, X_n$ be independent identically distributed random variables having unknown mean μ. For given constants $a < b$, we are interested in estimating $p = P\{a < \sum_{i=1}^{n} X_i/n - \mu < b\}$.

    (a) Explain how we can use the bootstrap approach to estimate p.

    (b) Estimate p if $n = 10$ and the values of the X_i are 56, 101, 78, 67, 93, 87, 64, 72, 80, and 69. Take $a = -5$, $b = 5$.

In the following three exercises $X_1, \ldots, X_n$ is a sample from a distribution whose variance is (the unknown) σ^2. We are planning to estimate σ^2 by the sample variance $S^2 = \sum_{i=1}^{n} (X_i - \bar{X})^2/(n - 1)$, and we want to use the bootstrap technique to estimate $\text{Var}(S^2)$.

14. If $n = 2$ and $X_1 = 1$ and $X_2 = 3$, what is the bootstrap estimate of $\text{Var}(S^2)$?

15. If $n = 15$ and the data are

$$5, 4, 9, 6, 21, 17, 11, 20, 7, 10, 21, 15, 13, 16, 8$$

approximate (by a simulation) the bootstrap estimate of $\text{Var}(S^2)$.

16. Consider a single-server system in which potential customers arrive in accordance with a Poisson process having rate 4.0. A potential customer will only enter if there are three or fewer other customers in the system when he or she arrives. The service time of a customer is exponential with rate 4.2. No additional customers are allowed in after time $T = 8$. (All time units are per hour.) Develop a simulation study to estimate the average amount of time that an entering customer spends in the system. Using the bootstrap approach, estimate the mean square error of your estimator.

References

Bratley, P., B. L. Fox, and L. E. Schrage, *A Guide to Simulation,* Second Ed., Springer Verlag, New York, 1988.

Crane, M. A., and A. J. Lemoine, *An Introducion to the Regenerative Method for Simulation Analysis,* Springer-Verlag, New York, 1977.

Efron, B., and R. Tibshirani, *Introduction to the Bootstrap,* Chapman-Hall, New York, 1993.

Kleijnen, J. P. C., *Statistical Techniques in Simulation,* Parts 1 and 2, Marcel Dekker, New York, 1974/1975.

Law, A. M., and W. D. Kelton, *Simulation Modelling and Analysis,* Second Ed., McGraw-Hill, New York, 1991.

Chapter 8 | Variance Reduction Techniques

Introduction

In a typical scenario for a simulation study, one is interested in determining θ, a parameter connected with some stochastic model. To estimate θ, the model is simulated to obtain, among other things, the output datum X which is such that $\theta = E[X]$. Repeated simulation runs, the ith one yielding the output variable X_i, are performed. The simulation study is then terminated when n runs have been performed and the estimate of θ is given by $\bar{X} = \sum_{i=1}^{n} X_i / n$. Because this results in an unbiased estimate of θ, it follows that its mean square error is equal to its variance. That is,

$$\text{MSE} = E[(\bar{X} - \theta)^2] = \text{Var}(\bar{X}) = \frac{\text{Var}(X)}{n}$$

Hence, if we can obtain a different unbiased estimate of θ having a smaller variance than does $\bar{X}$, we would obtain an improved estimator.

In this chapter we present a variety of different methods that one can attempt to use so as to reduce the variance of the (so-called raw) simulation estimate $\bar{X}$.

However, before presenting these variance reduction techniques, let us illustrate the potential pitfalls, even in quite simple models, of using the raw simulation estimator.

Example 8a Quality Control. Consider a process that produces items sequentially. Suppose that these items have measurable values attached to them and that when the process is "in control" these values (suitably normalized) come from a unit normal distribution. Suppose further that when the process goes "out of control" the distribution of these values changes from the unit normal to some other distribution.

To help detect when the process goes out of control the following type of procedure, called an exponentially weighted moving-average control rule, is often used. Let $X_1, X_2, \ldots$ denote the sequence of data values. For a fixed value α, $0 \le \alpha \le 1$, define the sequence S_n, $n \ge 0$, by

$$S_0 = 0$$

$$S_n = \alpha S_{n-1} + (1 - \alpha)X_n, \qquad n \ge 1$$

Now when the process is in control, all the X_n have mean 0, and thus it is easy to verify that, under this condition, the exponentially weighted moving-average values S_n also have mean 0. The moving-average control rule is to fix a constant B, along with the value of α, and then to declare the process "out of control" when $|S_n|$ exceeds B. That is, the process is declared out of control at the random time N, where

$$N = \text{Min}\{n: |S_n| > B\}$$

Now it is clear that eventually $|S_n|$ will exceed B and so the process will be declared out of control even if it is still working properly—that is, even when the data values are being generated by a unit normal distribution. To make sure that this does not occur too frequently, it is prudent to choose α and B so that, when the X_n, $n \ge 1$, are indeed coming from a unit normal distribution, $E[N]$ is large. Suppose that it has been decided that, under these conditions, a value for $E[N]$ of 800 is acceptable. Suppose further that it is claimed that the values $\alpha = 0.9$ and $B = 0.8$ achieve a value of $E[N]$ of around 800. How can we check this claim?

One way of verifying the above claim is by simulation. Namely, we can generate unit normals X_n, $n \ge 1$, until $|S_n|$ exceeds 0.8 (where $\alpha = 0.9$ in the defining equation for S_n). If N_1 denotes the number of normals needed until this occurs, then, for our first simulation run, we have the output variable N_1. We then generate other runs, and our estimate of $E[N]$ is the average value of the output data obtained over all runs.

However, let us suppose that we want to be 99 percent confident that our estimate of $E[N]$, under the in-control assumption, is accurate to within ± 0.1. Hence, since 99 percent of the time a normal random variable is within ± 2.33 standard deviations of its mean (i.e., $z_{.005} = 2.33$), it follows that the number of runs needed—call it n—is such that

$$\frac{2.33\sigma_n}{\sqrt{n}} \approx 0.1$$

where σ_n is the sample standard deviation based on the first n data values. Now σ_n will approximately equal $\sigma(N)$, the standard deviation of N, and we now argue that this is approximately equal to $E[N]$. The argument runs as follows: Since we are assuming that the process remains in control throughout, most of the time the value of the exponentially weighted moving average is near the origin. Occasionally, by chance, it gets large and approaches, in absolute value, B. At such times it may go beyond B and the run ends or there may be a string of normal data values which, after a short time, eliminate the fact that the moving average had been large (this is so because the old values of S_i are continually multiplied by 0.9 and so lose their effect). Hence, if we know that the process has not yet gone out of control by some fixed time k, then, no matter what the value of k, it would seem that the value of S_k is around the origin. In other words, it intuitively appears that the distribution of time until the moving average exceeds the control limits is approximately memoryless; that is, it is approximately an exponential random variable. But for an exponential random variable Y, $\text{Var}(Y) = (E[Y])^2$. Since the standard deviation is the square root of the variance, it thus seems intuitive that, when in control throughout, $\sigma(N) \approx E[N]$. Hence, if the original claim that $E[N] \approx 800$ is correct, the number of runs needed is such that

$$\sqrt{n} \approx 23.3 \times 800$$

or

$$n \approx (23.3 \times 800)^2 \approx 3.47 \times 10^8$$

In addition, because each run requires approximately 800 normal random variables (again assuming the claim is roughly correct), we see that to do this simulation would require approximately $800 \times 3.47 \times 10^8 \approx 2.77 \times 10^{11}$ normal random variables—a formidable task. ∎

8.1 The Use of Antithetic Variables

Suppose we are interested in using simulation to estimate $\theta = E[X]$ and suppose we have generated X_1 and X_2, identically distributed random variables having mean θ. Then

$$\text{Var}\left(\frac{X_1 + X_2}{2}\right) = \frac{1}{4}\left[\text{Var}(X_1) + \text{Var}(X_2) + 2\,\text{Cov}(X_1, X_2)\right]$$

Hence it would be advantageous (in the sense that the variance would be reduced) if X_1 and X_2 rather than being independent were negatively correlated.

To see how we might arrange for X_1 and X_2 to be negatively correlated, suppose that X_1 is a function of m random numbers: that is, suppose that

$$X_1 = h(U_1, U_2, \ldots, U_m)$$

where $U_1, \ldots, U_m$ are m independent random numbers. Now if U is a random number—that is, U is uniformly distributed on $(0, 1)$—then so is $1 - U$. Hence the random variable

$$X_2 = h(1 - U_1, 1 - U_2, \ldots, 1 - U_m)$$

has the same distribution as X_1. In addition, since $1 - U$ is clearly negatively correlated with U, we might hope that X_2 might be negatively correlated with X_1; and indeed this result can be proved in the special case where h is a monotone (either increasing or decreasing) function of each of its coordinates. [This result follows from a more general result which states that two increasing (or decreasing) functions of a set of independent random variables are positively correlated. Both results are presented in the Appendix.] Hence, in this case, after we have generated $U_1, \ldots, U_m$ so as to compute X_1, rather than generating a new independent set of m random numbers, we do better by just using the set $1 - U_1, \ldots,$ $1 - U_m$ to compute X_2. In addition, it should be noted that we obtain a double benefit: namely, not only does our resulting estimator have smaller variance (at least when h is a monotone function), but we are also saved the time of generating a second set of random numbers.

Example 8b Simulating the Reliability Function. Consider a system of n components, each of which is either functioning or failed. Letting

$$s_i = \begin{cases} 1 & \text{if component } i \text{ works} \\ 0 & \text{otherwise} \end{cases}$$

we call $s = (s_1, \ldots, s_n)$ the state vector. Suppose also that there is a nondecreasing function $\phi(s_1, \ldots, s_n)$ such that

$$\phi(s_1, \ldots, s_n) = \begin{cases} 1 & \text{if the system works under state vector } s_1, \ldots, s_n \\ 0 & \text{otherwise} \end{cases}$$

The function $\phi(s_1, \ldots, s_n)$ is called the structure function.

Some common structure functions are the following:

(a) *The series structure:* For the series structure

$$\phi(s_1, \ldots, s_n) = \underset{i}{\text{Min }} s_i$$

The series system works only if all its components function.

(b) *The parallel structure:* For the parallel structure

$$\phi(s_1, \ldots, s_n) = \underset{i}{\text{Max}} \; s_i$$

Hence the parallel system works if at least one of its components works.

(c) *The k-of-n system:* The structure function

$$\phi(s_1, \ldots, s_n) = \begin{cases} 1 & \text{if } \sum_{i=1}^{n} s_i \geq k \\ 0 & \text{otherwise} \end{cases}$$

is called a k-of-n structure function. Since $\sum_{i=1}^{n} s_i$ represents the number of functioning components, a k-of-n system works if at least k of the n components are working.

It should be noted that a series system is an n-of-n system, whereas a parallel system is a 1-of-n system.

(d) *The bridge structure:* A five-component system for which

$$\phi(s_1, s_2, s_3, s_4, s_5) = \text{Max}(s_1 s_3 s_5, \; s_2 s_3 s_4, \; s_1 s_4, \; s_2 s_5)$$

is said to have a bridge structure. Such a system can be represented schematically by Figure 8.1. The idea of the diagram is that the system functions if a signal can go, from left to right, through the system. The signal can go through any given node i provided that component i is functioning. We leave it as an exercise for the reader to verify the formula given for the bridge structure function.

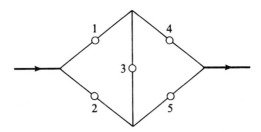

Figure 8.1   The bridge structure

Let us suppose now that the states of the components—call them S_i—$i = 1, \ldots n$, are independent random variables such that

$$P\{S_i = 1\} = p_i = 1 - P\{S_i = 0\} \qquad i = 1, \ldots, n$$

Let

$$r(p_1, \ldots, p_n) = P\{\phi(S_1, \ldots, S_n) = 1\}$$
$$= E[\phi(S_1, \ldots, S_n)]$$

The function $r(p_1, \ldots, p_n)$ is called the *reliability* function. It represents the probability that the system will work when the components are independent with component i functioning with probability p_i, $i = 1, \ldots, n$.

For a series system

$$r(p_1, \ldots, p_n) = P\{S_i = 1 \quad \text{for all } i = 1, \ldots, n\}$$

$$= \prod_{i=1}^{n} P\{S_i = 1\}$$

$$= \prod_{i=1}^{n} p_i$$

and for a parallel system

$$r(p_1, \ldots, p_n) = P\{S_i = 1 \quad \text{for at least one } i, i = 1, \ldots, n\}$$

$$= 1 - P\{S_i = 0 \quad \text{for all } i = 1, \ldots, n\}$$

$$= 1 - \prod_{i=1}^{n} P(S_i = 0)$$

$$= 1 - \prod_{i=1}^{n} (1 - p_i)$$

However, for most systems it remains a formidable problem to compute the reliability function (even for such small systems as a 5-of-10 system or the bridge system it can be quite tedious to compute). So let us suppose that for a given nondecreasing structure function ϕ and given probabilities $p_1, \ldots, p_n$, we are interested in using simulation to estimate

$$r(p_1, \ldots, p_n) = E[\phi(S_1, \ldots, S_n)]$$

Now we can simulate the S_i by generating uniform random numbers $U_1, \ldots,$ U_n and then setting

$$S_i = \begin{cases} 1 & \text{if } U_i < p_i \\ 0 & \text{otherwise} \end{cases}$$

Hence we see that

$$\phi(S_1, \ldots, S_m) = h(U_1, \ldots, U_n)$$

where h is a decreasing function of $U_1, \ldots, U_n$. Therefore

$$\text{Cov}(h(\mathbf{U}), h(\mathbf{1 - U})) \leq 0$$

and so the antithetic variable approach of using $U_1, \ldots, U_n$ to generate both $h(U_1, \ldots, U_n)$ and $h(1 - U_1, \ldots, 1 - U_n)$ results in a smaller variance than if an independent set of random numbers was used to generate the second value of h. ∎

Oftentimes the relevant output of a simulation is a function of the input random variables $Y_1, \ldots, Y_m$. That is, the relevant output is $X = h(Y_1, \ldots, Y_m)$. Suppose the Y_i having distribution $F_i, i = 1, \ldots, m$. If these input variables are generated by the inverse transform technique, we can write

$$X = h(F_1^{-1}(U_1), \ldots, F_m^{-1}(U_m))$$

where $U_1, \ldots, U_m$ are independent random numbers. Since a distribution function is increasing, it follows that its inverse is also increasing and thus if $h(y_1, \ldots, y_m)$ were a monotone function of its coordinates, then it follows that $h(F_1^{-1}(U_1), \ldots, F_m^{-1}(U_m))$ will be a monotone function of the U_i. Hence the method of antithetic variables, which would first generate $U_1, \ldots, U_m$ to compute X_1 and then use $1 - U_1, \ldots, 1 - U_m$ to compute X_2, would result in an estimator having a smaller variance than would have been obtained if a new set of random numbers were used for X_2.

Example 8c Simulating a Queueing System. Consider a given queueing system, and let D_i denote the delay in queue of the ith arriving customer, and suppose we are interested in simulating the system so as to estimate $\theta = E[X]$, where

$$X = D_1 + \cdots + D_n$$

is the sum of the delays in queue of the first n arrivals. Let $I_1, \ldots, I_n$ denote the first n interarrival times (i.e., I_j is the time between the arrivals of customers $j - 1$ and j), and let $S_1, \ldots, S_n$ denote the first n service times of this system, and suppose that these random variables are all independent. Now in many systems X is a function of the $2n$ random variables $I_1, \ldots, I_n, S_1, \ldots, S_n$, say,

$$X = h(I_1, \ldots, I_n, S_1, \ldots, S_n)$$

Also, as the delay in queue of a given customer usually increases (depending of course on the specifics of the model) as the service times of other customers increase and usually decreases as the times between arrivals increase, it follows that, for many models, h is a monotone function of its coordinates. Hence, if the inverse transform method is used to generate the random variables $I_1, \ldots, I_n$, $S_1, \ldots, S_n$, then the antithetic variable approach results in a smaller variance. That is, if we initially use the $2n$ random numbers $U_i, i = 1, \ldots, 2n$, to generate the interarrival and service times by setting $I_i = F_i^{-1}(U_i)$, $S_i = G_i^{-1}(U_{n+i})$, where F_i and G_i are, respectively, the distribution functions of I_i and S_i, then the second simulation run should be done in the same fashion, but using the random numbers $1 - U_i, i = 1, \ldots, 2n$. This results in a smaller variance than if a new set of $2n$ random numbers were generated for the second run. ∎

The following example illustrates the sort of improvement that can sometimes be gained by the use of antithetic variables.

Example 8d   Suppose we were interested in using simulation to estimate

$$\theta = E[e^U] = \int_0^1 e^x \, dx$$

(Of course, we know that $\theta = e-1$; however, the point of this example is to see what kind of improvement is possible by using antithetic variables.) Since the function $h(u) = e^u$ is clearly a monotone function, the antithetic variable approach leads to a variance reduction, whose value we now determine. To begin, note that

$$\text{Cov}(e^U, e^{1-U}) = E[e^U e^{1-U}] - E[e^U]E[e^{1-U}]$$
$$= e - (e - 1)^2 = -0.2342$$

Also, because

$$\text{Var}(e^U) = E[e^{2U}] - (E[e^U])^2$$
$$= \int_0^1 e^{2x} \, dx - (e - 1)^2$$

$$= \frac{[e^2 - 1]}{2} - (e - 1)^2 = 0.2420$$

we see that the use of independent random numbers results in a variance of

$$\text{Var}\left(\frac{\exp\{U_1\} + \exp\{U_2\}}{2}\right) = \frac{\text{Var}(e^U)}{2} = 0.1210$$

whereas the use of the antithetic variables U and $1 - U$ gives a variance of

$$\text{Var}\left(\frac{e^U + e^{1-U}}{2}\right) = \frac{\text{Var}(e^U)}{2} + \frac{\text{Cov}(e^U, e^{1-U})}{2} = 0.0039$$

a variance reduction of 96.7 percent. ■

Example 8e   Estimating e. Consider a sequence of random numbers and let N be the first one that is greater than its immediate predecessor. That is,

$$N = \min(n : n \geq 2, U_n > U_{n-1})$$

Now,

$$P\{N > n\} = P\{U_1 \geq U_2 \geq \cdots \geq U_n\}$$

$$= 1/n!$$

where the final equality follows because all possible orderings of $U_1, \ldots, U_n$ are equally likely. Hence,

$$P\{N = n\} = P\{N > n - 1\} - P\{N > n\} = \frac{1}{(n-1)!} - \frac{1}{n!} = \frac{n-1}{n!}$$

and so

$$E[N] = \sum_{n=2}^{\infty} \frac{1}{(n-2)!} = e$$

Also,

$$E[N^2] = \sum_{n=2}^{\infty} \frac{n}{(n-2)!} = \sum_{n=2}^{\infty} \frac{2}{(n-2)!} + \sum_{n=2}^{\infty} \frac{n-2}{(n-2)!}$$

$$= 2e + \sum_{n=3}^{\infty} \frac{1}{(n-3)!} = 3e$$

and so

$$\text{Var}(N) = 3e - e^2 \approx 0.7658$$

Hence, e can be estimated by generating random numbers and stopping the first time one exceeds its immediate predecessor.

If we employ antithetic variables then we could also let

$$M = \min(n : n \geq 2, 1 - U_n > 1 - U_{n-1}) = \min(n : n \geq 2, U_n < U_{n-1})$$

Since one of the values of N and M will equal 2 and the other will exceed 2, it would seem, even though they are not monotone functions of the U_n, that the estimator $(N + M)/2$ should have a smaller variance than the average of two independent random variables distributed according to N. Before determining $\text{Var}(N + M)$, it is useful to first consider the random variable N_a, whose distribution is the same as the conditional distribution of the number of additional random numbers that must be observed until one is observed greater than its predecessor, given that $U_2 \leq U_1$. Therefore, we may write

$$N = 2, \qquad \text{with probability } \frac{1}{2}$$

$$N = 2 + N_a, \qquad \text{with probability } \frac{1}{2}$$

Hence,

$$E[N] = 2 + \frac{1}{2} E[N_a]$$

$$E[N^2] = \frac{1}{2} 4 + \frac{1}{2} E[(2 + N_a)^2]$$

$$= 4 + 2E[N_a] + \frac{1}{2} E[N_a^2]$$

Using the previously obtained results for $E[N]$ and $\text{Var}(N)$ we obtain, after some algebra, that

$$E[N_a] = 2e - 4$$

$$E[N_a^2] = 8 - 2e$$

implying that

$$\text{Var}(N_a) = 14e - 4e^2 - 8 \approx 0.4997$$

Now consider the random variable N and M. It is easy to see that after the first two random numbers are observed, one of N and M will equal 2 and the other will equal 2 plus a random variable that has the same distribution as N_a. Hence,

$$\text{Var}(N + M) = \text{Var}(4 + N_a) = \text{Var}(N_a)$$

Hence,

$$\frac{\text{Var}(N_1 + N_2)}{\text{Var}(N + M)} \approx \frac{1.5316}{0.4997} \approx 3.065$$

Thus, the use of antithetic variables reduces the variance of the estimator by a factor of slightly more than 3. ∎

In the case of a normal random variable having mean μ and variance σ^2, we can use the antithetic variable approach by first generating such a random variable Y and then taking as the antithetic variable $2\mu - Y$, which is also normal with mean μ and variance σ^2 and is clearly negatively correlated with Y. If we were using simulation to compute $E[h(Y_1, \ldots, Y_n)]$, where the Y_i are independent normal random variables and h is a monotone function of its coordinates, then the antithetic approach of first generating the n normals $Y_1, \ldots, Y_n$ to compute $h(Y_1, \ldots, Y_n)$ and then using the antithetic variables $2\mu_i - Y_i, i = 1, \ldots,$ n, to compute the next simulated value of h would lead to a reduction in variance as compared with generating a second set of n normal random variables.

8.2 The Use of Control Variates

Again suppose that we want to use simulation to estimate $\theta = E[X]$, where X is the output of a simulation. Now suppose that for some other output variable Y, the expected value of Y is known—say, $E[Y] = \mu_y$. Then for any constant c, the quantity

$$X + c(Y - \mu_y)$$

is also an unbiased estimator of θ. To determine the best value of c, note that

$$\text{Var}(X + c(Y - \mu_y)) = \text{Var}(X + cY)$$
$$= \text{Var}(X) + c^2 \text{Var}(Y) + 2c \text{ Cov}(X, Y)$$

Simple calculus now shows that the above is minimized when $c = c^*$, where

$$c^* = -\frac{\text{Cov}(X, Y)}{\text{Var}(Y)} \tag{8.1}$$

and for this value the variance of the estimator is

$$\text{Var}(X + c^*(Y - \mu)) = \text{Var}(X) - \frac{[\text{Cov}(X, Y)]^2}{\text{Var}(Y)} \tag{8.2}$$

The quantity Y is called a *control variate* for the simulation estimator X. To see why it works, note that c^* is negative (positive) when X and Y are positively (negatively) correlated. So suppose that X and Y were positively correlated, meaning, roughly, that X is large when Y is large and vice versa. Hence, if a simulation run results in a large (small) value of Y—which is indicated by Y being larger than its known mean μ_y—then it is probably true that X is also larger (smaller) than its mean θ, and so we would like to correct for this by lowering (raising) the value of the estimator X, and this is done since c^* is negative (positive). A similar argument holds when X and Y are negatively correlated.

Upon dividing Equation (8.2) by $\text{Var}(X)$, we obtain that

$$\frac{\text{Var}(X + c^*(Y - \mu_y))}{\text{Var}(X)} = 1 - \text{Corr}^2(X, Y)$$

where

$$\text{Corr}(X, Y) = \frac{\text{Cov}(X, Y)}{\sqrt{\text{Var}(X)\text{Var}(Y)}}$$

is the correlation between X and Y. Hence, the variance reduction obtained in using the control variate Y is $100\,\text{Corr}^2(X, Y)$ percent.

The quantities $\text{Cov}(X, Y)$ and $\text{Var}(Y)$ are usually not known in advance and must be estimated from the simulated data. If n simulation runs are performed, and the output data $X_i, Y_i, i = 1, \ldots, n$, result, then using the estimators

$$\widehat{\text{Cov}}(X, Y) = \sum_{i=1}^{n} (X_i - \bar{X})(Y_i - \bar{Y})/(n - 1)$$

and

$$\widehat{\text{Var}}(Y) = \sum_{i=1}^{n} (Y_i - \bar{Y})^2/(n - 1),$$

we can approximate $c*$ by $\hat{c}*$, where

$$\hat{c}* = -\frac{\sum_{i=1}^{n} (X_i - \bar{X})(Y_i - \bar{Y})}{\sum_{i=1}^{n} (Y_i - \bar{Y})^2} .$$

The variance of the controlled estimator

$$\text{Var}(\bar{X} + c*(\bar{Y} - \mu_y)) = \frac{1}{n}\left(\text{Var}(X) - \frac{\text{Cov}^2(X, Y)}{\text{Var}(Y)}\right)$$

can then be estimated by using the estimator of $\text{Cov}(X,Y)$ along with the sample variance estimators of $\text{Var}(X)$ and $\text{Var}(Y)$.

Remark   Another way of doing the computations is to make use of a standard computer package for simple linear regression models. For if we consider the simple linear regression model

$$X = a + bY + e$$

where e is a random variable with mean 0 and variance σ^2, then $\hat{a}$ and $\hat{b}$, the least squares estimator of a and b based on the data X_i, Y_i, $i = 1, \ldots, n$, are

$$\hat{b} = \frac{\sum_{i=1}^{n} (X_i - \bar{X})(Y_i - \bar{Y})}{\sum_{i=1}^{n}(Y_i - \bar{Y})^2}$$

$$\hat{a} = \bar{X} - \hat{b}\bar{Y}$$

Therefore, $\hat{b} = -\hat{c}*$. In addition, since

$$\bar{X} + \hat{c}*(\bar{Y} - \mu_y) = \bar{X} - \hat{b}(\bar{Y} - \mu_y)$$
$$= \hat{a} + \hat{b}\mu_y$$

it follows that the control variate estimate is the evaluation of the estimated regression line at the value $Y = \mu_y$. Also, because $\hat{\sigma}^2$, the regression estimate of σ^2, is the estimate of $\text{Var}(X - \hat{b}Y) = \text{Var}(X + \hat{c}*Y)$, it follows that the estimated variance of the control variate estimator $\bar{X} + \hat{c}*(\bar{Y} - \mu_y)$ is $\hat{\sigma}^2/n$. ∎

Example 8f   Suppose, as in Example 8b, that we wanted to use simulation to estimate the reliability function

$$r(p_1, \ldots, p_n) = E[\phi(S_1, \ldots, S_n)]$$

where

$$S_i = \begin{cases} 1 & \text{if } U_i < p_i \\ 0 & \text{otherwise} \end{cases}$$

Since $E[S_i] = p_i$, it follows that

$$E\left[\sum_{i=1}^{n} S_i\right] = \sum_{i=1}^{n} p_i$$

Hence, we can use the number of working components, $Y \equiv \Sigma S_i$, as a control variate of the estimator $X \equiv \phi(S_1, \ldots, S_n)$. Since $\Sigma_{i=1}^{n} S_i$ and $\phi(S_1, \ldots, S_n)$ are both increasing functions of the S_i, they are positively correlated, and thus the sign of c^* is negative. ■

Example 8g   Consider a queueing system in which customers arrive in accordance with nonhomogeneous Poisson process with intensity function $\lambda(s)$, $s > 0$. Suppose that the service times are independent random variables having distribution G and are also independent of the arrival times. Suppose we were interested in estimating the total time spent in the system by all customers arriving before time t. That is, if we let W_i denote the amount of time that the ith entering customer spends in the system, then we are interested in $\theta = E[X]$, where

$$X = \sum_{i=1}^{N(t)} W_i$$

and where $N(t)$ is the number of arrivals by time t. A natural quantity to use as a control in this situation is the total of the service times of all these customers. That is, let S_i denote the service time of the ith customer and set

$$Y = \sum_{i=1}^{N(t)} S_i$$

Since the service times are independent of $N(t)$, it follows that

$$E[Y] = E[S]E[N(t)]$$

where $E[S]$, the mean service time, and $E[N(t)]$, the mean number of arrivals by t, are both known quantities. ■

Example 8h   As in Example 8d, suppose we were interested in using simulation to compute $\theta = E[e^U]$. Here, a natural variate to use as a control is the random number U. To see what sort of improvement over the raw estimator is possible, note that

$$\text{Cov}(e^U, U) = E[Ue^U] - E[U]E[e^U]$$

$$= \int_0^1 xe^x \, dx - \frac{(e-1)}{2}$$

$$= 1 - \frac{(e-1)}{2} = 0.14086$$

Because $\text{Var}(U) = \frac{1}{12}$ it follows from (8.2) that

$$\text{Var}\left(e^U + c^*\left(U - \frac{1}{2}\right)\right) = \text{Var}(e^U) - 12(0.14086)^2$$

$$= 0.2420 - 0.2380 = 0.0039$$

where the above used, from Example 8d, that $\text{Var}(e^U) = 0.2420$. Hence, in this case, the use of the control variate U can lead to a variance reduction of up to 98.4 percent. ∎

Example 8i A List Reordering Problem. Suppose we are given a set of n elements, numbered 1 through n, which are to be arranged in an ordered list. At each unit of time a request is made to retrieve one of these elements, with the request being for element i with probability $p(i)$, $\sum_{i=1}^n p(i) = 1$. After being requested, the element is put back in the list but not necessarily in the same position. For example, a common reordering rule is to interchange the requested element with the one immediately preceding it. Thus, if $n = 4$ and the present ordering is 1, 4, 2, 3, then under this rule a request for element 2 would result in the reorder 1, 2, 4, 3. Starting with an initial ordering that is equally likely to be any of the $n!$ orderings and using this interchange rule, suppose we are interested in determining the expected sum of the positions of the first N elements requested. How can we efficiently accomplish this by simulation?

One effective way is as follows. The "natural" way of simulating the above is first to generate a random permutation of 1, 2, . . . , n to establish the initial ordering, and then at each of the next N periods determine the element requested by generating a random number U and then letting the request be for element j if $\sum_{k=1}^{j-1} p(k) < U \leq \sum_{k=1}^j p(k)$. However, a better technique is to generate the element requested in such a way so that small values of U correspond to elements close to the front. Specifically, if the present ordering is $i_1, i_2, \ldots, i_n$, then generate the element requested by generating a random number U and then letting the selection be for i_j if $\sum_{k=1}^{j-1} p(i_k) < U \leq \sum_{k=1}^j p(i_k)$. For example, if $n = 4$ and the present ordering is 3, 1, 2, 4, then we should generate U and let the selection be for 3 if $U \le p(3)$, let it be for 1 if $p(3) < U \le p(3) + p(1)$, and so on. As small values of U thus correspond to elements near the front, we can use $\sum_{r=1}^{N} U_r$ as a control variables, where U_r is the random number used for the rth request in a run. That is, if P_r is the position of the rth selected element in a run, then rather than just using the raw estimator $\sum_{r=1}^{N} P_r$ we should use

$$\sum_{r=1}^{N} P_r + c^* \left(\sum_{r=1}^{N} U_r - \frac{N}{2} \right)$$

where

$$c^* = -\frac{\mathrm{Cov}\left(\sum_{r=1}^{N} P_r, \sum_{r=1}^{N} U_r \right)}{\dfrac{N}{12}}$$

and where the above covariance should be estimated using the data from all the simulated runs.

While the variance reduction obtained will, of course, depend on the probabilities $p(i)$, $i = 1, \ldots, n$, and the value of N, a small study indicates that when $n = 50$ and the $p(i)$ are approximately equal, then for $15 \le N \le 50$ the variance of the controlled estimator is less than $\frac{1}{2400}$ the variance of the raw simulation estimator. ■

Of course, one can use more than a single variable as a control. For example, if a simulation results in output variables Y_i, $i = 1, \ldots, k$, and $E[Y_i] = \mu_i$ is known, then for any constants c_i, $i = 1, \ldots, k$, we may use

$$X + \sum_{i=1}^{k} c_i(Y_i - \mu_i)$$

as an unbiased estimator of $E[X]$.

Example 8j Blackjack. The game of blackjack is often played with the dealer shuffling multiple decks of cards, putting aside used cards, and finally reshuffling when the number of remaining cards is below some limit. Let us say that a new round begins each time the dealer reshuffles, and suppose we are interested in using simulation to estimate $E[X]$, a player's expected winnings per round, where we assume that the player is employing some fixed strategy which might be of the type that "counts cards" that have already been played in the round and stakes different amounts depending on the "count." We will assume that the game consists of a single player against the dealer.

The randomness in this game results from the shuffling of the cards by the dealer. If the dealer uses k decks of 52 cards, then we can generate the shuffle by generating a random permutation of the numbers 1 through $52k$; let $I_1, \ldots,$ I_{52k} denote this permutation. If we now set

$$u_j = I_j \bmod 13 + 1$$

and let

$$v_j = \min(u_j, 10)$$

then $v_j, j = 1, \ldots, 52k$ represent the successive values of the shuffled cards, with 1 standing for an ace.

Let N denote the number of hands played in a round, and let B_j denote the amount bet on hand j. To reduce the variance, we can use a control variable that is large when the player is dealt more good hands than the dealer, and is small in the reverse case. Since being dealt 19 or better is good, let us define

$W_j = 1$ if the player's two dealt cards on deal j add to at least 19

and let W_j be 0 otherwise. Similarly, let

$Z_j = 1$ if the dealer's two dealt cards on deal j add to at least 19

and let Z_j be 0 otherwise. Since W_j and Z_j clearly have the same distribution it follows that $E[W_j - Z_j] = 0$, and it is not difficult to show that

$$E\left[\sum_{j=1}^{N} B_j(W_j - Z_j) \right] = 0$$

Thus, we recommend using $\sum_{j=1}^{N} B_j (W_j - Z_j)$ as a control variable. Of course, it is not clear that 19 is the best value, and one should experiment on letting 18 or even 20 be the critical value. However, some preliminary work indicates that 19 works best, and it has resulted in variance reductions of 15 percent or more depending on the strategy employed by the player. An even greater variance reduction should result if we use two control variables. One control variable is defined as before, with the exception that the W_j and Z_j are defined to be 1 if the hand is either 19 or 20. The second control variable is again similar, but this time its indicators are 1 when the hands consist of blackjacks. ■

When multiple control variates are used, the computations can be performed by using a computer program for the multiple linear regression model

$$X = a + \sum_{i=1}^{k} b_i Y_i + e$$

where e is a random variable with mean 0 and variance σ^2. Letting $\hat{c}_i^*$ be the estimate of the best c_i, for $i = 1, \ldots, k$, then

$$\hat{c}_i^* = -\hat{b}_i, \qquad i = 1, \ldots, k$$

where $\hat{b}_i$, $i = 1, \ldots, k$, are the least squares regression estimates of b_i, $i = 1, \ldots, k$. The value of the controlled estimate can be obtained from

$$\bar{X} + \sum_{i=1}^{k} \hat{c}_i^* (\bar{Y}_i - \mu_i) = \hat{a} + \sum_{i=1}^{k} \hat{b}_i \mu_i$$

That is, the controlled estimate is just the estimated multiple regression line evaluated at the point $(\mu_1, \ldots, \mu_k)$.

The variance of the controlled estimate can be obtained by dividing the regression estimate of σ^2 by the number of simulation runs.

Remarks

1. Since the variance of the controlled estimator is not known in advance, one often performs the simulation in two stages. In the first stage a small number of runs are performed so as to give a rough estimate of $\mathrm{Var}(X + c^* (Y - \mu_y))$. (This estimate can be obtained from a simple linear regression program, where Y is the independent and X is the dependent variable, by using the estimate of σ^2.) We can then fix the number of trials needed in the second run so that the variance of the final estimator is within an acceptable bound.

2. A valuable way of interpreting the control variable approach is that it combines estimators of θ. That is, suppose the values of X and W are both determined by the simulation, and suppose $E[X] = E[W] = \theta$. Then we may consider any unbiased estimator of the form

$$\alpha X + (1 - \alpha) W$$

The best such estimator, which is obtained by choosing α to minimize the variance, is given by letting $\alpha = \alpha^*$, where

$$\alpha^* = \frac{\mathrm{Var}(W) - \mathrm{Cov}(X, W)}{\mathrm{Var}(X) + \mathrm{Var}(W) - 2\,\mathrm{Cov}(X, W)} \tag{8.3}$$

Now if $E[Y] = \mu_y$ is known, we have the two unbiased estimators X and $X + Y - \mu_y$. The combined estimator can then be written as

$$(1 - c)X + c(X + Y - \mu_y) = X + c(Y - \mu_y)$$

To go the other way in the equivalence between control variates and combining estimators, suppose that $E[X] = E[W] = \theta$. Then if we use X, controling with the variable $Y = X - W$, which is known to have mean 0, we then obtain an estimator of the form

$$X + c(X - W) = (1 + c)X - cW$$

which is a combined estimator with $\alpha = 1 + c$.

3. With the interpretation given in Remark 2, the antithetic variable approach may be regarded as a special case of control variables. That is, if $E[X] = \theta$, where $X = h(U_1, \ldots, U_n)$, then also $E[W] = \theta$, where $W = h(1 - U_1, \ldots, 1 - U_n)$. Hence, we can combine to get an estimator of the form $\alpha X + (1 - \alpha)W$. Since $\text{Var}(X) = \text{Var}(W)$, as X and W have the same distribution, it follows from Equation (8.3) that the best value of α is $\alpha = \frac{1}{2}$, and this is the antithetic variable estimator. ■

8.3 Variance Reduction by Conditioning

Recall the conditional variance formula proved in Section 2.10 of Chapter 2.

$$\text{Var}(X) = E[\text{Var}(X|Y)] + \text{Var}(E[X|Y])$$

Since both terms on the right are nonnegative, because a variance is always nonnegative, we see that

$$\text{Var}(X) \geq \text{Var}(E[X|Y]) \tag{8.4}$$

Now suppose we are interested in performing a simulation study so as to ascertain the value of $\theta = E[X]$, where X is an output variable of a simulation run. Also, suppose there is a second variable Y, such that $E[X|Y]$ is known and takes on a value that can be determined from the simulation run. Since

$$E[E[X|Y]] = E[X] = \theta$$

it follows that $E[X|Y]$ is also an unbiased estimator of θ; thus, using (8.4) it follows that as an estimator of θ, $E[X|Y]$ is superior to the (raw) estimator X.

Remarks To understand why the conditional expectation estimator is superior to the raw estimator, note first that we are performing the simulation to estimate the unknown value of $E[X]$. We can now imagine that a simulation run proceeds in two stages: First, we observe the simulated value of the random variable Y and then the simulated value of X. However, after observing Y if we are now able to compute the (conditional) expected value of X, then by using this value we obtain an estimate of $E[X]$, which eliminates the additional variance involved in simulating the actual value of X. ∎

At this point one might consider further improvements by using an estimator of the type $\alpha X + (1 - \alpha) E[X|Y]$. However, by Equation (8.3) the best estimator of this type has $\alpha = \alpha^*$, where

$$\alpha^* = \frac{\text{Var}(E[X|Y]) - \text{Cov}(X, E[X|Y])}{\text{Var}(X) + \text{Var}(E[X|Y]) - 2\,\text{Cov}(X, E[X|Y])}$$

We now show that $\alpha^* = 0$, showing that combining the estimators X and $E[X|Y]$ does not improve on just using $E[X|Y]$.

First note that

$$\begin{aligned}
\text{Var}(E[X|Y]) &= E[(E[X|Y])^2] - (E[E[X|Y]])^2 \\
&= E[(E[X|Y])^2] - (E[X])^2
\end{aligned} \tag{8.5}$$

On the other hand,

$$\begin{aligned}
\text{Cov}(X, E[X|Y]) &= E[XE[X|Y]] - E[X]E[E[X|Y]] \\
&= E[XE[X|Y]] - (E[X])^2 \\
&= E[E[XE[X|Y]|Y]] - (E[X])^2 \\
&\quad \text{(conditioning on } Y) \\
&= E[E[X|Y]E[X|Y]] - (E[X])^2 \\
&\quad \text{(since given } Y,\ E[X|Y] \text{ is a constant)} \\
&= \text{Var}(E[X|Y]) \quad \text{[from (8.5)]}
\end{aligned}$$

Thus, we see that no additional variance reduction is possible by combining the estimators X and $E[X|Y]$.

We now illustrate the use of "conditioning" by a series of examples.

Example 8k Let us reconsider our use of simulation to estimate π. In Example 3a of Chapter 3, we showed how we can estimate π by determining how often a randomly chosen point in the square of area 4 centered around the origin falls within the inscribed circle of radius 1. Specifically, if we let $V_i = 2U_i - 1$, where U_i, $i = 1, 2$, are random numbers, and set

$$I = \begin{cases} 1 & \text{if } V_1^2 + V_2^2 \leq 1 \\ 0 & \text{otherwise} \end{cases}$$

then, as noted in Example 3a, $E[I] = \pi/4$.

The use of the average of successive values of I to estimate $\pi/4$ can be improved upon by using $E[I|V_1]$ rather than I. Now

$$E[I|V_1 = v] = P\{V_1^2 + V_2^2 \leq 1 | V_1 = v\}$$

$$= P\{v^2 + V_2^2 \leq 1 | V_1 = v\}$$

$$= P\{V_2^2 \leq 1 - v^2\} \qquad \text{by the independence of } V_1 \text{ and } V_2$$

$$= P\{-(1 - v^2)^{1/2} \leq V_2 \leq (1 - v^2)^{1/2}\}$$

$$= \int_{-(1-v^2)^{1/2}}^{(1-v^2)^{1/2}} \left(\frac{1}{2}\right) dx \qquad \text{since } V_2 \text{ is uniform over } (-1, 1)$$

$$= (1 - v^2)^{1/2}$$

Hence,

$$E[I|V_1] = (1 - V_1^2)^{1/2}$$

and so the estimator $(1 - V_1^2)^{1/2}$ also has mean $\pi/4$ and has a smaller variance than I. Since

$$E[(1 - V_1^2)^{1/2}] = \int_{-1}^{1} (1 - x^2)^{1/2} \left(\frac{1}{2}\right) dx$$

$$= \int_{0}^{1} (1 - x^2)^{1/2} dx$$

$$= E[(1 - U^2)^{1/2}]$$

we can simplify somewhat by using the estimator $(1 - U^2)^{1/2}$, where U is a random number.

The improvement in variance obtained by using the estimator $(1 - U^2)^{1/2}$ over the estimator I is easily determined.

$$\text{Var}[(1 - U^2)^{1/2}] = E[1 - U^2] - \left(\frac{\pi}{4}\right)^2$$

$$= \frac{2}{3} - \left(\frac{\pi}{4}\right)^2 = 0.0498$$

where the first inequality used the identity $\text{Var}(W) = E[W^2] - (E[W])^2$. On the other hand, because I is a Bernoulli random variable having mean $\pi/4$, we have

$$\text{Var}(I) = \left(\frac{\pi}{4}\right)\left(1 - \frac{\pi}{4}\right) = 0.1686$$

thus showing that conditioning results in a 70.44 percent reduction in variance. (In addition, only one rather than two random numbers is needed for each simulation run, although a computational cost of having to compute a square root must be paid.)

Since the function $(1 - u^2)^{1/2}$ is clearly a monotone decreasing function of u in the region $0 < u < 1$, it follows that the estimator $(1 - U^2)^{1/2}$ can be improved upon by using antithetic variables. That is, the estimator

$$\frac{1}{2}[(1 - U^2)^{1/2} + (1 - (1 - U)^2)^{1/2}]$$

has smaller variance than $\frac{1}{2}[(1 - U_1^2)^{1/2} + (1 - U_2^2)^{1/2}]$.

Another way of improving the estimator $(1 - U^2)^{1/2}$ is by using a control variable. A natural control variable in this case is U^2 and, because $E[U^2] = \frac{1}{3}$, we could use an estimator of the type

$$(1 - U^2)^{1/2} + c\left(U^2 - \frac{1}{3}\right)$$

The best c—namely, $c^* = -\text{Cov}[(1 - U^2)^{1/2}, U^2]/\text{Var}(U^2)$—can be estimated by using the simulation to estimate the covariance term. (We could also have tried to use U as a control variable; it makes a difference because a correlation between two random variables is only a measure of their "linear dependence" rather than of their total dependence. But the use of U^2 leads to a greater improvement; see Exercise 16.) ∎

Example 8l The Reliability Function Revisited. Suppose, as in Example 8b, that $S_j, j = 1, \ldots, n$, are independent with

$$P\{S_j = 1\} = 1 - P\{S_j = 0\} = p_j$$

and suppose we are interested in estimating the reliability function $E[\phi(S_1, \ldots, S_n)]$, where ϕ is an increasing binary (i.e., its only possible values are 0 and 1) function. If we generate the values of $S_1, \ldots, S_n$, then an improvement over the raw estimator $\phi(S_1, \ldots, S_n)$ is to take its conditional expectation given all of the S_j except one. That is, for fixed i,

$$E[\phi(S_1, \ldots, S_n)|S_1, \ldots, S_{i-1}, S_{i+1}, \ldots, S_n] \qquad (8.6)$$

will be an improved estimator. (To use the above estimator we would, on any given simulation run, simulate all the component states S_j except for S_i. The estimate for that simulation run will take on one of three possible values: either it will equal 1 if, given the states S_j, $j \neq i$, the system would function even if component i did not function; or it will equal 0 if the system will not function even if component i did function; or it will equal p_i if the system will function if i functions and would be failed otherwise.)

The above estimator, given by (8.6), can now be further improved upon either by using antithetic variables—since the estimator is still a monotone function—or by controlling on $\Sigma_{j \neq i} S_j$ the number of the simulated components that work.   ∎

Example 8m   A Finite Capacity Queueing Model. Consider a queueing system in which arrivals enter only if there are fewer than N other customers in the system when they arrive. Any customer encountering N others upon arrival is deemed to be lost to the system. Suppose further that potential customers arrive in accordance with a Poisson process having rate λ; and suppose we are interested in using simulation to estimate the expected number of lost customers by some fixed time t.

A simulation run would consist of simulating the above system up to time t. If, for a given run, we let L denote the number of lost customers, then the average value of L, over all simulation runs, is the (raw) simulation estimator of the desired quantity $E[L]$. However, we can improve upon this estimator by conditioning upon the amount of time that the system is at capacity. That is, rather than using L, the actual number of lost customers up to time t, we consider $E[L|T_C]$, where T_C is the total amount of time in the interval $(0, t)$ that there are N customers in the system. Since customers are always arriving at the Poisson rate λ no matter what is happening within the system, it follows that

$$E[L|T_C] = \lambda T_C$$

Hence an improved estimator is obtained by ascertaining, for each run, the total time in which there are N customers in the system—say, $T_{C,i}$ is the time at capacity during the ith run. Then the improved estimator of $E[L]$ is $\lambda \Sigma_{i=1}^k T_{C,i}/k$, where k is the number of simulation runs. (In effect, since the expected number of lost customers given the time at capacity T_c is just λT_c, what this estimator does is use the actual conditional expectation rather than simulating

—and increasing the variance of the estimator—a Poisson random variable having this mean.)

If the arrival process were a nonhomogeneous Poisson process having intensity function $\lambda(s)$, $0 \leq s \leq t$, then we would not be able to compute the conditional expected number of lost customers if we were given only the total time at capacity. What we now need is the actual times at which the system was at capacity. So let us condition on the intervals during which the system was at capacity. Now letting N_C denote the number of intervals during $(0, t)$ during which the system is at capacity, and letting those intervals be designated by $I_1, \ldots, I_{N_C}$, then

$$E[L|N_C, I_1, \ldots, I_{N_C}] = \sum_{i=1}^{N_C} \int_{I_i} \lambda(s) \, ds$$

The use of the average value, over all simulation runs, of the above quantity leads to a better estimator—in the sense of having a smaller mean square error—of $E[L]$ than the raw simulation estimator of the average number lost per run.

One can combine the preceding with other variance reduction techniques in estimating $E[L]$. For instance, if we let M denote the number of customers that actually enter service by time t, then with $N(t)$ equal to the number of arrivals by time t we have that

$$N(t) = M + L$$

Taking expectations gives that

$$\int_0^t \lambda(s) \, ds = E[M] + E[L]$$

Therefore, $\int_0^t \lambda(s)ds - M$ is also an unbiased estimator of $E[L]$, which suggests the use of the combined estimator

$$\alpha \sum_{i=1}^{N_C} \int_{I_i} \lambda(s) \, ds + (1 - \alpha)\left(\int_0^t \lambda(s) \, ds - M\right)$$

The value of α to be used is given by Equation (8.3) and can be estimated from the simulation. ∎

Example 8n Suppose we wanted to estimate the expected sum of the times in the system of the first n customers in a queueing system. That is, if W_i is the time that the ith customer spends in the system, we are interested in estimating

$$\theta = E\left[\sum_{i=1}^n W_i\right]$$

Let S_i denote the "state of the system" at the moment that the ith customer arrives, and consider the estimator

$$\sum_{i=1}^{n} E[W_i|S_i]$$

Since

$$E\left[\sum_{i=1}^{n} E[W_i|S_i]\right] = \sum_{i=1}^{n} E[E[W_i|S_i]] = \sum_{i=1}^{n} E[W_i] = \theta$$

it follows that this is an unbiased estimator of θ. It can be shown[†] that, in a wide class of models, this estimator has a smaller variance than the raw simulation estimator $\sum_{i=1}^{n} W_i$. (It should be noted that whereas it is immediate that $E[W_i|S_i]$ has smaller variance than W_i, this does not imply, because of the covariance terms, that $\sum_{i=1}^{n} E[W_i|S_i]$ has smaller variance than $\sum_{i=1}^{n} W_i$.)

The quantity S_i, which refers to the state of the system as seen by the ith customer upon its arrival, is supposed to represent the least amount of information that enables us to compute the conditional expected time that the customer spends in the system. For example, if there is a single server and the service times are all exponential with mean μ, then S_i would refer to N_i, the number of customers in the system encountered by the ith arrival. In this case,

$$E[W_i|S_i] = E[W_i|N_i] = (N_i + 1)\mu$$

which follows since the ith arrival will have to wait for N_i service times (one of which is the completion of service of the customer presently being served when customer i arrives—but, by the memoryless property of the exponential, that remaining time will also be exponential with mean μ) all having mean μ, and then to this we must add its own service time. Thus, the estimator that takes the average value, over all simulation runs, of the quantity $\sum_{i=1}^{n}(N_i + 1)\mu$ is a better estimator than the average value of $\sum_{i=1}^{n} W_i$. ∎

ESTIMATING THE EXPECTED NUMBER OF RENEWALS BY TIME t

Suppose that "events" are occurring randomly in time. Let T_1 denote the time of the first event, T_2 the time between the first and second event, and,

[†] S. M. Ross, "Simulating Average Delay—Variance Reduction by Conditioning," *Probability in the Engineering and Informational Sciences,* Vol. 2, No. 3, 1988.

in general, T_n the time between the $(n - 1)$st and the nth event, $n \geq 1$. If we let

$$S_n = \sum_{i=1}^{n} T_i$$

the first event occurs at time S_1, the second at time S_2, and, in general, the nth event occurs at time S_n (see Figure 8.2). Let $N(t)$ denote the number of events that occur by time t; that is, $N(t)$ is the largest n for which the nth event occurs by time t, or, equivalently,

$$N(t) = \text{Max}\{n: S_n \leq t\}$$

If the interevent times $T_1, T_2, \ldots$ are independent and identically distributed according to some distribution function F, then the process $\{N(t), t \geq 0\}$ is called a *renewal process*.

A renewal process is easily simulated by generating the interarrival times. Suppose now that we wanted to use simulation to estimate $\theta = E[N(t)]$, the mean number of events by some fixed time t. To do so we would successively simulate the interevent times, keeping track of their sum (which represent the times at which events occur) until that sum exceeds t. That is, we keep on generating interevent times until we reach the first event time after t. Letting $N(t)$—the raw simulation estimator—denote the number of simulated events by time t, we find that a natural quantity to use as a control variable is the sequence of $N(t) + 1$ interevent times that were generated. That is, if we let μ denote the mean interevent time, then as the random variables $T_i - \mu$ have mean 0 it follows that

$$E\left[\sum_{i=1}^{N(t)+1} (T_i - \mu)\right] = 0$$

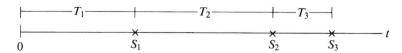

Figure 8.2 $x = $ event

Hence, we can control by using an estimator of the type

$$N(t) + c\left[\sum_{i=1}^{N(t)+1}(T_i - \mu)\right] = N(t) + c\left[\sum_{i=1}^{N(t)+1}T_i - \mu(N(t) + 1)\right]$$

$$= N(t) + c[S_{N(t)+1} - \mu N(t) - \mu]$$

Now since S_n represents the time of the nth event and $N(t) + 1$ represents the number of events by time t plus 1, it follows that $S_{N(t)+1}$ represents the time of the first event after time t. Hence, if we let $Y(t)$ denote the time from t until the next event [$Y(t)$ is commonly called the excess life at t], then

$$S_{N(t)+1} = t + Y(t)$$

and so the above controlled estimator can be written

$$N(t) + c[t + Y(t) - \mu N(t) - \mu]$$

The best c is given by

$$c^* = -\frac{\text{Cov}[N(t), Y(t) - \mu N(t)]}{\text{Var}[Y(t) - \mu N(t)]}$$

Now for t large, it can be shown that the terms involving $N(t)$ dominate—because their variance will grow linearly with t, whereas the other terms will remain bounded—and so for t large

$$c^* \approx -\frac{\text{Cov}[N(t), -\mu N(t)]}{\text{Var}[-\mu N(t)]} = \frac{\mu \, \text{Var}[N(t)]}{\mu^2 \, \text{Var}[N(t)]} = \frac{1}{\mu}$$

Thus, for t large, the best controlled estimator of the above type is close to

$$N(t) + \frac{1}{\mu}(t + Y(t) - \mu N(t) - \mu) = \frac{Y(t)}{\mu} + \frac{t}{\mu} - 1 \tag{8.7}$$

In other words, for t large, the critical value to be determined from the simulation is $Y(t)$, the time from t until the next renewal.

The above estimator can further be improved upon by the use of "condition-ing." Namely, rather than using the actual observed time of the first event after t, we can condition on $A(t)$, the time at t since the last event (see Figure 8.3). The quantity $A(t)$ is often called the age of the renewal process at t. [If we imagine a system consisting of a single item that functions for a random time having distribution F and then fails and is immediately replaced by a new item, then we have a renewal process with each event corresponding to the failure of

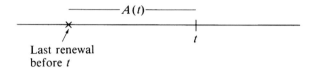

Figure 8.3 Age at t

an item. The variable $A(t)$ would then refer to the age of the item in use at time t, where by age we mean the amount of time it has already been in use.]

Now if the age of the process at time t is x, the expected remaining life of the item is just the expected amount by which an interevent time exceeds x given that it is greater than x. That is,

$$E[Y(t)|A(t) = x] = E[T - x|T > x]$$

$$= \int_x^\infty (y - x) \frac{f(x)\,dx}{1 - F(x)}$$

$$\equiv \mu[x]$$

where the above supposes that F is a continuous distribution with density function f. Hence, with $\mu[x]$ defined as above to equal $E[T - x \mid T > x]$, we see that

$$E[Y(t)|A(t)] = \mu[A(t)]$$

Thus, for large t, a better estimator of $E[N(t)]$ than the one given in Equation (8.7) is

$$\frac{\mu[A(t)]}{\mu} + \frac{t}{\mu} - 1 \tag{8.8}$$

8.4 Stratified Sampling

Consider a finite capacity queueing system which has the property that it empties at the end of each day and then begins anew at the beginning of the next day. Customers arrive daily in accordance with a Poisson process, but suppose that the rate of that process can change each day. Specifically, suppose that for any given day the Poisson arrival rate, independently of what occurred on prior days, is either λ_1, λ_2, or λ_3, each with probability $\frac{1}{3}$. We are interested in simulating this system so as to estimate the average number of customers that are lost (because they arrived when the system was at capacity) during a day.

To simulate the above we begin each run by generating a random variable I which is equally likely to be 1, 2, or 3. We then simulate one day of the above system under the assumption that customers arrive in accordance with a Poisson process having rate λ_I. Intuitively, however, since we know that each day is equally likely to have Poisson arrivals at rate λ_i, $i = 1, 2, 3$, it seems that it might be preferable to perform exactly one-third of our simulation runs using each of these three rates.

To verify the above intuition, let, for $i = 1, 2, 3$, L_i^* denote the number of lost customers in a day given that the arrivals during that day are Poisson with mean λ_i. Also, let L denote the number of lost customers in a day. Then, upon conditioning upon what the daily arrival rate is, we see that

$$E[L] = \frac{1}{3} (E[L_1^*] + E[L_2^*] + E[L_3^*]) \tag{8.9}$$

Now let L_i, having the same distribution as L, denote the number of lost customers on day i. We now argue that

$$\text{Var}(L_1^* + L_2^* + L_3^*) \leq \text{Var}(L_1 + L_2 + L_3) \tag{8.10}$$

Since $(L_1^* + L_2^* + L_3^*)/3$ is by (8.9) an unbiased estimator of $E[L]$, it thus follows from (8.10) that using each λ_i in exactly one-third of the simulation runs (as opposed to a random choosing at the beginning of each run) results in an unbiased estimator having smaller variance.

To prove the inequality (8.10) we make use of the conditional variance formula

$$\text{Var}(X) = E[\text{Var}(X|Y)] + \text{Var}(E[X|Y])$$

Because both terms on the right are nonnegative, we see that

$$\text{Var}(X) \geq E[\text{Var}(X|Y)]$$

Hence, with L representing the number of lost customers in a day and I being the index of the Poisson arrival rate for that day, we see that

$$\text{Var}(L) \geq E[\text{Var}(L|I)]$$

$$= \sum_{i=1}^{3} \text{Var}(L|I = i)P\{I = i\}$$

$$= \frac{1}{3} \sum_{i=1}^{3} \mathrm{Var}(L_i^*)$$

$$= \frac{1}{3} \mathrm{Var}(L_1^* + L_2^* + L_3^*)$$

which, since $\mathrm{Var}(L_1 + L_2 + L_3) = 3\,\mathrm{Var}(L)$ establishes (8.10).

Example 8o   On good days customers arrive at an infinite server queue according to a Poisson process with rate 12 per hour, whereas on other days they arrive according to a Poisson process with rate 4 per hour. The service times, on all days, are exponentially distributed with rate 1 per hour. Every day at time 10 hours the system is shut down and all those presently in service are forced to leave without completing service. Suppose that each day is, independently, a good day with probability 0.5 and that we want to use simulation to estimate θ, the mean number of customers per day that do not have their services completed.

Let L denote the number of customers whose service is not completed on a randomly selected day, and let L_g and L_o denote the number on a good and on an ordinary day respectively. Now, it can be shown that L_g and L_o are both Poisson random variables with respective means $12(1 - e^{-10})$ and $4(1 - e^{-10})$. Hence, since the variance of a Poisson random variable is equal to its mean, we see that

$$\mathrm{Var}(L_g) \approx 12, \qquad \mathrm{Var}(L_o) \approx 4$$

Also, since L is equal to L_g with probability $\frac{1}{2}$ and is equal to L_o with probability $\frac{1}{2}$, it follows that

$$\theta = E[L] = \frac{1}{2} E[L_g] + \frac{1}{2} E[L_o] \approx 8$$

$$E[L^2] = \frac{1}{2} E[L_g^2] + \frac{1}{2} E[L_o^2] \approx \frac{(12 + 144 + 4 + 16)}{2} = 88$$

where the preceding used the identity $E[X^2] = \mathrm{Var}(X) + (E[X])^2$. Hence,

$$\mathrm{Var}(L) \approx 88 - 64 = 24$$

Thus, if we first simulate L_g and then L_o, then the variance of the estimator $(L_g + L_o)/2$ is

$$\mathrm{Var}\!\left(\frac{L_g + L_o}{2}\right) = \frac{[\mathrm{Var}(L_g) + \mathrm{Var}(L_o)]}{4} \approx 4$$

On the other hand, if we simulate two iterations of L, then the variance of the estimator $(L_1 + L_2)/2$ is

$$\text{Var}[(L_1 + L_2)/2] \approx \frac{24}{2} = 12$$

which is larger than that of the preceding estimator by a factor approximately equal to 3. ■

In the more general case, suppose that the possible arrival rates on each day are λ_i, with respective probabilities p_i, $\sum_{i=1}^k p_i = 1$. In this case we would have that

$$E[L] = \sum_{i=1}^k E[L_i^*] p_i$$

where L_i^* is the number lost on a day in which customers arrive at rate λ_i. Hence, rather than randomly choosing an arrival rate on each day, a similar argument to the one presented shows that it is better to perform $100 p_i\%$ of the runs with the arrival rate λ_i, $i = 1, \ldots, k$. If $\overline{L}_i^*$ is the average number of lost customers in those runs that use the arrival rate λ_i, then the estimator of $\theta = E[L]$ based on n runs is

$$\hat{\theta} = \sum_{i=1}^k p_i \overline{L}_i^*$$

The variance of the estimator is given by

$$\text{Var}(\hat{\theta}) = \sum_{i=1}^k \frac{p_i^2 \text{Var}(L_i^*)}{n_i} \tag{8.11}$$

where $n_i = np_i$ is the number of runs that use the arrival rate λ_i. If we let S_i^2 denote the sample variance of the number of lost customers on the days that use the arrival rate λ_i, then $\text{Var}(\hat{\theta})$ can be estimated by $\sum_{i=1}^k p_i^2 S_i^2/n_i$.

Although performing np_i of the n runs with the arrival rate λ_i, $i = 1, \ldots, k$, is better than randomly choosing the rate at the beginning of each day, this is not necessarily the optimal number of runs to perform using each of these rates. Suppose that we plan to perform n simulation runs. If we let n_i denote the number of these runs that use the arrival rate λ_i, $i = 1, \ldots, k$, then the estimator of $E[L]$ will be $\sum_{i=1}^k p_i \overline{L}_i^*$, with its variance given by (8.11). Whereas the variances of L_i^*, $i = 1, \ldots, k$, will be initially unknown, we could perform a small simulation study to estimate them—say we use the estimators s_i^2. We could then choose n_i by solving the following optimization problem:

$$\text{choose} \quad n_1, \ldots, n_k, \quad \sum_{i=1}^{k} n_i = n \quad \text{to}$$

$$\min \sum_{i=1}^{k} p_i^2 s_i^2/n_i$$

Once the n_i are chosen we would estimate $E[L]$ by $\sum_{i=1}^{k} p_i \bar{L}_i^*$ and we would estimate its variance by $\sum_{i=1}^{k} p_i^2 S_i^2/n_i$ where, as before, S_i^2 is the sample variance for the n_i runs that use λ_i.

For instance, suppose that $k = 2$ and that we make nx runs using λ_1 and $n(1 - x)$ runs using λ_2. Then, letting $p = p_1$, we would then want to choose x, $0 \le x \le 1$, to minimize

$$\frac{ps_1^2}{nx} + \frac{(1 - p)s_2^2}{n(1 - x)}$$

and this is easily accomplished by using calculus. If, as in Example 8n, $p = \frac{1}{2}$, $s_1^2 = 12$, $s_2^2 = 4$, then solving the preceding gives the minimizing value $x \approx 0.634$, thus showing that we should do approximately 63.4 percent of the runs using $\lambda = 12$ and 36.6 percent with $\lambda = 4$.

In general, if we want to estimate $E[X]$ in a situation where X depends on a random variable S that takes on one of the values $1, \ldots, k$ with known probabilities, then the technique of stratifying the simulation runs into k groups, with the ith group having $S = i$, letting $\bar{X}_i$ be the average value of X in those runs with $S = i$, and then estimating $E[X] = \sum_{i=1}^{k} E[X|S = i] P\{S = i\}$ by $\sum_{i=1}^{k} \bar{X}_i P\{S = i\}$, is called *stratified sampling*.

Remark   It is interesting that the proof that stratified sampling leads to a reduction in variance uses the conditional variance formula to assert that

$$\text{Var}(X) \ge E[\text{Var}(X|Y)]$$

whereas the proof that "conditioning" always reduces the variance of an estimator (see Section 8.3) uses the conditional variance formula to assert that

$$\text{Var}(X) \ge \text{Var}(E[X|Y]) \qquad \blacksquare$$

For another illustration of stratified sampling, suppose that we want to use n simulation runs to estimate

$$\theta = E[h(U)] = \int_0^1 h(x) \, dx$$

If we let

$$S = j \quad \text{if} \quad \frac{j-1}{n} \le U < \frac{j}{n}, \quad j = 1, \ldots, n$$

then

$$\theta = \frac{1}{n} \sum_{j=1}^{n} E[h(U)|S = j]$$

$$= \frac{1}{n} \sum_{j=1}^{n} E[h(U_{(j)}]$$

where $U_{(j)}$ is uniform on $((j-1)/n, j/n)$. Hence, by the preceding, it follows that rather than generating $U_1, \ldots, U_n$ and then using $\sum_{j=1}^{n} h(U_j)/n$ to estimate θ, a better estimator is obtained by using

$$\hat{\theta} = \frac{1}{n} \sum_{j=1}^{n} h\left(\frac{U_j + j - 1}{n}\right)$$

Example 8p In Example 8k we showed that

$$\frac{\pi}{4} = E[\sqrt{(1 - U^2}]$$

Hence, we can estimate π by generating $U_1, \ldots, U_n$ and using the estimator

$$\text{est} = \frac{4}{n} \sum_{j=1}^{n} \sqrt{1 - [(U_j + j - 1)/n]^2}$$

In fact, we can improve the preceding by making use of antithetic variables to obtain the estimator

$$\hat{\pi} = \frac{2}{n} \sum_{j=1}^{n} \left(\sqrt{1 - [(U_j + j - 1)/n]^2} + \sqrt{1 - [(j - U_j)/n]^2} \right)$$

A simulation using the estimator $\hat{\pi}$ yielded the following results:

n	$\hat{\pi}$
5	3.161211
10	3.148751
100	3.141734
500	3.141615
1000	3.141601
5000	3.141593

When $n = 5000$, the estimator $\hat{\pi}$ is correct to six decimal places. ■

Suppose again that we are interested in estimating $\theta = E[X]$, where X is dependent on the random variable S, which takes on one of the values $1, 2, \ldots, k$ with respective probabilities p_i, $i = 1, \ldots, k$. Then

$$E[X] = p_1 E[X|S = 1] + p_2 E[X|S = 2] + \cdots + p_k E[X|S = k]$$

If all of the quantities $E[X|S = i]$ are known (that is, if $E[X|S]$ is known), but the p_i are not, then we can estimate θ by generating the value of S and then using the conditional expectation estimator $E[X|S]$. On the other hand, if it is the p_i that are known and we can generate from the conditional distribution of X given the value of S, then we can use simulation to obtain estimators $\hat{E}[X|S = i]$ of the quantities $E[X|S = i]$ and then use the stratified sampling estimator $\Sigma_{i=1}^{k} p_i \hat{E}[X|S = i]$ to estimate $E[X]$. When some of the p_i and some of the $E[X|S = i]$ are known, we can use a combination of these approaches.

Example 8q In the game of video poker a player inserts one dollar into a machine, which then deals the player a random hand of 5 cards. The player is then allowed to discard certain of these cards, with the discarded cards replaced by new ones from the remaining 47 cards. The player is then returned a certain amount depending on the makeup of her or his final cards. The following is a typical payoff scheme:

Hand	Payoff
Royal flush	800
Straight flush	50
Four of a kind	25
Full house	8
Flush	5
Straight	4
Three of a kind	3
Two pair	2
High pair (jacks or better)	1
Anything else	0

In the preceding, a hand is characterized as being in a certain category if it is of that type and not of any higher type. That is, for instance, by a flush we mean 5 cards of the same suit that are not consecutive.

Consider a strategy that never takes any additional cards (that is, the player stands pat) if the original cards constitute a straight or higher, and that always retains whatever pairs or triplets that it is dealt. For a given strategy of this type let X denote the player's winnings on a single hand, and suppose we are interested in estimating $\theta = E[X]$. Rather than just using X as the estimator, let us start by conditioning on the type of hand that is initially dealt to the player. Let R represent a royal flush, S represent a straight flush, 4 represent four of a kind, 3 represent three of a kind, 2 represent two pair, 1 represent a high pair, 0 represent a low pair, and "other" represent all other hands not mentioned. We then have

$$E[X] = E[X|R]P\{R\} + E[X|S]P\{S\} + E[X|4]P\{4\} + E[X|full]P\{full\} +$$
$$E[X|flush]P\{flush\} + E[X|straight]P\{straight\} + E[X|3]P\{3\} +$$
$$E[X|2]P\{2\} + E[X|1]P\{1\} + E[X|0]P\{0\} + E[X|other]P\{other\}$$

Now, with $C = \binom{52}{5}^{-1}$, we have

$$P\{R\} = 4C = 1.539 \times 10^{-6}$$
$$P\{S\} = 4 \cdot 9 \cdot C = 1.3851 \times 10^{-4}$$
$$P\{4\} = 13 \cdot 48 \cdot C = 2.40096 \times 10^{-4}$$

$$P\{full\} = 13 \cdot 12\binom{4}{3}\binom{4}{2}C = 1.440576 \times 10^{-3}$$

$$P\{flush\} = 4\left(\binom{13}{5} - 10\right)C = 1.965402 \times 10^{-3}$$

$$P\{straight\} = 10(4^5 - 4)C = 3.924647 \times 10^{-3}$$

$$P\{3\} = 13\binom{12}{2}4^3C = 2.1128451 \times 10^{-2}$$

$$P\{2\} = \binom{13}{2}44\binom{4}{2}\binom{4}{2}C = 4.7539016 \times 10^{-2}$$

$$P\{1\} = 4\binom{4}{2}\binom{12}{3}4^3C = 0.130021239$$

$$P\{0\} = 9\binom{4}{2}\binom{12}{3}4^3C = 0.292547788$$

$$P\{other\} = 1 - P\{R\} - P\{S\} - P\{full\} - P\{flush\}$$
$$- P\{straight\} - \sum_{i=0}^{4} P\{i\} = 0.5010527$$

Therefore, we see that

$$E[X] = 0.0512903 + \sum_{i=0}^{3} E[X|i]P\{i\} + E[X|other]0.5010527$$

Now, $E[X|3]$ can be analytically computed by noting that the 2 new cards will come from a subdeck of 47 cards that contains 1 card of one denomination (namely the denomination to which your three of a kind belong), 3 cards of two denominations, and 4 cards of the other 10 denominations. Thus, letting F be the final hand, we have that

$$P\{F = 4|\text{dealt } 3\} = \frac{46}{\binom{47}{2}} = 0.042553191$$

$$P\{F = \text{full}|\text{dealt } 3\} = \frac{2 \cdot 3 + 10 \cdot 6}{\binom{47}{2}} = 0.061054579$$

$$P\{F = 3|\text{dealt } 3\} = 1 - 0.042553191 - 0.061054579 = 0.89639223$$

Hence,

$$E[X|3] = 25(0.042553191) + 8(0.061054579) + 3(0.89639223)$$
$$= 4.241443097$$

Similarly, we can analytically derive (and the derivation is left as an exercise) $E[X|i]$ for $i = 0, 1, 2)$.

In running the simulation, we should thus generate a hand. If it contains at least one pair or a higher hand then it should be discarded and the process begun again. When we are dealt a hand that does not contain a pair (or any higher hand), we should use whatever strategy we are employing to discard and receive new cards. If X_o is the payoff on this hand, then X_o is the estimator of $E[X|\text{other}]$, and the estimator of $\theta = E[X]$ based on this single run is

$$\hat{\theta} = 0.0512903 + 0.021128451(4.241443097) + 0.047539016E[X|2]$$
$$+ 0.130021239E[X|1] + 0.292547788E[X|0] + 0.5010527X_o$$

Note that the variance of the estimator is

$$\text{Var}(\hat{\theta}) = (0.5010527)^2\text{Var}(X_o)$$

Remarks

1. We have supposed that the strategy employed always sticks with a pat hand and always keeps whatever pairs it has. However, for the payoffs given this is not an optimal strategy. For instance, if one is dealt 2, 10, Jack, Queen, King, all of spades, then rather than standing with this flush it is better to discard the 2 and draw another card (why is that?). Also, if dealt 10, Jack, Queen, King, all of spades, along with the 10 of hearts, it is better to discard the 10 of hearts and draw 1 card than it is to keep the pair of 10s.

2. We could have made further use of stratified sampling by breaking up the "other" category into, say, those "other" hands that contain four cards of the same suit, and those that do not. It is not difficult to analytically compute the probability that a hand will be without a pair and with four cards of the same suit. We could then use simulation to estimate the conditional expected payoffs in these two "other" cases. ∎

8.5 Importance Sampling

Let $\mathbf{X} = (X_1, \ldots, X_n)$ denote a vector of random variables having a joint density function (or joint mass function in the discrete case) $f(\mathbf{x}) = f(x_1, \ldots, x_n)$, and suppose that we are interested in estimating

$$\theta = E[h(\mathbf{X})] = \int h(\mathbf{x})f(\mathbf{x}) \, d\mathbf{x}$$

where the preceding is an n-dimensional integral. (If the X_i are discrete, then interpret the integral as an n-fold summation.)

Suppose that a direct simulation of the random vector $\mathbf{X}$, so as to compute values of $h(\mathbf{X})$, is inefficient, possibly because (a) it is difficult to simulate a random vector having density function $f(\mathbf{x})$, or (b) the variance of $h(\mathbf{X})$ is large, or (c) a combination of (a) and (b).

Another way in which we can use simulation to estimate θ is to note that if $g(\mathbf{x})$ is another probability density such that $f(\mathbf{x}) = 0$ whenever $g(\mathbf{x}) = 0$, then we can express θ as

$$\begin{aligned} \theta &= \int \frac{h(\mathbf{x})f(\mathbf{x})}{g(\mathbf{x})} \, g(\mathbf{x}) \, d\mathbf{x} \\ &= E_g\left[\frac{h(\mathbf{X})f(\mathbf{X})}{g(\mathbf{X})}\right] \end{aligned} \tag{8.12}$$

where we have written E_g to emphasize that the random vector $\mathbf{X}$ has joint density $g(\mathbf{x})$.

It follows from Equation (8.12) that θ can be estimated by successively generating values of a random vector $\mathbf{X}$ having density function $g(\mathbf{x})$ and then using as the estimator the average of the values of $h(\mathbf{X})f(\mathbf{X})/g(\mathbf{X})$. If a density function $g(\mathbf{x})$ can be chosen so that the random variable $h(\mathbf{X})f(\mathbf{X})/g(\mathbf{X})$ has a small variance, then this approach—referred to as *importance sampling*—can result in an efficient estimator of θ.

Let us now try to obtain a feel for why importance sampling can be useful. To begin, note that $f(\mathbf{X})$ and $g(\mathbf{X})$ represent the respective likelihoods of obtaining the vector $\mathbf{X}$ when $\mathbf{X}$ is a random vector with respective densities f and g. Hence, if $\mathbf{X}$ is distributed according to g, then it will usually be the case that $f(\mathbf{X})$ will be small in relation to $g(\mathbf{X})$, and thus when $\mathbf{X}$ is simulated according to g the likelihood ratio $f(\mathbf{X})/g(\mathbf{X})$ will usually be small in comparison to 1. However, it is easy to check that its mean is 1:

$$E_g\left[\frac{f(\mathbf{X})}{g(\mathbf{X})}\right] = \int \frac{f(\mathbf{x})}{g(\mathbf{x})} g(\mathbf{x})\, d\mathbf{x} = \int f(\mathbf{x})\, d\mathbf{x} = 1$$

Thus we see that even though $f(\mathbf{X})/g(\mathbf{X})$ is usually smaller than 1, its mean is equal to 1, thus implying that it is occasionally large and so will tend to have a large variance. So how can $h(\mathbf{X})f(\mathbf{X})/g(\mathbf{X})$ have a small variance? The answer is that we can sometimes arrange to choose a density g such that those values of $\mathbf{x}$ for which $f(\mathbf{x})/g(\mathbf{x})$ is large are precisely the values for which $h(\mathbf{x})$ is exceedingly small, and thus the ratio $h(\mathbf{X})f(\mathbf{X})/g(\mathbf{X})$ is always small. Since this will require that $h(\mathbf{x})$ is sometimes small, importance sampling seems to work best when estimating a small probability, for in this case the function $h(\mathbf{x})$ is equal to 1 when $\mathbf{x}$ lies in some set and is equal to 0 otherwise.

We will now consider how to select an appropriate density g. We fill find that the so-called tilted densities are useful. Let $M(t) = E_f[e^{tX}] = \int e^{tx}f(x)\, dx$ be the moment generating function corresponding to a one-dimensional density f.

Definition   *A density function*

$$f_t(x) = \frac{e^{tx}f(x)}{M(t)}$$

is called a tilted density of f, $-\infty < t < \infty$.

A random variable with density f_t tends to be larger than one with density f when $t > 0$ and tends to be smaller when $t < 0$.

In certain cases the tilted densities f_t have the same parametric form as does f.

Examples 8r   If f is the exponential density with rate λ, then

$$f_t(x) = Ce^{tx}\lambda e^{-\lambda x} = Ce^{-(\lambda-t)x}$$

where $C = 1/M(t)$ does not depend on x. Therefore, for $t < \lambda$, f_t is an exponential density with rate $\lambda - t$.

If f is a Bernoulli probability mass function with parameter p, then

$$f(x) = p^x(1 - p)^{1-x}, \qquad x = 0, 1$$

Hence, $M(t) = E_f[e^{tX}] = pe^t + 1 - p$, and so

$$f_t(x) = \frac{1}{M(t)} (pe^t)^x(1 - p)^{1-x}$$

$$= \left(\frac{pe^t}{pe^t + 1 - p}\right)^x \left(\frac{1 - p}{pe^t + 1 - p}\right)^{1-x}$$

That is, f_t is the probability mass function of a Bernoulli random variable with parameter $p_t = (pe^t)/(pe^t + 1 - p)$.

We leave it as an exercise to show that if f is a normal density with parameters μ and σ^2 then f_t is a normal density having mean $\mu + \sigma^2 t$ and variance σ^2. ■

In certain situations the quantity of interest is the sum of the independent random variables $X_1, \ldots, X_n$. In this case the joint density f is the product of one-dimensional densities. That is,

$$f(x_1, \ldots, x_n) = f_1(x_1) \cdots f_n(x_n)$$

where f_i is the density function of X_i. In this situation it is often useful to generate the X_i according to their tilted densities, with a common choice of t employed.

Example 8s Let $X_1, \ldots, X_n$ be independent random variables having respective probability density (or mass) functions f_i, for $i = 1, \ldots, n$. Suppose we are interested in approximating the probability that their sum is at least as large as a, where a is much larger than the mean of the sum. That is, we are interested in

$$\theta = P\{S \geq a\}$$

where $S = \sum_{i=1}^{n} X_i$, and where $a > \sum_{i=1}^{n} E[X_i]$. Letting $I\{S \geq a\}$ equal 1 if $S \geq a$ and letting it be 0 otherwise, we have that

$$\theta = E_f[I\{S \geq a\}]$$

where $\mathbf{f} = (f_1, \ldots, f_n)$. Suppose now that we simulate X_i according to the tilted mass function $f_{i,t}$, $i = 1, \ldots, n$, with the value of t, $t > 0$, left to be determined. The importance sampling estimator of θ would then be

$$\hat{\theta} = I\{S \geq a\} \prod \frac{f_i(X_i)}{f_{i,t}(X_i)}$$

Now,

$$\frac{f_i(X_i)}{f_{i,t}(X_i)} = M_i(t)e^{-tX_i}$$

and so,

$$\hat{\theta} = I\{S \geq a\}M(t)e^{-tS}$$

where $M(t) = \prod M_i(t)$ is the moment generating function of S. Since $t > 0$ and $I\{S \geq a\}$ is equal to 0 when $S < a$, it follows that

$$I\{S \geq a\}e^{-tS} \leq e^{-ta}$$

and so

$$\hat{\theta} \leq M(t)e^{-ta}$$

To make the bound on the estimator as small as possible we thus choose t, $t > 0$, to minimize $M(t)e^{-ta}$. In doing so, we will obtain an estimator whose value on each iteration is between 0 and $\min_t M(t)e^{-ta}$. It can be shown that the minimizing t—call it t^*— is such that

$$E_{t*}[S] = E_{t*}\left[\sum_{i=1}^{n} X_i\right] = a$$

where, in the preceding, we mean that the expected value is to be taken under the assumption that the distribution of X_i is $f_{i,t*}$ for $i = 1, \ldots, n$.

For instance, suppose that $X_1, \ldots, X_n$ are independent Bernoulli random variables having respective parameters p_i, for $i = 1, \ldots, n$. Then, if we generate the X_i according to their tilted mass functions $p_{i,t}$, $i = 1, \ldots, n$, then the importance sampling estimator of $\theta = P\{S \geq \alpha\}$ is

$$\hat{\theta} = I\{S \geq a\}e^{-tS} \prod_{i-1}^{n} (p_ie^t + 1 - p_i)$$

Since $p_{i,t}$ is the mass function of Bernoulli random variable with parameter $(p_ie^t)/(p_ie^t + 1 - p_i)$, it follows that

$$E_t\left[\sum_{i=1}^{n} X_i\right] = \sum_{i=1}^{n} \frac{p_ie^t}{p_ie^t + 1 - p_i}$$

The value of t that makes the preceding equal to a can be numerically approximated and the t utilized in the simulation.

As an illustration, suppose that $n = 20$, $p_i = 0.4$, $a = 16$. Then

$$E_t[S] = 20 \, \frac{0.4e^t}{0.4e^t + 0.6}$$

Setting this equal to 16 yields after a little algebra that

$$e^{t^*} = 6$$

Thus, if we generate the Bernoullis using the parameter $(0.4e^{t^*})/(0.4e^{t^*} + 0.6)$ $= 0.8$, then as

$$M(t^*) = (0.4e^{t^*} + 0.6)^{20} \qquad \text{and} \qquad e^{-t^*S} = (1/6)^S$$

we see that the importance sampling estimator is

$$\hat{\theta} = I\{S \geq 16\}(1/6)^S 3^{20}$$

It follows from the preceding that

$$\hat{\theta} \leq (1/6)^{16} 3^{20} = 81/2^{16} = 0.001236$$

That is, on each iteration the value of estimator is between 0 and 0.001236. Since, in this case, θ is the probability that a binomial random variable with parameters 20, 0.4 is at least 16, it can be explicitly computed with the result α $= 0.000317$. Hence, the raw simulation estimator I, which on each iteration takes the value 0 if the sum of the Bernoullis with parameter 0.4 is less than 16 and takes the value 1 otherwise, will have variance

$$\text{Var}(I) = \theta(1 - \theta) = 3.169 \times 10^{-4}$$

On the other hand, it follows from the fact that $0 \leq \theta \leq 0.001236$ that (see Exercise 22)

$$\text{Var}(\hat{\theta}) \leq 2.9131 \times 10^{-7} \qquad\qquad \blacksquare$$

Example 8t Consider a single server queue in which the times between successive customer arrivals have density function f and the service times have density g. Let D_n denote the amount of time that nth arrival spends waiting in queue and suppose we are interested in estimating $\alpha = P\{D_n \geq a\}$ when a is much larger than $E[D_n]$. Rather than generating the successive interarrival and service times according to f and g, respectively, we should generate them according to the densities f_{-t} and g_t, where t is a positive number to be determined. Note that using these distributions as opposed to f and g will result in smaller interarrival times (since $-t < 0$) and larger service times. Hence, there will be a greater chance that $D_n > a$ than if we had simulated using the densities f and g. The importance sampling estimator of α would then be

$$\hat{\alpha} = I\{D_n > a\}e^{t(S_n - Y_n)}[M_f(-t)M_g(t)]^n$$

where S_n is the sum of the first n interarrival times, Y_n is the sum of the first n service times, and M_f and M_g are the moment generating functions of the densities f and g, respectively. The value of t used should be determined by experimenting with a variety of different choices. ■

Example 8u   Let $X_1, X_2, \ldots$ be a sequence of independent and identically distributed normal random variables having mean μ and variance 1, where $\mu < 0$. An important problem in the theory of quality control (specifically in the analysis of the so-called cumulative sum charts) is to determine the probability that the partial sums of these values exceeds B before going below $-A$. That is, let

$$S_n = \sum_{i=1}^{n} X_i$$

and define

$$N = \text{Min}\{n: \text{ either } S_n < -A, \text{ or } S_n > B\}$$

where A and B are fixed positive numbers. We are now interested in estimating

$$\theta = P\{S_N > B\}$$

An effective way of estimating θ is by simulating the X_i as if they were normal with mean $-\mu$ and variance 1, stopping again when their sum either exceeds B or falls below $-A$. (Since $-\mu$ is positive, the stopped sum is greater than B more often than if we were simulating with the original negative mean.) If $X_1, \ldots, X_N$ denote the simulated variables (each being normal with mean $-\mu$ and variance 1) and

$$I = \begin{cases} 1 & \text{if } \sum_{i=1}^{N} X_i > B \\ 0 & \text{otherwise} \end{cases}$$

then the estimate of θ from this run is

$$I \prod_{i=1}^{N} \left[\frac{f_\mu(X_i)}{f_{-\mu}(X_i)}\right] \tag{8.13}$$

where f_c is the normal density with mean c and variance 1. Since

$$\frac{f_\mu(x)}{f_{-\mu}(x)} = \frac{\exp\left\{-\dfrac{(x-\mu)^2}{2}\right\}}{\exp\left\{-\dfrac{(x+\mu)^2}{2}\right\}} = e^{2\mu x}$$

it follows from (8.13) that the estimator of θ based on this run is

$$I \exp\left\{2\mu \sum_{i=1}^{N} X_i\right\} = I \exp\{2\mu S_N\}$$

When I is equal to 1, S_N exceeds B and, since $\mu < 0$, the estimator in this case is less than $e^{2\mu B}$. That is, rather than obtaining from each run either the value 0 or 1—as would occur if we did a straight simulation—we obtain in this case either the value 0 or a value that is less than $e^{2\mu B}$, which strongly indicates why this importance sampling approach results in a reduced variance. For example, if $\mu = -0.1$ and $B = 5$, then the estimate from each run lies between 0 and $e^{-1} = 0.3679$. In addition, the above is theoretically important because it shows that

$$P\{\text{cross } B \text{ before } -A\} \le e^{2\mu B}$$

Since the above is true for all positive A, we obtain the interesting result

$$P\{\text{ever cross } B\} \le e^{2\mu B} \qquad ■$$

Example 8v   Let $\mathbf{X} = (X_1, \ldots, X_{100})$ be a random permutation of $(1, 2, \ldots, 100)$. That is $\mathbf{X}$ is equally likely to be any of the $(100)!$ permutations. Suppose we are interested in using simulation to estimate

$$\theta = P\left\{\sum_{j=1}^{100} jX_j > 290{,}000\right\}$$

To obtain a feel for the magnitude of θ, we can start by computing the mean and standard deviation of $\sum_{j=1}^{100} jX_j$. Indeed, it is not difficult to show that

$$E\left[\sum_{j=1}^{100} jX_j\right] = 100(101)^2/4 = 255{,}025$$

$$\text{SD}\left(\sum_{j=1}^{100} jX_j\right) = \sqrt{(99)(100)^2(101)^2/144} = 8374.478$$

Hence, if we suppose that $\Sigma_{j=1}^{100} jX_j$ is roughly normally distributed then, with Z representing a standard normal random variable, we have that

$$\theta \approx P\left\{Z > \frac{290{,}000 - 255{,}025}{8374.478}\right\}$$

$$= P\{Z > 4.1764\}$$

$$= 0.00001481$$

Thus, θ is clearly a small probability and so an importance sampling estimator is worth considering.

To utilize importance sampling we would want to generate the permutation **X** so that there is a much larger probability that $\Sigma_{j=1}^{100} jX_j > 290{,}000$. Indeed, we should try for a probability of about .5. Now, $\Sigma_{j=1}^{100} jX_j$ will attain its largest value when $X_j = j$, $j = 1, \ldots, 100$, and indeed it will tend to be large when X_j tends to be large when j is large and small when j is small. One way to generate a permutation **X** that will tend to be of this type is as follows: Generate independent exponential random variables Y_j, $j = 1, \ldots, 100$, with respective rates λ_j, $j = 1, \ldots, 100$ where λ_j, $j = 1, \ldots, 100$, is an increasing sequence whose values will soon be specified. Now, for $j = 1, \ldots, 100$, let X_j be the index of the jth largest of these generated values. That is,

$$Y_{X_1} > Y_{X_2} > \cdots > Y_{X_{100}}$$

Since, for j large, Y_j will tend to be one of the smaller Y's, it follows that X_j will tend to be large when j is large and so $\Sigma_{j=1}^{100} jX_j$ will tend to be larger than if X were a uniformly distributed permutation.

Let us now compute $E[\Sigma_{j=1}^{100} jX_j]$. To do so, let $R(j)$ denote the rank of Y_j, $j = 1, \ldots, 100$, where rank 1 signifies the largest, rank 2 the second largest, and so on until rank 100, which is the smallest. Note that since X_j is the index of the jth largest of the Y's, it follows that $R(X_j) = j$. Hence,

$$\sum_{j=1}^{100} jX_j = \sum_{j=1}^{100} R(X_j)X_j = \sum_{j=1}^{100} jR(j)$$

where the final equality follows since $X_1, \ldots, X_{100}$ is a permutation of $1, \ldots, 100$. Therefore, we see that

$$E\left[\sum_{j=1}^{100} jX_j\right] = \sum_{j=1}^{100} jE[R(j)]$$

To compute $E[R_j]$, let $I(i, j) = 1$ if $Y_j < Y_i$ and let it be 0 otherwise, and note that

$$R_j = 1 + \sum_{i:i \neq j} I(i, j)$$

In words, the preceding equation states that the rank of Y_j is 1 plus the number of the Y_i that are larger than it. Hence, taking expectations and using the fact that

$$P\{Y_j < Y_i\} = \frac{\lambda_j}{\lambda_i + \lambda_j},$$

we obtain that

$$E[R_j] = 1 + \sum_{i:i \neq j} \frac{\lambda_j}{\lambda_i + \lambda_j}$$

and thus

$$E\left[\sum_{j=1}^{100} jX_j\right] = \sum_{j=1}^{100} j\left(1 + \sum_{i:i \neq j} \frac{\lambda_j}{\lambda_i + \lambda_j}\right)$$

If we let $\lambda_j = j^{0.7}$, $j = 1, \ldots, 100$, then a computation shows that $E[\sum_{j=1}^{100} jX_j] = 290{,}293.6$, and so when $\mathbf{X}$ is generated using these rates it would seem that

$$P\left\{\sum_{j=1}^{100} jX_j > 290{,}000\right\} \approx 0.5$$

Thus, we suggest that the simulation estimator should be obtained by first generating independent exponentials Y_j with respective rates $j^{.7}$, and then letting X_j be the index of the jth largest, $j = 1, \ldots, 100$. Let $I = 1$ if $\sum_{j=1}^{100} jX_j > 290{,}000$ and let it be 0 otherwise. Now, the outcome will be $\mathbf{X}$ when $Y_{X_{100}}$ is the smallest Y, $Y_{X_{99}}$ is the second smallest, and so on. The probability of this outcome is $1/(100)!$ when $\mathbf{X}$ is equally likely to be any of the permutations, whereas its probability when the simulation is as performed is

$$\frac{(X_{100})^{0.7}}{\sum_{j=1}^{100} (X_j)^{0.7}} \frac{(X_{99})^{0.7}}{\sum_{j=1}^{99} (X_j)^{0.7}} \cdots \frac{(X_2)^{0.7}}{\sum_{j=1}^{2} (X_j)^{0.7}} \frac{(X_1)^{0.7}}{(X_1)^{0.7}}$$

Therefore, the importance sampling estimator from a single run is

$$\hat{\theta} = \frac{I}{(100)!} \frac{\prod_{n=1}^{100} \left(\sum_{j=1}^{n} (X_j)^{0.7}\right)}{\left(\prod_{n=1}^{100} n\right)^{0.7}} = \frac{I \prod_{n=1}^{100} \left(\sum_{j=1}^{n} (X_j)^{0.7}\right)}{\left(\prod_{n=1}^{100} n\right)^{1.7}}$$

Before the simulation is begun, the values of $C = 1.7 \sum_{n=1}^{100} \log(n)$ and $a(j) = -j^{-0.7}, j = 1, \ldots, 100$, should be computed. A simulation run can then be obtained as follows:

> For $j = 1$ to 100
>
> Generate a random number U
>
> $Y_j = a(j) \log U$
>
> Next
>
> Let $X_j, j = 1, \ldots, 100$, be such that Y_{X_j} is the jth largest Y
>
> If $\sum_{j=1}^{n} jX_j \leq 290{,}000$ set $\hat{\theta} = 0$ and stop
>
> $S = 0, P = 0$
>
> For $n = 1$ to 100
>
> $S = S + (X_n)^{0.7}$
>
> $P = P + \log(S)$
>
> Next
>
> $\hat{\theta} = e^{P-C}$

A sample of 50,000 simulation runs yielded the estimate $\hat{\theta} = 3.77 \times 10^{-6}$, with a sample variance 1.89×10^{-8}. Since the variance of the raw simulation estimator, which is equal to 1 if $\sum_{j=1}^{100} jX_j > 290{,}000$ and is equal to 0 otherwise, is $\text{Var}(I) = \theta(1 - \theta) \approx 3.77 \times 10^{-6}$, we see that

$$\frac{\text{Var}(I)}{\text{Var}(\hat{\theta})} \approx 199.47 \qquad \blacksquare$$

Importance sampling is also quite useful in estimating a conditional expectation when one is conditioning on a rare event. That is, suppose $\mathbf{X}$ is a random vector with density function f and that we are interested in estimating

$$\theta = E[h(\mathbf{X})|\mathbf{X} \in \mathcal{A}]$$

where $h(\mathbf{x})$ is an arbitrary real valued function and where $P\{\mathbf{X} \in \mathcal{A}\}$ is a small unknown probability. Since the conditional density of $\mathbf{X}$ given that it lies in $\mathcal{A}$ is

$$f(\mathbf{x}|\mathbf{X} \in \mathcal{A}) = \frac{f(\mathbf{x})}{P\{\mathbf{X} \in \mathcal{A}\}}, \qquad \mathbf{x} \in \mathcal{A}$$

we have that

$$\theta = \frac{\int_{\mathbf{x} \in \mathcal{A}} h(\mathbf{x})f(\mathbf{x})d(\mathbf{x})}{P\{\mathbf{X} \in \mathcal{A}\}}$$

$$= \frac{E[h(\mathbf{X})I(\mathbf{X} \in \mathcal{A})]}{E[I(\mathbf{X} \in \mathcal{A})]}$$

$$= \frac{E[N]}{E[D]}$$

where $E[N]$ and $E[D]$ are defined to equal the numerator and denominator in the preceding, and $I(\mathbf{X} \in \mathcal{A})$ is defined to be 1 if $\mathbf{X} \in \mathcal{A}$ and 0 otherwise. Hence, rather than simulating $\mathbf{X}$ according to the density f, which would make it very unlikely to be in $\mathcal{A}$, we can simulate it according to some other density g which makes this event more likely. If we simulate k random vectors $\mathbf{X}^1, \ldots, \mathbf{X}^k$ according to g, then we can estimate $E[N]$ by $1/k \sum_{i=1}^{k} N_i$ and $E[D]$ by $1/k \sum_{i=1}^{k} D_i$, where

$$N_i = \frac{h(\mathbf{X}^i)I(\mathbf{X}^i \in \mathcal{A})f(\mathbf{X}^i)}{g(\mathbf{X}^i)}$$

and

$$D_i = \frac{I(\mathbf{X}^i \in \mathcal{A})f(\mathbf{X}^i)}{g(\mathbf{X}^i)}$$

Thus, we obtain the following estimator of θ:

$$\hat{\theta} = \frac{\sum_{i=1}^{k} h(\mathbf{X}^i)I(\mathbf{X}^i \in \mathcal{A})f(\mathbf{X}^i)/g(\mathbf{X}^i)}{\sum_{i=1}^{k} I(\mathbf{X}^i \in \mathcal{A})f(\mathbf{X}^i)/g(\mathbf{X}^i)} \tag{8.14}$$

The mean square error of this estimator can then be estimated by the bootstrap approach (see, for instance, Example 7e).

Example 8w Let X_i be independent exponential random variables with respective rates $1/(i + 2)$, $i = 1, 2, 3, 4$. Let $S = \sum_{i=1}^{4} X_i$, and suppose that we want to estimate $\theta = E[S|S > 62]$. To accomplish this, we can use importance sampling with the tilted distributions. That is, we can choose a value t and then simulate the X_i with rates $1/(i + 2) - t$. If we choose $t = 0.14$, then $E_t[S] = 68.43$. So, let us generate k sets of exponential random variables X_i with rates $1/(i + 2) - 0.14$, $i = 1,2,3,4$, and let S_j be the sum of the jth set, $j = 1, \ldots, k$. Then we can estimate

$$E[SI(S > 62)] \quad \text{by} \quad \frac{C}{k} \sum_{j=1}^{k} S_j I(S_j > 62)e^{-0.14S_j}$$

$$E[I(S > 62)] \quad \text{by} \quad \frac{C}{k} \sum_{j=1}^{k} I(S_j > 62)e^{-0.14S_j}$$

where $C = \Pi_{i=1}^4 \dfrac{1}{1 - 0.14(i + 2)} = 81.635$. The estimator of θ is

$$\hat{\theta} = \frac{\sum_{j=1}^k S_j I(S_j > 62)e^{-0.14S_j}}{\sum_{j=1}^k I(S_j > 62)e^{-0.14S_j}}$$

∎

The importance sampling approach is also useful in that it enables us to estimate two (or more) distinct quantities in a single simulation. For example, suppose that

$$\theta_1 = E[h(\mathbf{Y})] \qquad \text{and} \qquad \theta_2 = E[h(\mathbf{W})]$$

where $\mathbf{Y}$ and $\mathbf{W}$ are random vectors having joint density functions f and g, respectively. If we now simulate $\mathbf{W}$, we can simultaneously use $h(\mathbf{W})$ and $h(\mathbf{W})f(\mathbf{W})/g(\mathbf{W})$ as estimators of θ_2 and θ_1, respectively. For example, suppose we simulate T, the total time in the system of the first r customers in a queueing system in which the service distribution is exponential with mean 2. If we now decide that we really should have considered the same system but with a service distribution that is gamma distributed with parameters $(2, 1)$, then it is not necessary to repeat the simulation, because we can just use the estimator

$$T\frac{\displaystyle\prod_{i=1}^r S_i\exp\{-S_i\}}{\displaystyle\prod_{i=1}^r \left(\frac{1}{2}\exp\{-S_i/2\}\right)} = 2^r T \exp\left\{-\sum_{i=1}^r \frac{S_i}{2}\right\} \prod_{i=1}^r S_i$$

where S_i is the (exponentially) generated service time of customer i. [The above follows since the exponential service time density is $g(s) = \frac{1}{2}\,e^{-s/2}$, whereas the gamma $(2,1)$ density is $f(s) = se^{-s}$.]

8.6   Using Common Random Numbers

Suppose that a set of n jobs are to be processed by either of a pair of identical machines. Let T_i denote the processing time for job i, $i = 1, \ldots, n$. We are interested in comparing the time it takes to complete the processing of all the jobs under two different policies for deciding the order in which to process jobs. Whenever a machine becomes free, the first policy, called longest job first, always chooses the remaining job having the longest processing time, whereas the second policy, called shortest job first, always selects the one having the shortest processing time. For example, if $n = 3$ and $T_1 = 2$, $T_2 = 5$, and $T_3 = 3$, then the longest job first would complete processing at time 5, whereas the shortest job first would not get done until time 7. We would like to use simulation to compare the expected difference in the completion times under these two policies when the times to process jobs, $T_1, \ldots, T_n$, are random variables having a given distribution F.

In other words, if $g(t_1, \ldots, t_n)$ is the time it takes to process the n jobs having processing times $t_1, \ldots, t_n$ when we use the longest job first policy and if $h(t_1, \ldots, t_n)$ is the time when we use the shortest first policy, then we are interested in using simulation to estimate

$$\theta = \theta_1 - \theta_2$$

where

$$\theta_1 = E[g(\mathbf{T})], \qquad \theta_2 = E[h(\mathbf{T})], \qquad \mathbf{T} = (T_1, \ldots, T_n)$$

If we now generate the vector $\mathbf{T}$ to compute $g(\mathbf{T})$, the question arises whether we should use those same generated values to compute $h(\mathbf{T})$ or whether it is more efficient to generate an independent set to estimate θ_2. To answer this question suppose that we used $\mathbf{T}^* = (T_1^*, \ldots, T_n^*)$, having the same distribution as $\mathbf{T}$, to estimate θ_2. Then the variance of the estimator $g(\mathbf{T}) - h(\mathbf{T}^*)$ of θ is

$$\mathrm{Var}(g(\mathbf{T}) - h(\mathbf{T}^*)) = \mathrm{Var}(g(\mathbf{T})) + \mathrm{Var}(h(\mathbf{T}^*)) - 2\,\mathrm{Cov}(g(\mathbf{T}), h(\mathbf{T}^*))$$
$$= \mathrm{Var}(g(\mathbf{T})) + \mathrm{Var}(h(\mathbf{T})) - 2\,\mathrm{Cov}(g(\mathbf{T}), h(\mathbf{T}^*)) \tag{8.15}$$

Hence, if $g(\mathbf{T})$ and $h(\mathbf{T})$ are positively correlated—that is, if their covariance is positive—then the variance of the estimator of θ is smaller if we use the same set of generated random values $\mathbf{T}$ to compute both $g(\mathbf{T})$ and $h(\mathbf{T})$ than it would be if we used an independent set $\mathbf{T}^*$ to compute $h(\mathbf{T}^*)$ [in this latter case the covariance in (8.15) would be 0].

Since both g and h are increasing functions of their arguments, it follows, because increasing functions of independent random variables are positively correlated (see the Appendix of this chapter for a proof), that in the above case it is more efficient to successively compare the policies by always using the same set of generated job times for both policies.

As a general rule of thumb when comparing different operating policies in a randomly determined environment, after the environmental state has been simulated one should then evaluate all the policies for this environment. That is, if the environment is determined by the vector $\mathbf{T}$ and $g_i(\mathbf{T})$ is the return from policy *i* under the environmental state **T,** then after simulating the value of the random vector **T** one should then evaluate, for that value of **T,** all the returns $g_i(T)$.

Appendix: Verification of Antithetic Variable Approach When Estimating the Expected Value of Monotone Functions

The following theorem is the key to showing that the use of antithetic variables will lead to a reduction in variance in comparison with generating a new independent set of random numbers whenever the function *h* is monotone in each of its coordinates.

Theorem   *If* $X_1, \ldots, X_n$ *are independent, then for any increasing functions f and g of n variables*

$$E[f(\mathbf{X})g(\mathbf{X})] \geq E[f(\mathbf{X})]E[g(\mathbf{X})] \tag{8.16}$$

where $\mathbf{X} = (X_1, \ldots, X_n)$.

Proof   The proof is by induction on *n*. To prove it when $n = 1$, let *f* and *g* be increasing functions of a single variable. Then for any *x* and *y*

$$[f(x) - f(y)][g(x) - g(y)] \geq 0$$

since if $x \geq y$ $(x \leq y)$ then both factors are nonnegative (nonpositive). Hence, for any random variables *X* and *Y*,

$$[f(X) - f(Y)][g(X) - g(Y)] \geq 0$$

implying that

$$E\{[f(X) - f(Y)][g(X) - g(Y)]\} \geq 0$$

or, equivalently,

$$E[f(X)g(X)] + E[f(Y)g(Y)] \geq E[f(X)g(Y)] + E[f(Y)g(X)]$$

If we now suppose that *X* and *Y* are independent and identically distributed then, as in this case,

$$E[f(X)g(X)] = E[f(Y)g(Y)]$$

$$E[f(X)g(Y)] = E[f(Y)g(X)] = E[f(X)]E[g(X)]$$

we obtain the result when $n = 1$.

So assume that Equation (8.16) holds for $n - 1$ variables, and now suppose that $X_1, \ldots, X_n$ are independent and f and g are increasing functions. Then

$E[f(\mathbf{X})g(\mathbf{X})|X_n = x_n]$

$$= E[f(X_1, \ldots, X_{n-1}, x_n)g(X_1, \ldots, X_{n-1}, x_n)|X_n = x]$$

$$= E[f(X_1, \ldots, X_{n-1}, x_n)g(X_1, \ldots, X_{n-1}, x_n)]$$

by independence

$$\geq E[f(X_1, \ldots, X_{n-1}, x_n)]E[g(X_1, \ldots, X_{n-1}, x_n)]$$

by the induction hypothesis

$$= E[f(\mathbf{X})|X_n = x_n]E[g(\mathbf{X})|X_n = x_n]$$

Hence,

$$E[f(\mathbf{X})g(\mathbf{X})|X_n] \geq E[f(\mathbf{X})|X_n]E[g(\mathbf{X})|X_n]$$

and, upon taking expectations of both sides,

$$E[f(\mathbf{X})g(\mathbf{X})] \geq E[E[f(\mathbf{X})|X_n]E[g(\mathbf{X})|X_n]]$$

$$\geq E[f(\mathbf{X})]E[g(\mathbf{X})]$$

The last inequality follows because $E[f(\mathbf{X})|X_n]$ and $E[g(\mathbf{X})|X_n]$ are both increasing functions of X_n, and so, by the result for $n = 1$,

$$E[E[f(\mathbf{X})|X_n]E[g(\mathbf{X})|X_n]] \geq E[E[f(\mathbf{X})|X_n]]E[E[g(\mathbf{X})|X_n]]$$

$$= E[f(\mathbf{X})]E[g(\mathbf{X})] \qquad \blacksquare$$

Corollary   *If $h(x_1, \ldots, x_n)$ is a monotone function of each of its arguments, then, for a set $U_1, \ldots, U_n$ of independent random numbers,*

$$\text{Cov}[h(U_1, \ldots, U_n), h(1 - U_1, \ldots, 1 - U_n)] \leq 0$$

Proof   By redefining h we can assume, without loss of generality, that h is increasing in its first r arguments and decreasing in its final $n - r$. Hence, letting

$$f(x_1, \ldots, x_n) = h(x_1, \ldots, x_r, 1 - x_{r+1}, \ldots, 1 - x_n)$$

$$g(x_1, \ldots, x_n) = -h(1 - x_1, \ldots, 1 - x_r, x_{r+1}, \ldots, x_n)$$

it follows that f and g are both increasing functions. Thus, by the preceding theorem,

$$\text{Cov}[f(U_1, \ldots, U_n), g(U_1, \ldots, U_n)] \geq 0$$

or, equivalently,

$$\text{Cov}[h(U_1, \ldots, U_r, 1 - U_{r+1}, \ldots, 1 - U_n), h(1 - U_1, \ldots, \\ 1 - U_r, U_{r+1}, \ldots, U_n)] \le 0$$

The result now follows since the random vector $h(U_1, \ldots, U_n)$, $h(1 - U_1, \ldots, 1 - U_n)$ has the same joint distribution as does the random vector

$$h(U_1, \ldots, U_r, 1 - U_{r+1}, \ldots, 1 - U_n), \\ h(1 - U_1, \ldots, 1 - U_r, U_{r+1}, \ldots, U_n) \quad \blacksquare$$

Exercises

1. Suppose we wanted to estimate θ, where

$$\theta = \int_0^1 e^{x^2} \, dx$$

   Show that generating a random number U and then using the estimator $e^{U^2}(1 + e^{1-2U})/2$ is better than generating two random numbers U_1 and U_2 and using $[\exp(U_1^2) + \exp(U_2^2)]/2$.

2. Explain how antithetic variables can be used in obtaining a simulation estimate of the quantity

$$\theta = \int_0^1 \int_0^1 e^{(x+y)^2} \, dy \, dx$$

   Is it clear in this case that using antithetic variables is more efficient than generating a new pair of random numbers?

3. Let X_i, $i = 1, \ldots, 5$, be independent exponential random variables each with mean 1, and consider the quantity θ defined by

$$\theta = P\left\{ \sum_{i=1}^{5} iX_i \ge 21.6 \right\}$$

   (a) Explain how we can use simulation to estimate θ.
   (b) Give the antithetic variable estimator.
   (c) Is the use of antithetic variables efficient in this case?

4. Show that if X and Y have the same distribution then $\text{Var}[(X + Y)/2] \le \text{Var}(X)$, and conclude that the use of antithetic variables can never increase variance (although it need not be as efficient as generating an independent set of random numbers).

5. (a) If Z is a unit normal random variable, design a study using antithetic variables to estimate $\theta = E[Z^3 e^Z]$.

(b) Using the above, do the simulation to obtain an interval of length no greater than 0.1 that you can assert, with 95 percent confidence, contains the value of θ.

6. Suppose that X is an exponential random variable with mean 1. Give another random variable that is negatively correlated with X and that is also exponential with mean 1.

7. Verify Equation (8.1).

8. Verify Equation (8.2).

9. Explain why it is unusual to obtain a large increase in efficiency from using both control variables and antithetic variables as opposed to just using one or the other.

10. Let U_n, $n \geq 1$, be a sequence of independent uniform $(0, 1)$ random variables. Define

$$S = \min(n{:}U_1 + \cdots + U_n > 1)$$

It can be shown that S has the same distribution as does N in Example 3e, and so $E[S] = e$. In addition, if we let

$$T = \min(n{:}1 - U_1 + \cdots + 1 - U_n > 1)$$

then it can be shown that $S + T$ has the same distribution as does $N + M$ in Example 3e. This suggests the use of $(S + T + N + M)/4$ to estimate e. Use simulation to estimate $\text{Var}(N + M + S + T)/4$.

11. In certain situations a random variable X, whose mean is known, is simulated so as to obtain an estimate of $P\{X \leq a\}$ for a given constant a. The raw simulation estimator from a single run is I, where

$$I = \begin{cases} 1 & \text{if } X \leq a \\ 0 & \text{if } X > a \end{cases}$$

Because I and X are clearly negatively correlated, a natural attempt to reduce the variance is to use X as a control—and so use an estimator of the form $I + c(X - E[X])$.

(a) Determine the percentage of variance reduction over the raw estimator I that is possible (by using the best c) if X were uniform on $(0, 1)$.

(b) Repeat (a) if X were exponential with mean 1.

(c) Explain why we knew that I and X were negatively correlated.

12. Show that $\text{Var}(\alpha X + (1 - \alpha)W)$ is minimized by α being equal to the value given in Equation (8.3) and determine the resulting variance.

13. (a) Explain how control variables may be used to estimate θ in Exercise 1.

   (b) Do 100 simulation runs, using the control given in (a), to estimate first c^* and then the variance of the estimator.

   (c) Using the same data as in Part (b), determine the variance of the antithetic variable estimator.

   (d) Which of the two types of variance reduction technique worked better in this example?

14. Repeat Exercise 13 for θ as given in Exercise 2.

15. Repeat Exercise 13 for θ as given in Exercise 3.

16. Show that in estimating $\theta = E[(1 - U^2)^{1/2}]$ it is better to use U^2 rather than U as the control variate. To do this, use simulation to approximate the necessary covariances.

17. Five elements, numbered 1, 2, 3, 4, 5, are initially arranged in a random order (i.e., the initial ordering is a random permutation of 1, 2, 3, 4, 5). At each stage one of the elements is selected and put at the front of the list. That is, if the present order is 2, 3, 4, 1, 5 and element 1 is chosen, then the new ordering is 1, 2, 3, 4, 5. Suppose that each selection is, independently, element i with probability p_i, where $p_1 = \frac{1}{15}$, $p_2 = \frac{2}{15}$, $p_3 = \frac{3}{15}$, $p_4 = \frac{4}{15}$, $p_5 = \frac{5}{15}$. Let L_j denote the position of the jth element to be selected, and let $L = \sum_{j=1}^{100} L_j$. We are interested in using simulation to estimate $E[L]$.

   (a) Explain how we could use simulation to estimate $E[L]$.

   (b) Compute $E[N_i]$, where N_i is the number of times element i is chosen in the 100 selections.

   (c) Let $Y = \sum_{i=1}^{5} iN_i$. Do you think Y is positively or negatively correlated with L?

   (d) Develop a study to estimate L, using Y as a control variable.

   (e) Give a different approach using the idea of Example 8i, and develop a study to determine the efficiency of this approach.

18. Let X and Y be independent with respective distributions F and G and with expected values μ_x and μ_y. For a given value t, we are interested in estimating $\theta = P\{X + Y \le t\}$.

   (a) Give the raw simulation approach to estimating θ.

   (b) Use "conditioning" to obtain an improved estimator.

   (c) Give a control variable that can be used to further improve upon the estimator in (b).

19. (The Hit–Miss Method.) Let g be a bounded function over the interval $[0, 1]$—for example, suppose $0 \le g(x) \le b$ whenever $0 \le x \le 1$—and suppose we are interested in using simulation to approximate $\theta =$

$\int_0^1 g(x)\,dx$. The hit–miss method for accomplishing this is to generate a pair of independent random numbers U_1 and U_2. Now set $X = U_1$, $Y = bU_2$ so that the random point (X, Y) is uniformly distributed in a rectangle of length 1 and and height b. Now set

$$I = \begin{cases} 1 & \text{if } Y < g(x) \\ 0 & \text{otherwise} \end{cases}$$

That is, I is equal to 1 if the random point (X, Y) falls within the shaded area of Figure 8.4.

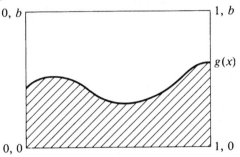

Figure 8.4

(a) Show that $E[I] = [\int_0^1 g(x)\,dx]/b$.

(b) Show that $\mathrm{Var}(bI) \geq \mathrm{Var}(g(U))$ and so the hit-miss estimator has a larger variance than simply computing g of a random number.

20. Suppose that X is exponential with mean 1; and given that $X = x$, Y is exponential with mean x. (Thus, X and Y are dependent random variables.) Give an efficient way to estimate $P\{XY \leq 3\}$.

21. Let X and Y be independent exponentials with X having mean 1 and Y having mean 2, and suppose we want to use simulation to estimate $P\{X + Y > 4\}$. If you were going to use conditional expectation to reduce the variance of the estimator, would you condition on X or on Y? Explain your reasoning.

22. Let X and Y be independent normal random variables both having mean 1 and variance 1, and let $\theta = E[e^{XY}]$.

(a) Explain the simulation approach to estimate θ.

(b) Give a control variate and explain how to utilize it to obtain an estimator having a smaller variance than the raw simulation estimator in Part (a).

(c) Give a different control variate which intuitively should perform better than the one given in Part (b). *Hint:* Recall the series expansion of $f(x) = e^x$.

(d) Suppose you have generated X and Y. What would be the antithetic variable estimator of θ?

(e) Would the estimator in Part (d) necessarily have a smaller variance than the raw simulation estimator based on two pairs of values X and Y? Why or why not?

(f) Use conditional expectation to improve on the raw simulation estimator. *Hint:* If W is normal with mean μ and variance σ^2, then $E[e^W] = e^{\mu + \sigma^2/2}$.

(g) Improve upon the estimator in Part (f) by using a control variate.

(h) Estimate θ in an efficient manner. Stop the simulation when you are at least 95 percent confident that your estimate is correct to within 0.1.

23. Suppose that customers arrive at a single-server queuing station in accordance with a Poisson process with rate λ. Upon arrival they either enter service, if the server is free, or join the queue. Upon a service completion the customer first in queue, if there are any customers in queue, enters service. All service times are independent random variables with distribution G. Suppose that the server is scheduled to take a break either at time T if the system is empty at that time or at the first moment past T that the system becomes empty. Let X denote the amount of time past T that the server goes on break, and suppose that we want to use simulation to estimate $E[X]$. Explain how to utilize conditional expectation to obtain an efficient estimator of $E[X]$.

   Hint: Consider the situation at time T regarding the remaining service time of the customer presently in service and the number waiting in queue. (This problem requires some knowledge of the theory of the $M/G/1$ busy period.)

24. Consider a single server queue where customers arrive according to a Poisson process with rate 2 per minute and the service times are exponentially distributed with mean 1 minute. Let T_i denote the amount of time that customer i spends in the system. We are interested in using simulation to estimate $\theta = E[T_1 + \cdots + T_{10}]$.

(a) Do a simulation to estimate the variance of the raw simulation estimator. That is, estimate $\text{Var}(T_1 + \cdots + T_{10})$.

(b) Do a simulation to determine the improvement over the raw estimator obtained by using antithetic variables.

(c) Do a simulation to determine the improvement over the raw estimator obtained by using $\sum_{i=1}^{10} S_i$ as a control variate, where S_i is the ith service time.

(d) Do a simulation to determine the improvement over the raw estimator obtained by using $\sum_{i=1}^{10} S_i - \sum_{i=1}^{9} I_i$ as a control variate, where I_i is the time between the ith and $(i + 1)$st arrival.

(e) Do a simulation to determine the improvement over the raw estimator obtained by using the estimator $\sum_{i=1}^{10} E[T_i | N_i]$, where N_i is the number in the system when customer i arrives (and so $N_1 = 0$).

25. In Example 8q, compute $E[X|i]$ for $i = 0, 1, 2$.

26. Estimate the variance of the raw simulation estimator of the expected payoff in the video poker model described in Example 8q. Then estimate the variance using the variance reduction suggested in that example. What is your estimate of the expected payoff? (If it is less than 1, then the game is unfair to the player.)

27. Consider a system of 20 independent components, with component i being nonfunctional with probability $0.5 + i/50, i = 1, \ldots, 20$. Let X denote the number of nonfunctional components. Use simulation to efficiently estimate $P\{X \leq 5\}$.

28. Estimate $P\{X = 5 | X \leq 5\}$ in the preceding exercise.

29. If X is such that $P\{0 \leq X \leq a\} = 1$, show that
    (a) $E[X^2] \leq aE[X]$.
    (b) $\text{Var}(X) \leq E[X](a - E[X])$.
    (c) $\text{Var}(X) \leq a^2/4$.
    Hint: Recall that $\max_{0 \leq p \leq 1} p(1 - p) = \frac{1}{4}$.

30. In Example 8w, give an analytic upper bound on $P\{S > 62\}$.

31. Use simulation to estimate $E[S|S > 200]$ in Example 8w.

32. Suppose we have a "black box" which on command can generate the value of a gamma random variable with parameters $\frac{3}{2}$ and 1. Explain how we can use this black box to approximate $E[e^X/(X + 1)]$, where X is an exponential random variable with mean 1.

33. Suppose in Exercise 13 of Chapter 6 that we are interested in using simulation to estimate p, the probability that the system fails by some fixed time t. If p is very small, explain how we could use importance sampling to obtain a more efficient estimator than the raw simulation one. Choose some values for α, C, and t that make p small, and do a simulation to estimate the variance of an importance sampling estimator as well as the raw simulation estimator of p.

34. Consider two different approaches for manufacturing a product. The profit from these approaches depends on the value of a parameter α, and let $v_i(\alpha)$ denote the profit of approach i as a function of α. Suppose that approach 1 works best for small values of α in that $v_1(\alpha)$ is a decreasing function of α, whereas approach 2 works best for large values of α in that $v_2(\alpha)$ is an increasing function of α. If the daily value of α is a random variable coming from the distribution F, then in comparing the average profit of these two approaches should we generate a single value

of α and compute the profits for this α, or should we generate α_1 and α_2 and then compute $v_i(\alpha_i)$, $i = 1, 2$?

35. Consider a list of n names, where n is very large and suppose that a given name may appear many times on the list. Let $N(i)$ denote the number of times the name in position i appears on the list, $i = 1, \ldots, n$, and let D denote the number of distinct names on the list. We are interested in using simulation to estimate $\theta = E[D]$.

    (a) Argue that $D = \sum_{i=1}^{n} \frac{1}{N(i)}$.

    Let X be equally likely to be $1, \ldots, n$. Determine the name in position X and go through the list starting from the beginning, stopping when you reach that name. Let $Y = 1$ if the name is first reached at position X and let $Y = 0$ otherwise. (That is, $Y = 1$ if the first appearance of the name is at position X.)

    (b) Argue that $E[Y|N(X)] = \frac{1}{N(X)}$.

    (c) Argue that $E[nY] = \theta$.

    (d) Now, let $W = 1$ if position X is the last time that the name in that position appears on the list, and let it be 0 otherwise. (That is, $W = 1$ if going from the back to the front of the list, the name is first reached at position X.) Argue that $n(W + Y)/2$ is an unbiased estimator of θ.

    (e) Argue that if every name on the list appears at least twice, then the estimator in Part (d) is a better estimator of θ than is $(nY_1 + nY_2)/2$ where Y_1 and Y_2 are independent and distributed as is Y.

    (f) Argue that $n/(N(X))$ has smaller variance than the estimator in Part (e), although the estimator in Part (e) may still be more efficient when replication is very high because its search process is quicker.

References

Hammersley, J. M., and D. C. Handscomb, *Monte Carlo Methods,* Wiley, New York, 1964.

Hammersley, J. M., and K. W. Morton, "A New Monte Carlo Technique: Antithetic Variables," *Proc. Cambridge Phil. Soc.,* **52,** 449–474, 1956.

Lavenberg, S. S., and P. D. Welch, "A Perspective on the Use of Control Variables to Increase the Efficiency of Monte Carlo Simulations," *Management Science,* **27,** 322–335, 1981.

Morgan, B. J. T., *Elements of Simulation,* Chapman and Hall, London, 1983.

Ripley, B., *Stochastic Simulation,* Wiley, New York, 1986.

Rubenstein, R. Y., *Simulation and the Monte Carlo Method,* Wiley, New York, 1981.

Siegmund, D., "Importance Sampling in the Monte Carlo Study of Sequential Tests." *Annals of Statistics,* **4,** 673–684, 1976.

Chapter 9 | Statistical Validation Techniques

Introduction

In this chapter we consider some statistical procedures that are useful in validating simulation models. Sections 9.1 and 9.2 consider goodness of fit tests, which are useful in ascertaining whether an assumed probability distribution is consistent with a given set of data. In Section 9.1 we suppose that the assumed distribution is totally specified, whereas in Section 9.2 we suppose that it is only specified up to certain parameters—for example, it may be Poisson having an unknown mean. In Section 9.3 we show how one can test the hypothesis that two separate samples of data come from the same underlying population—as would be the case with real and simulated data when the assumed mathematical model being simulated is an accurate representation of reality. The results of Section 9.3 are particularly useful in testing the validity of a simulation model. A generalization to the case of many samples is also presented in this section. Finally, in Section 9.4, we show how to use real data to test the hypothesis that the process generating the data constitutes a nonhomogeneous Poisson process. The case of a homogeneous Poisson process is also considered in this section.

9.1 Goodness of Fit Tests

One often begins a probabilistic analysis of a given phenomenon by hypothesizing that certain of its random elements have a particular probability distribution. For example, we might begin an analysis of a traffic network by supposing that the daily number of accidents has a Poisson distribution. Such hypotheses can be statistically tested by observing data and then seeing whether the assumption of a particular probability distribution is consistent with this data. These statistical tests are called *goodness of fit* tests.

One way of performing a goodness of fit test is to first partition the possible values of a random quantity into a finite number of regions. A sample of values of this quantity is then observed and a comparison is made between the numbers of them that fall into each of the regions and the theoretical expected numbers when the specified probability distribution is indeed governing the data.

In this section we consider goodness of fit tests when all the parameters of the hypothesized distribution are specified; in the following section we consider such tests when certain of the parameters are unspecified. We first consider the case of a discrete and then a continuous hypothesized distribution.

THE CHI-SQUARE GOODNESS OF FIT TEST FOR DISCRETE DATA

Suppose that n independent random variables—$Y_1, \ldots, Y_n$—each taking on one of the values 1, 2, . . . , k, are to be observed, and that we are interested in testing the hypothesis that $\{p_i, i = 1, \ldots, k\}$ is the probability mass function of these random variables. That is, if Y represents any of the Y_j, the hypothesis to be tested, which we denote by H_0 and refer to as the *null hypothesis,* is

$$H_0: P\{Y = i\} = p_i, \qquad i = 1, \ldots, k$$

To test the foregoing hypothesis, let $N_i, i = 1, \ldots, k$, denote the number of the Y_j's that equal i. Because each Y_j independently equals i with probability $P\{Y = i\}$, it follows that, under H_0, N_i is binomial with parameters n and p_i. Hence, when H_0 is true,

$$E[N_i] = np_i$$

and so $(N_i - np_i)^2$ is an indication as to how likely it appears that p_i indeed equals the probability that $Y = i$. When this is large, say, in relation to np_i, then it is an indication that H_0 is not correct. Indeed, such reasoning leads us to consider the quantity

$$T = \sum_{i=1}^{k} \frac{(N_i - np_i)^2}{np_i}$$

and to reject the null hypothesis when T is large.

Whereas small values of the test quantity T are evidence in favor of the hypothesis H_0, large ones are indicative of its falsity. Suppose now that the actual data result in the test quantity T taking on the value t. To see how unlikely such a large outcome would have been if the null hypothesis had been true, we define the so-called p-value by

$$p\text{-value} = P_{H_0}\{T \geq t\}$$

where we have used the notation P_{H_0} to indicate that the probability is to be computed under the assumption that H_0 is correct. Hence, the p-value gives the probability that such a large value of T as the one observed would have occurred if the null hypothesis were true. It is typical to reject the null hypothesis—saying that it appears to be inconsistent with the data—when a small p-value results (a value less than 0.05, or more conservatively, 0.01 is usually taken to be critical) and to accept the null hypothesis—saying that it appears to be consistent with the data—otherwise.

After observing the value—call it t—of the test quantity, it thus remains to determine the probability

$$p\text{-value} = P_{H_0}\{T \geq t\}$$

A reasonably good approximation to this probability can be obtained by using the classical result that, for large values of n, T has approximately a chi-square distribution with $k - 1$ degrees of freedom when H_0 is true. Hence,

$$p\text{-value} \approx P\{X^2_{k-1} \geq t\} \tag{9.1}$$

where X^2_{k-1} is a chi-square random variable with $k - 1$ degrees of freedom. The chi-square probability can then be obtained by running Program 9-1 in the Appendix.

Example 9a   Consider a random quantity which can take on any of the possible values 1, 2, 3, 4, 5, and suppose we want to test the hypothesis that these values are equally likely to occur. That is, we want to test

$$H_0: p_i = 0.2, \qquad i = 1, \ldots, 5$$

If a sample of size 50 yielded the following values of N_i:

$$12, 5, 19, 7, 7$$

then the approximate p-value is obtained as follows. The value of the test statistic T is given by

$$T = \frac{4 + 25 + 81 + 9 + 9}{10} = 12.8$$

Running Program 9-1 yields that

$$p\text{-value} \approx P\{X_4^2 > 12.8\} = 0.0122$$

For such a low p-value the hypothesis that all outcomes are equally likely would be rejected. ■

If the p-value approximation given by Equation (9.1) is not too small—say, of the order of 0.15 or larger—then it is clear that the null hypothesis is not going to be rejected, and so there is no need to look for a better approximation. However, when the p-value is closer to a critical value (such as 0.05 or 0.01) we would probably want a more accurate estimate of its value than the one given by the chi-square approximate distribution. Fortunately, a more accurate estimator can be obtained via a simulation study.

The simulation approach to estimating the p-value of the outcome $T = t$ is as follows. To determine the probability that T would have been at least as large as t when H_0 is true, we generate n independent random variables $Y_1^{(1)}, \ldots, Y_n^{(1)}$, each having the probability mass function $\{p_i, i = 1, \ldots, k\}$—that is,

$$P\{Y_j^{(1)} = i\} = p_i, \quad i = 1, \ldots, k, \quad j = 1, \ldots, n$$

Now let

$$N_i^{(1)} = \text{number } j: Y_j^{(1)} = i$$

and set

$$T^{(1)} = \sum_{i=1}^{k} \frac{(N_i^{(1)} - np_i)^2}{np_i}$$

Now repeat this procedure by simulating a second set, independent of the first set, of n independent random variables $Y_1^{(2)}, \ldots, Y_n^{(2)}$ each having the probability mass function $\{p_i, i = 1, \ldots, k\}$ and then, as for the first set, determining $T^{(2)}$. Repeating this a large number of times, say r, yields r independent random variables $T^{(1)}, T^{(2)}, \ldots, T^{(r)}$, each of which has the same distribution as does the test statistic T when H_0 is true. Hence, by the law of large numbers, the proportion of the T_i that are as large as t will be very nearly equal to the probability that T is as large as t when H_0 is true—that is,

$$\frac{\text{number } l: T^{(l)} \geq t}{r} \approx P_{H_0}\{T \geq t\}$$

Program 9-2 in the Appendix uses simulation to approximate the p-value. The user must input the probabilities, $p_i, i = 1, \ldots, k$, the sample size n, the value of the observed test quantity T, and the number of simulation runs desired.

Example 9b Let us consider Example 9a and this time employ simulation to approximate the p-value. To do so we run Program 9-2.

```
RUN
THIS PROGRAM USES SIMULATION TO APPROXIMATE THE p-value IN
   THE GOODNESS OF FIT TEST
Random number seed (−32768 to 32767)? 6867
ENTER THE NUMBER OF POSSIBLE VALUES
? 5
ENTER THE PROBABILITIES ONE AT A TIME
? .2
? .2
? .2
? .2
? .2
ENTER THE SAMPLE SIZE
? 50
ENTER THE DESIRED NUMBER OF SIMULATION RUNS
? 1000
ENTER THE VALUE OF THE TEST STATISTIC
? 12.8
THE ESTIMATE OF THE p-value IS .011
OK                                                              ■
```

THE KOLMOGOROV–SMIRNOV TEST FOR CONTINUOUS DATA

Now consider the situation where $Y_1, \ldots, Y_n$ are independent random variables, and we are interested in testing the null hypothesis H_0 that they have the common distribution function F, where F is a given continuous distribution function. One approach to testing H_0 is to break up the set of possible values of the Y_j into k distinct intervals, say,

$$(y_0, y_1), (y_1, y_2), \ldots, (y_{k-1}, y_k), \qquad \text{where } y_0 = -\infty, y_k = +\infty$$

and then consider the discretized random variables $Y_j^d, j = 1, \ldots, n$, defined by

$$Y_j^d = i \qquad \text{if } Y_j \text{ lies in the interval } (y_{i-1}, y_i)$$

The null hypothesis then implies that

$$P\{Y_j^d = i\} = F(y_i) - F(y_{i-1}), \qquad i = 1, \ldots, k$$

and this can be tested by the chi-square goodness of fit test already presented.

There is, however, another way of testing that the Y_j come from the continuous distribution function F which is generally more efficient than discretizing; it works as follows. After observing $Y_1, \ldots, Y_n$, let F_e be the empirical distribution function defined by

$$F_e(x) = \frac{\#i: Y_i \le x}{n}$$

That is, $F_e(x)$ is the proportion of the observed values that are less than or equal to x. Because $F_e(x)$ is a natural estimator of the probability that an observation is less than or equal to x, it follows that, if the null hypothesis that F is the underlying distribution is correct, it should be close to $F(x)$. Since this is so for all x, a natural quantity on which to base a test of H_0 is the test quantity

$$D \equiv \underset{x}{\text{Maximum}} \, |F_e(x) - F(x)|$$

where the maximum (the more mathematically sophisticated readers will recognize that technically we should have written supremum rather than maximum) is over all values of x from $-\infty$ to $+\infty$. The quantity D is called the *Kolmogorov–Smirnov test statistic*.

To compute the value of D for a given data set $Y_j = y_j, j = 1, \ldots, n$, let $y_{(1)}, y_{(2)}, \ldots, y_{(n)}$ denote the values of the y_j in increasing order. That is,

$$y_{(j)} = j\text{th smallest of } y_1, \ldots, y_n$$

For example, if $n = 3$ and $y_1 = 3, y_2 = 5, y_3 = 1$, then $y_{(1)} = 1, y_{(2)} = 3, y_{(3)} = 5$. Since $F_e(x)$ can be written

$$F_e(x) = \begin{cases} 0 & \text{if } x < y_{(1)} \\ \dfrac{1}{n} & \text{if } y_{(1)} \le x < y_{(2)} \\ \vdots & \\ \dfrac{j}{n} & \text{if } y_{(j)} \le x < y_{(j+1)} \\ \vdots & \\ 1 & \text{if } y_{(n)} \le x \end{cases}$$

we see that $F_e(x)$ is constant within the intervals $(y_{(j-1)}, y_{(j)})$ and then jumps by $1/n$ at the points $y_{(1)}, \ldots, y_{(n)}$. Since $F(x)$ is an increasing function of x which is bounded by 1, it follows that the maximum value of $F_e(x) - F(x)$ is nonnegative and occurs at one of the points $y_{(j)}, j = 1, \ldots, n$ (see Figure 9.1). That is,

$$\text{Maximum}_{x} \{F_e(x) - F(x)\} = \text{Maximum}_{j = 1, \ldots, n} \left\{ \frac{j}{n} - F(y_{(j)}) \right\} \qquad (9.2)$$

Similarly, the maximum (supremum) value of $F(x) - F_e(x)$ is also nonnegative and occurs immediately before one of the jump points $y_{(j)}$, and so

$$\text{Maximum}_{x} \{F(x) - F_e(x)\} = \text{Maximum}_{j=1, \ldots, n} \left\{ F(y_{(j)}) - \frac{(j - 1)}{n} \right\} \qquad (9.3)$$

From Equations (9.2) and (9.3) we see that

$$D = \text{Maximum}_{x} |F_e(x) - F(x)|$$

$$= \text{Maximum} \{\text{Maximum}\{F_e(x) - F(x)\}, \text{Maximum}\{F(x) - F_e(x)\}\}$$

$$= \text{Maximum} \left\{ \frac{j}{n} - F(y_{(j)}), F(y_{(j)}) - \frac{(j - 1)}{n}, j = 1, \ldots, n \right\} \qquad (9.4)$$

Equation (9.4) can be used to compute the value of D.

Suppose now that the Y_j are observed and their values are such that $D = d$. Since a large value of D would appear to be inconsistent with the null hypothesis

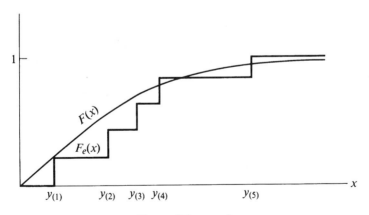

Figure 9.1 $n = 5$

that F is the underlying distribution, it follows that the p-value for this data set is given by

$$p\text{-value} = P_F\{D \geq d\}$$

where we have written P_F to make explicit that this probability is to be computed under the assumption that H_0 is correct (and so F is the underlying distribution).

The above p-value can be approximated by a simulation that is made easier by the following proposition, which shows that $P_F\{D \geq d\}$ does not depend on the underlying distribution F. This result enables us to estimate the p-value by doing the simulation with any continuous distribution F we choose [thus allowing us to use the uniform (0, 1) distribution].

Proposition $P_F\{D \geq d\}$ *is the same for any continuous distribution F.*

Proof

$$P_F\{D \geq d\} = P_F\left\{\underset{x}{\text{Maximum}} \left| \frac{\#i: Y_i \leq x}{n} - F(x) \right| \geq d\right\}$$

$$= P_F\left\{\underset{x}{\text{Maximum}} \left| \frac{\#i: F(Y_i) \leq F(x)}{n} - F(x) \right| \geq d\right\}$$

$$= P\left\{\underset{x}{\text{Maximum}} \left| \frac{\#i: U_i \leq F(x)}{n} - F(x) \right| \geq d\right\}$$

where $U_1, \ldots, U_n$ are independent uniform (0, 1) random variables: the first equality following because F is an increasing function and so $Y \leq x$ is equivalent to $F(Y) \leq F(x)$, and the second because of the result (whose proof is left as an exercise) that if Y has the continuous distribution F then the random variable $F(Y)$ is uniform on (0, 1).

Continuing the above, we see by letting $y = F(x)$ and noting that as x ranges from $-\infty$ to $+\infty$, $F(x)$ ranges from 0 to 1, that

$$P_F\{D \geq d\} = P\left\{\underset{0 \leq y \leq 1}{\text{Maximum}} \left| \frac{\#i: U_i \leq y}{n} - y \right| \geq d\right\}$$

which shows that the distribution of D, when H_0 is true, does not depend on the actual distribution F. ∎

It follows from the preceding proposition that after the value of D is determined from the data, say, $D = d$, the p-value can be obtained by doing a simulation with the uniform $(0, 1)$ distribution. That is, we generate a set of n random numbers $U_1, \ldots, U_n$ and then check whether or not the inequality

$$\underset{0 \le y \le 1}{\text{Maximum}} \left| \frac{\#i \colon U_i \le y}{n} - y \right| \ge d \tag{9.5}$$

is valid. This is then repeated many times and the proportion of times that it is valid is our estimate of the p-value of the data set. As noted earlier, the left side of the inequality (9.5) can be computed by ordering the random numbers and then using the identity

$$\text{Max} \left| \frac{\#i \colon U_i \le y}{n} - y \right|$$

$$= \text{Max} \left\{ \frac{j}{n} - U_{(j)}, \ U_{(j)} - \frac{(j-1)}{n}, \quad j = 1, \ldots, n \right\}$$

where $U_{(j)}$ is the jth smallest value of $U_1, \ldots, U_n$. For example, if $n = 3$ and $U_1 = 0.7$, $U_2 = 0.6$, $U_3 = 0.4$, then $U_{(1)} = 0.4$, $U_{(2)} = 0.6$, $U_{(3)} = 0.7$ and the value of D for this data set is

$$D = \text{Max} \left\{ \frac{1}{3} - 0.4, \ \frac{2}{3} - 0.6, \ 1 - 0.7, \ 0.4, \ 0.6 - \frac{1}{3}, \ 0.7 - \frac{2}{3} \right\} = 0.4$$

Program 9-3 uses simulation to approximate the p-value for the Kolmogorov–Smirnov test quantity D. The user must input n, the size of the data set; d, the value of D based on the data; and the required number of simulation runs. The program generates the ordered values of a set of random numbers by using the approach outlined in Exercise 8.

Example 9c Suppose we want to test the hypothesis that a given population distribution is exponential with mean 100; that is, $F(x) = 1 - e^{-x/100}$. If the (ordered) values from a sample of size 10 from this distribution are

$$66, 72, 81, 94, 112, 116, 124, 140, 145, 155$$

what conclusion can be drawn?

To answer the above, we first employ Equation (9.4) to compute the value of the Kolmogorov–Smirnov test quantity D. After some computation this gives the result $D = 0.4831487$. To obtain the approximate p-value we now run Program 9-3, which gives the following output:

```
RUN
THIS PROGRAM USES SIMULATION TO APPROXIMATE THE p-value
   OF THE KOLMOGOROV–SMIRNOV TEST
Random number seed (−32768 to 32767) ? 4567
ENTER THE VALUE OF THE TEST QUANTITY
? 0.4831487
ENTER THE SAMPLE SIZE
? 10
ENTER THE DESIRED NUMBER OF SIMULATION RUNS
? 500
THE APPROXIMATE p-value IS 0.012
OK
```

Because the p-value is so low (it is extremely unlikely that the smallest of a set of 10 values from the exponential distribution with mean 100 would be as large as 66), the hypothesis would be rejected. ■

9.2   Goodness of Fit Tests When Some Parameters Are Unspecified

THE DISCRETE DATA CASE

We can also perform a goodness of fit test of a null hypothesis that does not completely specify the probabilities $\{p_i, i = 1, \ldots, k\}$. For example, suppose we are interested in testing whether the daily number of traffic accidents in a certain region has a Poisson distribution with some unspecified mean. To test this hypothesis, suppose that data are obtained over n days and let Y_i represent the number of accidents in day i, for $i = 1, \ldots, n$. To determine whether these data are consistent with the assumption of an underlying Poisson distribution, we must first address the difficulty that, if the Poisson assumption is correct, these data can assume an infinite number of possible values. However, this is accomplished by breaking up the set of possible values into a finite number of, say, k regions and then seeing in which of the regions the n data points lie. For instance, if the geographical area of interest is small, and so there are not too many accidents in a day, we might say that the number of accidents in a given day falls in region i, $i = 1, 2, 3, 4, 5$, when there are $i - 1$ accidents on that day, and in region 6 when there are 5 or more accidents. Hence, if the underlying distribution is indeed Poisson with mean λ, then

$$p_i = P\{Y = i - 1\} = \frac{e^{-\lambda}\lambda^{i-1}}{(i-1)!}, \qquad i = 1, 2, 3, 4, 5 \qquad (9.6)$$

$$p_6 = 1 - \sum_{j=0}^{4} \frac{e^{-\lambda}\lambda^j}{j!}$$

Another difficulty we face in obtaining a goodness of fit test of the hypothesis that the underlying distribution is Poisson is that the mean value λ is not specified. Now, the intuitive thing to do when λ is unspecified is clearly to estimate its value from the data—call $\hat{\lambda}$ the estimate—and then compute the value of the test statistic

$$T = \sum_{i=1}^{k} \frac{(N_i - n\hat{p}_i)^2}{n\hat{p}_i}$$

where N_i is the number of the Y_j that fall in region i, and where $\hat{p}_i$ is the estimated probability, under H_0, that Y_j falls in region i, $i = 1. \ldots, k$, which is obtained by substituting $\hat{\lambda}$ for λ in the expression (9.6).

The above approach can be used whenever there are unspecified parameters in the null hypothesis that are needed to compute the quantities p_i, $i = 1, \ldots,$ k. Suppose now that there are m such unspecified parameters. It can be proved that, for reasonable estimators of these parameters, when n is large the test quantity T has, when H_0 is true, approximately a chi-square distribution with $k - 1 - m$ degrees of freedom. (In other words, one degree of freedom is lost for each parameter that needs to be estimated.)

If the test quantity takes on the value, say, $T = t$, then, using the above, the p-value can be approximated by

$$p\text{-value} \approx P\{X^2_{k-1-m} \geq t\}$$

where X^2_{k-1-m} is a chi-square random variable with $k - 1 - m$ degrees of freedom.

Example 9d Suppose that over a 30-day period there are 6 days in which no accidents occurred, 2 in which 1 accident occurred, 1 in which 2 accidents occurred, 9 in which 3 occurred, 7 in which 4 occurred, 4 in which 5 occurred, and 1 in which 8 occurred. To test whether these data are consistent with the hypothesis of an underlying Poisson distribution, note first that since there were a total of 87 accidents, the estimate of the mean of the Poisson distribution is

$$\hat{\lambda} = \frac{87}{30} = 2.9$$

Since the estimate of $P\{Y = i\}$ is thus $e^{-2.9} (2.9)^i/i!$, we obtain that with the six regions as given at the beginning of this section

$$\hat{p}_1 = 0.0500, \quad \hat{p}_2 = 0.1596, \quad \hat{p}_3 = 0.2312,$$
$$\hat{p}_4 = 0.2237, \quad \hat{p}_5 = 0.1622, \quad \hat{p}_6 = 0.1682$$

Using the data values $N_1 = 6, N_2 = 2, N_3 = 1, N_4 = 9, N_5 = 7, N_6 = 5$, we see that the value of the test statistic is

$$T = \sum_{i=1}^{6} \frac{(N_i - 30\hat{p}_i)^2}{30\hat{p}_i} = 19.887$$

To determine the p-value we run Program 9-1, which yields

$$p\text{-value} \approx P\{X_4^2 > 19.887\} = 0.0005$$

and so the hypothesis of an underlying Poisson distribution is rejected. ∎

We can also use simulation to estimate the p-value. However, since the null hypothesis no longer completely specifies the probability model, the use of simulation to determine the p-value of the test statistic is somewhat trickier than before. The way it should be done is as follows.

(a) *The Model.* Suppose that the null hypothesis is that the data values $Y_1, \ldots, Y_n$ constitute a random sample from a distribution that is specified up to a set of unknown parameters $\theta_1, \ldots, \theta_m$. Suppose also that when this hypothesis is true, the possible values of the Y_i are $1, \ldots, k$.

(b) *The Initial Step.* Use the data to estimate the unknown parameters. Specifically, let $\hat{\theta}_j$ denote the value of the estimator of θ_j, $j = 1, \ldots, m$. Now compute the value of the test statistic

$$T = \sum_{i=1}^{k} \frac{(N_i - n\hat{p}_i)^2}{n\hat{p}_i}$$

where N_i is the number of the data values that are equal to i, $i = 1, \ldots, k$, and $\hat{p}_i$ is the estimate of p_i that results when $\hat{\theta}_j$ is substituted for θ_j, for $j = 1, \ldots, m$. Let t denote the value of the test quantity T.

(c) *The Simulation Step.* We now do a series of simulations to estimate the p-value of the data. First note that all simulations are to be obtained by using the population distribution that results when the null hypothesis is true and θ_j is equal to its estimate $\hat{\theta}_j$, $j = 1, \ldots, m$, determined in step (b).

Simulate a sample of size n from the aforementioned population distribution and let $\hat{\theta}_j(\text{sim})$ denote the estimate of θ_j, $j = 1, \ldots, m$, based on the simulated data. Now determine the value of

$$T_{\text{sim}} = \sum_{i=1}^{k} \frac{[N_i - n\hat{p}_i(\text{sim})]^2}{n\hat{p}_i(\text{sim})}$$

where N_i is the number of the simulated data values equal to i, $i = 1, \ldots, k$, and $\hat{p}_i(\text{sim})$ is the value of p_i when θ_j is equal to $\theta_j(\text{sim})$, $j = 1, \ldots, m$.

The simulation step should then be repeated many times. The estimate of the p-value is then equal to the proportion of the values of T_{sim} that are at least as large as t.

Example 9e Let us reconsider Example 9d. The data presented in this example resulted in the estimate $\hat{\lambda} = 2.9$ and the test quantity value $T = 19.887$. The simulation step now consists of generating 30 independent Poisson random variables each having mean 2.9 and then computing the value of

$$T^* \equiv \sum_{i=1}^{6} \frac{(X_i - 30p_i^*)^2}{30p_i^*}$$

where X_i is the number of the 30 values that fall into region i, and p_i^* is the probability that a Poisson random variable with a mean equal to the average of the 30 generated values would fall into region i. This simulation step should be repeated many times, and the estimated p-value is the proportion of times it results in a T^* at least as large as 19.887. ■

THE CONTINUOUS DATA CASE

Now consider the situation where we want to test the hypothesis that the random variables $Y_1, \ldots, Y_n$ have the continuous distribution function F_θ, where $\theta = (\theta_1, \ldots, \theta_m)$ is a vector of unknown parameters. For example, we might be interested in testing that the Y_j come from a normally distributed population. To employ the Kolmogorov–Smirnov test we first use the data to estimate the parameter vector $\boldsymbol{\theta}$, say, by the vector of estimators $\hat{\boldsymbol{\theta}}$. The value of the test statistic D is now computed by

$$D = \underset{x}{\text{Maximum}} \left| F_e(x) - F_{\hat{\theta}}(x) \right|$$

where $F_{\hat{\theta}}$ is the distribution function obtained from F_θ when $\boldsymbol{\theta}$ is estimated by $\hat{\boldsymbol{\theta}}$.

If the value of the test quantity is $D = d$, then the p-value can be *roughly* approximated by $P_{F_{\hat{\theta}}}\{D \geq d\} = P_U\{D \geq d\}$. That is, after determining the value of D, a rough approximation, which actually overestimates the p-value, is obtained. If this does not result in a small estimate for the p-value, then, as the hypothesis is not going to be rejected, we might as well stop. However, if this estimated p-value is small, then a more accurate way of using simulation to estimate the true p-value is necessary. We now describe how this should be done.

STEP 1:   Use the data to estimate $\boldsymbol{\theta}$, say, by $\hat{\boldsymbol{\theta}}$. Compute the value of D as described above.

STEP 2:   All simulations are to be done using the distribution $F_{\hat{\theta}}$. Generate a sample of size n from this distribution and let $\hat{\boldsymbol{\theta}}(\text{sim})$ be the estimate of $\boldsymbol{\theta}$ based on this simulation run. Compute the value of

$$\underset{x}{\text{Maximum}} \left| F_{e,\text{sim}}(x) - F_{\hat{\theta}(\text{sim})}(x) \right|$$

where $F_{e,\text{sim}}$ is the empirical distribution function of the simulated data; and note whether it is at least as large as d. Repeat this many times and use the proportion of times that this test quantity is at least as large as d as the estimate of the p-value.

9.3   The Two-Sample Problem

Suppose we have formulated a mathematical model for a service system which clears all its customers at the end of a day; also suppose that our model assumes that each day is probabilistically alike in that the probability laws for each day are identical and independent. Some of the individual assumptions of the model—such as, for example, that the service times are all independent with the common distribution G, or that the arrivals of customers constitute a Poisson process—can be individually tested by using the results of Sections 9.1 and 9.2. Suppose that none of these individual tests results in a particularly small p-value and so all the parts of the model, taken individually, do not appear to be inconsistent with the real data we have about the system. [We must be careful here in what we mean by a small p-value because, even if the model is correct, if we perform a large number of tests then, by chance, some of the resulting p-values may be small. For example, if we perform r separate tests on independent data, then the probability that at least one of the resulting p-values is as small as α is $1 - (1 - \alpha)^r$, which even for small α will become large as r increases.]

At this stage, however, we are still not justified in asserting that our model is correct and has been validated by the real data; for the totality of the model, including not only all the individual parts but also our assumptions about the ways in which these parts interact, may still be inaccurate. One way of testing the model in its entirety is to consider some random quantity that is a complicated function of the entire model. For example, we could consider the total amount of waiting time of all customers that enter the system in a given day. Suppose that we have observed the real system for m days and let Y_i, $i = 1, \ldots, m,$ denote the sum of these waiting times for day i. If we now simulate the proposed mathematical model for n days, we can let X_i, $i = 1, \ldots, n,$ be the sum of the waiting times of all customers arriving on the (simulated) day i. Since the mathematical model supposes that all days are probabilistically alike and independent, it follows that all the random variables $X_1, \ldots, X_m$ have some common distribution, which we denote by F. Now if the mathematical model is an accurate representation of the real system, then the real data $Y_1, \ldots, Y_m$ also have the distribution F. That is, if the mathematical model is accurate, one should not be able to tell the simulated data apart from the real data. From this it follows that one way of testing the accuracy of the model in its entirety is to test the null hypothesis H_0 that $X_1, \ldots, X_n, Y_1, \ldots, Y_m$ are independent random variables having a common distribution. We now show how such a hypothesis can be tested.

Suppose we have two sets of data—$X_1, \ldots, X_n$ and $Y_1, \ldots, Y_m$—and we want to test the hypothesis H_0 that these $n + m$ random variables are all independent and identically distributed. This statistical hypothesis testing problem is called the two-sample problem.

To test H_0, order the $n + m$ values $X_1, \ldots, X_n, Y_1, \ldots, Y_m$ and suppose for the time being that all $n + m$ values are distinct and so the ordering is unique. Now for $i = 1, \ldots, n,$ let R_i denote the rank of X_i among the $n + m$ data values; that is, $R_i = j$ if X_i is the jth smallest among the $n + m$ values. The quantity

$$R = \sum_{i=1}^{n} R_i$$

equal to the sum of the ranks of the first data set, is used as our test quantity. (Either of the two data sets can be considered as the "first" set.)

If R is either very large (indicating that the first data set tends to be larger than the second) or very small (indicating the reverse), then this would be strong evidence against the null hypothesis. Specifically, if $R = r$, we reject the null hypothesis if either

$$P_{H_0}\{R \le r\} \quad \text{or} \quad P_{H_0}\{R \ge r\}$$

is very low. Indeed, the p-value of the test data which results in $R = r$ is given by

$$p\text{-value} = 2 \text{ Minimum } (P_{H_0}\{R \le r\}, P_{H_0}\{R \ge r\}) \tag{9.7}$$

[It is twice the minimum of the probabilities because we reject either if R is too small or too large. For example, suppose r_* and r^* were such that the probability, under H_0, of obtaining a value less (greater) than or equal to r_* (r^*) is 0.05. Since the probability of either event occurring is, under H_0, 0.1 it follows that if the outcome is r_* (or r^*) the p-value is 0.1.]

The hypothesis test resulting from the above p-value—that is, the test that calls for rejection of the null hypothesis when the p-value is sufficiently small—is called the *two-sample rank sum test*. (Other names that have also been used to designate this test are the Wilcoxon two-sample test and the Mann–Whitney two-sample test.)

Example 9f Suppose that direct observation of a system over 5 days has yielded that a certain quantity has taken on the successive values

$$342, 448, 504, 361, 453$$

whereas a 10-day simulation of a mathematical model proposed for the system has resulted in the following values:

$$186, 220, 225, 456, 276, 199, 371, 426, 242, 311$$

Because the five data values from the first set have ranks 8, 12, 15, 9, 13, it follows that the value of the test quantity is $R = 57$. ■

We can explicitly compute the p-value given in Equation (9.7) when n and m are not too large and all the data are distinct. To do so let

$$P_{n,m}(r) = P_{H_0}\{R \le r\}$$

Hence $P_{n,m}(r)$ is the probability that from two identically distributed data sets of sizes n and m, the sum of the ranks of the data values from the first set is less than or equal to r. We can obtain a recursive equation for these probabilities by conditioning on whether the largest data value comes from the first or the second set. If the largest value is indeed contained in the first data set, the sum of the ranks of this set equals $n + m$ (the rank of the largest value) plus the sum of the ranks of the other $n - 1$ values from this set when considered along with the m values from the other set. Hence, when the largest is contained in the first data set, the sum of the ranks of that set is less than or equal to r if the sum of the ranks of the remaining $n - 1$ elements is less than or equal to $r - n - m$, and this is true with probability $P_{n-1,m}(r - n - m)$. By a similar argument we can show that if the largest value is contained in the second set, the sum of the ranks of the first set is less than or equal to r with probability $P_{n,m-1}(r)$. Finally, since the largest value is equally likely to be any of the $n + m$ values, it follows that it is a member of the first set with probability $n/(n + m)$. Putting this together yields the following recursive equation:

$$P_{n,m}(r) = \frac{n}{n + m} P_{n-1,m}(r - n - m) + \frac{m}{n + m} P_{n,m-1}(r) \qquad (9.8)$$

Starting with the boundary conditions

$$P_{1,0}(k) = \begin{cases} 0, & k \le 0 \\ 1, & k > 0 \end{cases} \quad \text{and} \quad P_{0,1}(k) = \begin{cases} 0, & k < 0 \\ 1, & k \ge 0 \end{cases}$$

Equation (9.8) can be recursively solved to obtain $P_{n,m}(r) = P_{H_0} \{R \le r\}$ and $P_{n,m}(r - 1) = 1 - P_{H_0} \{R \ge r\}$.

Program 9-4 uses the recursion presented in Equation (9.8) to compute the p-value for the rank sum test. The inputs needed are the sizes of the first and second data sets and the sum of the ranks of the elements of the first set. Whereas either set can be designated as the first set, the program runs fastest if the first set is the one whose sum of ranks is smallest.

Example 9g Five days of observation of a system yielded the following values of a certain quantity of interest:

$$132, 104, 162, 171, 129$$

A 10-day simulation of a proposed model of this system yielded the values

$$107, 94, 136, 99, 114, 122, 108, 130, 106, 88$$

Suppose the formulated model implies that these daily values should be independent and have a common distribution. To determine the p-value that results from the above data, note first that R, the sum of the ranks of the first sample, is

$$R = 12 + 4 + 14 + 15 + 10 = 55$$

To determine the p-value we now run Program 9-4, which yields

```
RUN
THIS PROGRAM COMPUTES THE p-value FOR THE TWO-SAMPLE RANK
    SUM TEST
THIS PROGRAM WILL RUN FASTEST IF YOU DESIGNATE AS THE FIRST
    SAMPLE THE SAMPLE HAVING THE SMALLER SUM OF RANKS
ENTER THE SIZE OF THE FIRST SAMPLE
? 5
ENTER THE SIZE OF THE SECOND SAMPLE
? 10
ENTER THE SUM OF THE RANKS OF THE FIRST SAMPLE
? 55
The p-value IS 0.0752579
OK                                                            ■
```

The difficulty with employing the recursion (9.8) to compute the p-value is that the amount of computation needed grows enormously as the sample sizes increase. For example, if $n = m = 20$, even if we choose the test quantity to be the smaller sum of ranks, then since the sum of all the ranks is $1 + 2 + \cdots + 40 = 820$, it is possible that the test statistic could have a value as large as 410. Hence, there can be as many as $20 \times 20 \times 410 = 164,000$ values of $P_{n,m}(r)$ that would have to be computed to determine the p-value. Thus, for large samples, the use of the recursion provided by (9.8) may not be viable. Two different approximation methods that can be used in such cases are (a) a classical approach based on approximating the distribution of R and (b) simulation.

To use the classical approach for approximating the p-value we make use of the fact that under H_0 all possible orderings of the $n + m$ values are equally likely. Using this fact it is easy to show that

$$E_{H_0}[R] = n \frac{(n + m + 1)}{2}$$

$$\mathrm{Var}_{H_0}(R) = nm \frac{(n + m + 1)}{12}$$

Now it can be shown that, under H_0, when n and m are large, R is approximately normally distributed. Hence, when H_0 is true,

$$\frac{R - n(n + m + 1)/2}{\sqrt{nm(n + m + 1)/12}} \text{ is approximately a unit normal.}$$

Since, for a normal random variable W, the minimum of $P\{W \le r\}$ and $P\{W \ge r\}$ is the former when $r \le E[W]$, and the latter otherwise, it thus follows that when n and m are not too small (both being greater than 7 should suffice), we can approximate the p-value of the test result $R = r$ by

$$p\text{-value} \approx \begin{cases} 2\, P\{Z < r^*\} & \text{if } r \le n\dfrac{(n + m + 1)}{2} \\ 2\, P\{Z > r^*\} & \text{otherwise} \end{cases} \tag{9.9}$$

where

$$r^* = \frac{r - \dfrac{n(n + m + 1)}{2}}{\sqrt{\dfrac{nm(n + m + 1)}{12}}}$$

and where Z is a unit normal random variable.

Example 9h Let us see how well the classical approximation works for the data of Example 9g. In this case, since $n = 5$ and $m = 10$, we have that

$$p\text{-value} = 2\, P_{H_0}\{R \ge 55\}$$

$$\approx 2\, P\left\{ Z \ge \frac{55 - 40}{\sqrt{\dfrac{50 \times 16}{12}}} \right\}$$

$$= 2\, P\{Z \ge 1.8371\}$$

$$= 0.066$$

which should be compared with the exact answer 0.075. ∎

The p-value of the two-sample rank test can also be approximated by simulation. To see how this is accomplished, recall that if the observed value of the test quantity R is $R = r$, then the p-value is given by

$$p\text{-value} = 2\, \text{Minimum}(P_{H_0}\{R \ge r\}, P_{H_0}\{R \le r\})$$

Now, under H_0, provided that all the $n + m$ data values are distinct, it follows that all orderings among these data values are equally likely, and thus the ranks of the first data set of size n have the same distribution as a random selection of n of the values $1, 2, \ldots, n + m$. Thus, under H_0, the probability distribution of R can be approximated by continually simulating a random subset of n of the integers $1, 2, \ldots, n + m$ and determining the sum of the elements in the subset. The value of $P_{H_0}\{R \leq r\}$ can be approximated by the proportion of simulations that result in a sum less than or equal to r, and the value of $P_{H_0}\{R \geq r\}$ by the proportion of simulations that result in a sum greater than or equal to r.

Program 9-5 approximates the p-value by performing the preceding simulation. It operates by continually summing the last n terms of a random permutation of the numbers $1, 2, \ldots, n + m$. (The method used to simulate a random permutation is explained in Example 3a of Chapter 3.) The program runs most efficiently when the data set of smallest size is designated as the first sample.

Example 9i Using Program 9-5 with 1000 runs for the data in Example 9g yields the following:

```
RUN
THIS PROGRAM APPROXIMATES THE p-value IN THE TWO-SAMPLE
    RANK SUM TEST BY A SIMULATION STUDY
Random number seed (-32768 to 32767)? 4566
ENTER THE SIZE OF THE FIRST SAMPLE
? 5
ENTER THE SIZE OF THE SECOND SAMPLE
? 10
ENTER THE SUM OF THE RANKS OF THE FIRST SAMPLE
? 55
ENTER THE DESIRED NUMBER OF SIMULATION RUNS
? 1000
THE APPROXIMATE p-value IS 0.07
OK                                                             ■
```

The above analysis supposes that all the $n + m$ data values are distinct. When certain of the values have a common value, one should take as the rank of a data value the average of the ranks of the values equal to it. For example, if the first data set is 2, 3, 4 and the second 3, 5, 7, then the sum of the ranks of the first set is $1 + 2.5 + 4 = 7.5$. The p-value should be approximated by using the normal approximation via Equation (9.9).

A generalization of the two-sample problem is the multisample problem, where one has the following m data sets:

$$
\begin{array}{cccc}
X_{1,1}, & X_{1,2}, & \ldots, & X_{1,n_1} \\
X_{2,1}, & X_{2,2}, & \ldots, & X_{2,n_2} \\
\vdots & \vdots & \vdots & \vdots \\
X_{m,1}, & X_{m,2}, & \ldots, & X_{m,n_m}
\end{array}
$$

and we are interested in testing the null hypothesis H_0 that all the $n = \sum_{i=1}^{m} n_i$ random variables are independent and have a common distribution. A generalization of the two-sample rank test, called the multisample rank test (or often referred to as the Kruskal–Wallis test), is obtained by first ranking all the n data values. Then let R_i, $i = 1, \ldots, m$, denote the sum of the ranks of all the n_i data values from the ith set. (Note that with this notation R_i is a sum of ranks and not an individual rank as previously.) Since, under H_0, all orderings are equally likely (provided all the data values are distinct), it follows exactly as before that

$$
E[R_i] = n_i \frac{(n + 1)}{2}
$$

Using the above, the multisample rank sum test is based on the test quantity

$$
R = \frac{12}{n(n + 1)} \sum_{i=1}^{m} \frac{[R_i - n_i(n + 1)/2]^2}{n_i}
$$

Since small values of R indicate a good fit to H_0, the test based on the quantity R rejects H_0 for sufficiently large values of R. Indeed, if the observed value of R is $R = y$, the p-value of this result is given by

$$
p\text{-value} = P_{H_0}\{R \geq y\}
$$

This value can be approximated by using the result that for large values of $n_1, \ldots, n_m$, R has approximately a chi-square distribution with $m - 1$ degrees of freedom [this latter result being the reason why we include the term $12/n(n + 1)$ in the definition of R]. Hence, if $R = y$,

$$
p\text{-value} \approx P\{X^2_{m-1} \geq y\}
$$

Simulation can also be used to evaluate the p-value (see Exercise 14).

Even when the data values are not all distinct, the above approximation for the p-value should be used. In computing the value of R the rank of an individual data value should be, as before, the average of all the ranks of the data equal to it.

9.4   Validating the Assumption of a Nonhomogeneous Poisson Process

Consider a mathematical model which supposes that the daily arrivals to a system occur in accordance with a nonhomogeneous Poisson process, with the arrival process from day to day being independent and having a common, but unspecified, intensity function.

To validate such an assumption, suppose that we observe the system over r days, noting the arrival times. Let N_i, $i = 1, \ldots, r$, denote the number of arrivals on day i, and note that if the arrival process is indeed a nonhomogeneous Poisson process, then these quantities are independent Poisson random variables with the same mean. Now whereas this consequence could be tested by using the goodness of fit approach, as is done in Example 9a, we present an alternative approach that is sometimes more efficient. This alternative approach is based on the fact that the mean and variance of a Poisson random variable are equal. Hence, if the N_i are indeed a sample from a Poisson distribution, the sample mean

$$\bar{N} = \sum_{i=1}^{r} \frac{N_i}{r}$$

and the sample variance

$$S^2 = \sum_{i=1}^{r} \frac{(N_i - \bar{N})^2}{r - 1}$$

should be roughly equal. Motivated by this, we base our test of the hypothesis $H_0 : N_i$ are independent Poisson random variables with a common mean on the test quantity

$$T = \frac{S^2}{\bar{N}} \tag{9.10}$$

Because either a very small or very large value of T would be inconsistent with H_0, the p-value for the outcome $T = t$ would be

$$p\text{-value} = 2 \text{ Minimum}(P_{H_0}\{T \leq t\}, P_{H_0}\{T \geq t\})$$

However, since H_0 does not specify the mean of the Poisson distribution, we cannot immediately compute the above probabilities; rather, we must first use the observed data to estimate the mean. By using the estimator $\bar{N}$, it follows that if the observed value of $\bar{N}$ is $\bar{N} = m$, the p-value can be approximated by

$$p\text{-value} \approx 2 \text{ Minimum}(P_m\{T \le t\}, P_m\{T \ge t\})$$

where T is defined by Equation (9.10) with $N_1, \ldots, N_r$ being independent Poisson random variables each with mean m. We can now approximate $P_m\{T \le t\}$ and $P_m\{T \ge t\}$ via a simulation. That is, we continually generate r independent Poisson random variables with mean m and compute the resulting value of T. The proportion of these for which $T \le t$ is our estimate of $P\{T \le t\}$, and the proportion for which $T \ge t$ is our estimate of $P\{T \ge t\}$.

If the above p-value is quite small, we reject the null hypothesis that the daily arrivals constitute a nonhomogeneous Poisson process. However, if the p-value is not small, this only implies that the assumption that the number of arrivals each day has a Poisson distribution is a viable assumption and does not by itself validate the stronger assumption that the actual arrival pattern (as determined by the nonhomogeneous intensity function) is the same from day to day. To complete our validation we must now consider the actual arrival times for each of the r days observed. Suppose that the arrival times on day j, $j = 1, \ldots, r$, are $X_{j,1}$, $X_{j,2}, \ldots, X_{j,N_j}$. Now if the arrival process is indeed a nonhomogeneous Poisson process, it can be shown that each of these r sets of arrival times constitutes a sample from a common distribution. That is, under the null hypothesis, the r sets of data $X_{j,1}, \ldots, X_{j,N_j}$, $j = 1, \ldots, r$, are all independent random variables from a common distribution.

The above consequence, however, can be tested by the multisample rank test given in Section 9.3. That is, first rank all the $N \equiv \sum_{j=1}^{r} N_j$ data values, and then let R_j denote the sum of the ranks of all the N_j data values from the jth set. The test quantity

$$R = \frac{12}{N(N + 1)} \sum_{j=1}^{r} \frac{\left(R_j - N_j \frac{(N + 1)}{2} \right)^2}{N_j}$$

can now be employed by using the fact that, when H_0 is true, R has approximately a chi-square distribution with $r - 1$ degrees of freedom. Hence, if the observed value of R is $R = y$, the resulting p-value can be approximated by

$$p\text{-value} = 2 \text{ Minimum}(P_{H_0}\{R \le y\}, P_{H_0}\{R \ge y\})$$

$$\approx 2 \text{ Minimum}(P\{X_{r-1}^2 \le y\}, 1 - P\{X_{r-1}^2 \le y\})$$

where X_{r-1}^2 is a chi-square random variable with $r - 1$ degrees of freedom. (Of course, we could also approximate the p-value by a simulation.) If the above p-value, along with the previous p-value considered, is not too small, we may conclude that the data are not inconsistent with our assumption that daily arrivals constitute a nonhomogeneous Poisson process.

Example 9j   Suppose that the daily times at which deliveries are made at a certain plant are noted over 5 days. During this time the numbers of deliveries during each of the days are as follows:

$$18, 24, 16, 19, 25$$

Suppose also that when the 102 delivery times are ranked according to the time of day they arrived, the sums of the ranks of the deliveries from each day are

$$1010, 960, 1180, 985, 1118$$

Using the above data, let us test the hypothesis that the daily arrival process of deliveries is a nonhomogeneous Poisson process.

We first test that the first data set of the daily number of deliveries consists of a set of five independent and identically distributed Poisson random variables. Now the sample mean and sample variance are equal to

$$\bar{N} = 20.4 \quad \text{and} \quad S^2 = 15.3$$

and so the value of the test quantity is $T = 0.75$. To determine the approximate p-value of the test that the N_i are independent Poisson random variables, we then simulated 500 sets of five Poisson random variables with mean 20.4 and then computed the resulting value of $T = S^2/\bar{N}$. The output of this simulation indicated a p-value of approximately 0.84, and so it is clear that the assumption that the numbers of daily deliveries are independent Poisson random variables having a common mean is consistent with the data.

To continue our test of the null hypothesis of a nonhomogeneous Poisson process, we compute the value of the test quantity R, which is seen to be equal to 14.425. Because the probability that a chi-square random variable with four degrees of freedom is as large as 14.425 is (from Program 9-1) 0.006, it follows that the p-value is 0.012. For such a small p-value we must reject the null hypothesis. ■

If we wanted to test the assumption that the daily arrival process constituted a *homogeneous* Poisson process, we would proceed as above and first test the hypothesis that the numbers of arrivals each day are independent and identically distributed Poisson random variables. If the hypothesis remains plausible after we perform this test, we again continue as in the nonhomogeneous case by considering the actual set of $N = \sum_{j=1}^{r} N_j$ arrival times. However, we now use the result that, under a homogeneous Poisson process, it can be shown that, given the number of arrivals in a day, the actual arrivals are independently and uniformly distributed over $(0, T)$, where T is the length of a day. This consequence, however, can be tested by the Kolmogorov–Smirnov goodness of fit test presented in Section 9.1. That is, if the arrivals constitute a homogeneous Poisson process, the N random variables $X_{j,i}$, $i = 1, \ldots, N_j$, $j = 1, \ldots, r$, where $X_{j,i}$ represents the ith arrival time on day j, can be regarded as constituting a set of N independent and uniformly distributed random variables over $(0, T)$. Hence, if we define the empirical distribution function F_e by letting $F_e(x)$ be the proportion of the N data values that are less than or equal to x—that is,

$$F_e(x) = \sum_{j=1}^{r} \sum_{i=1}^{N_j} \frac{I_{j,i}}{N}$$

where

$$I_{j,i} = \begin{cases} 1 & \text{if } X_{j,i} \leq x \\ 0 & \text{otherwise} \end{cases}$$

then the value of the test quantity is

$$D = \frac{\text{Maximum}}{0 \leq x \leq T} \left| F_e(x) - \frac{x}{T} \right|$$

Once the value of the test statistic D is determined, we can then find the resulting p-value by simulation, as is shown in Section 9.1.

If the hypothesis of a nonhomogeneous Poisson process is shown to be consistent with the data, we face the problem of estimating the intensity function $\lambda(t)$, $0 \leq t \leq T$, of this process. [In the homogeneous case the obvious estimator is $\lambda(t) = \hat{\lambda}/T$, where $\hat{\lambda}$ is the estimate of the mean number of arrivals in a day of length T.] To estimate the intensity function, order the $N = \sum_{j=1}^{r} N_j$ daily arrival times. Let $y_0 = 0$, and for $k = 1, \ldots, N$, let y_k denote the kth smallest of these N arrival times. Because there has been a total of 1 arrival over r days within the time interval (y_{k-1}, y_k), $k = 1, \ldots, N$, a reasonable estimate of $\lambda(t)$ would be

$$\hat{\lambda}(t) = \frac{1}{r(y_k - y_{k-1})} \qquad \text{for} \quad y_{k-1} < t < y_k$$

[To understand the above estimator, note that if $\hat{\lambda}(t)$ were the intensity function, the expected number of daily arrivals that occur at a time point t such that $y_{k-1} < t \le y_k$ would be given by

$$E[N(y_k) - N(y_{k-1})] = \int_{y_{k-1}}^{y_k} \hat{\lambda}(t)\, dt = \frac{1}{r}$$

and hence the expected number of arrivals within that interval over r days would be 1, which coincides with the actual observed number of arrivals in that interval.]

Exercises

1. According to the Mendelian theory of genetics, a certain garden pea plant should produce white, pink, or red flowers, with respective probabilities $\frac{1}{4}, \frac{1}{2}, \frac{1}{4}$. To test this theory a sample of 564 peas was studied with the result that 141 produced white, 291 produced pink, and 132 produced red flowers. Approximate the p-value of this data set

   (a) by using the chi-square approximation, and
   (b) by using a simulation.

2. To ascertain whether a certain die was fair, 1000 rolls of the die were recorded, with the result that the numbers of times the die landed i, $i = 1, 2, 3, 4, 5, 6$ were, respectively, 158, 172, 164, 181, 160, 165. Approximate the p-value of the test that the die was fair

   (a) by using the chi-square approximation, and
   (b) by using simulation.

3. Approximate the p-value of the hypothesis that the following 10 values are random numbers: 0.12, 0.18, 0.06, 0.33, 0.72, 0.83, 0.36, 0.27, 0.77, 0.74.

4. Approximate the p-value of the hypothesis that the following data set of 14 points is a sample from a uniform distribution over (50, 200):

   164, 142, 110, 153, 103, 52, 174, 88, 178, 184, 58, 62, 132, 128

5. Approximate the p-value of the hypothesis that the following 13 data values come from an exponential distribution with mean 50:

   86, 133, 75, 22, 11, 144, 78, 122, 8, 146, 33, 41, 99

6. Approximate the p-value of the test that the following data come from a binomial distribution with parameters $(8, p)$, where p is unknown:

$$6, 7, 3, 4, 7, 3, 7, 2, 6, 3, 7, 8, 2\ 1, 3, 5, 8, 7$$

7. Approximate the p-value of the test that the following data set comes from an exponentially distributed population: 122, 133, 106, 128, 135, 126.

8. To generate the ordered values of n random numbers we could generate n random numbers and then order, or sort, them. Another approach makes use of the result that given that the $(n + 1)$st event of a Poisson process occurs at time t, the first n event times are distributed as the set of ordered values of n uniform $(0, t)$ random variables. Using this result, explain why, in the following algorithm, $y_1, \ldots, y_n$ denote the ordered values of n random numbers.

$$\text{Generate } n + 1 \text{ random numbers } U_1, \ldots, U_{n+1}$$
$$X_i = -\log U_i, \qquad i = 1, \ldots, n + 1$$
$$t = \sum_{i=1}^{n+1} X_i, \qquad c = \frac{1}{t}$$
$$y_i = y_{i-1} + cX_i, \qquad i = 1, \ldots, n \text{ (with } y_0 = 0)$$

9. Generate the values of 10 independent exponential random variables each having mean 1. Then, based on the Kolmogorov–Smirnov test quantity, approximate the p-value of the test that the data do indeed come from an exponential distribution with mean 1.

10. An experiment designed to compare two treatments against corrosion yielded the following data (representing the maximum depth of pits in units of one-thousandth of an inch) in pieces of wire subjected to one or the other of the two treatments:

Treatment 1:	65.2	67.1	69.4	78.4	74.0	80.3
Treatment 2:	59.4	72.1	68.0	66.2	58.5	

Compute the exact p-value of this data set when testing the hypothesis that the two treatments have identical results.

11. In Exercise 10, compute the approximate p-value based on

(a) the normal approximation, and

(b) a simulation.

12. Fourteen cities, of roughly equal size, are chosen for a traffic safety study. Seven of them are randomly chosen, and in these cities a series of newspaper articles dealing with traffic safety are run over a 1-month period.

The numbers of traffic accidents reported in the month following this campaign are as follows:

Treatment group:	19	31	39	45	47	66	75
Control group:	28	36	44	49	52	72	72

Determine the exact p-value when testing the hypothesis that the articles have not had any effect.

13. Approximate the p-value in Exercise 12

(a) by using the normal approximation, and

(b) by using a simulation.

14. Explain how simulation can be employed to approximate the p-value in the multisample problem—that is, when testing that a set of m samples all come from the same probability distribution.

15. Consider the following data resulting from three samples:

Sample 1:	121	144	158	169	194	211	242
Sample 2:	99	128	165	193	242	265	302
Sample 3:	129	134	137	143	152	159	170

Compute the approximate p-value of the test that all the data come from a single probability distribution

(a) by using the chi-square approximation, and

(b) by using a simulation.

16. The number of daily arrivals over an 8-day interval are as follows:

$$122, 118, 120, 116, 125, 119, 124, 130$$

Do you think the daily arrivals could be independent and identically distributed as nonhomogeneous Poisson processes?

17. Over an interval of length 100 there have been 18 arrivals at the following times:

$$12, 20, 33, 44, 55, 56, 61, 63, 66, 70, 73, 75, 78, 80, 82, 85, 87, 90$$

Approximate the p-value of the test that the arrival process is a (homogeneous) Poisson process.

References

Diaconis, P., and B. Efron, "Computer Intensive Methods in Statistics," *Scientific American,* **248**:(5), 96–109, 1983.

Fishman, G. S., *Concepts and Methods in Discrete Event Digital Simulations,* Wiley, New York, 1973.

Kendall, M., and A. Stuart, *The Advanced Theory of Statistics,* Fourth Ed., MacMillan, New York, 1979.

Mihram, G. A., *Simulation—Statistical Foundations and Methodology,* Academic Press, New York, 1972.

Sargent, R. G., "A Tutorial on Validation and Verification of Simulation Models," *Proc. 1988 Winter Simulation Conf.,* San Diego, pp. 33–39, 1988.

Schruben, L. W., "Establishing the Credibility of Simulations," *Simulation,* **34,** 101–105, 1980.

Chapter 10 | Markov Chain Monte Carlo Methods

Introduction

It is, in general, very difficult to simulate the value of a random vector $\mathbf{X}$ whose component random variables are dependent. In this chapter we present a powerful approach for generating a vector whose distribution is approximately that of $\mathbf{X}$. This approach, called the Markov chain Monte Carlo method, has the added significance of only requiring that the mass (or density) function of $\mathbf{X}$ be specified up to a multiplicative constant, and this, we will see, is of great importance in applications.

In Section 10.1 we introduce and give the needed results about Markov chains. In Section 10.2 we present the Hastings–Metropolis algorithm for constructing a Markov chain having a specified probability mass function as its limiting distribution. A special case of this algorithm, referred to as the Gibbs sampler, is studied in Section 10.3. The Gibbs sampler is probably the most widely used Markov chain Monte Carlo method. An application of the preceding methods to deterministic optimization problems, known as simulated annealing, is presented in Section 10.4. In Section 10.5 we present the sampling importance resampling (SIR) technique. While not strictly a Markov chain Monte Carlo algorithm, it also results in approximately simulating a random vector whose mass function is specified up to a multiplicative constant.

10.1 Markov Chains

Consider a collection of random variables $X_0, X_1, \ldots$. Interpret X_n as the "state of the system at time n," and suppose that the set of possible values of the X_n—that is, the possible states of the system—is the set $1, \ldots, N$. If there exists a set of numbers P_{ij}, $i, j = 1, \ldots, N$, such that whenever the process is in state i then, independent of the past states, the probability that the next state is j is P_{ij}, then we say that the collection $\{X_n, n \geq 0\}$ constitutes a *Markov chain* having transition probabilities P_{ij}, $i, j = 1, \ldots, N$. Since the process must be in some state after it leaves states i, these transition probabilities satisfy

$$\sum_{j=1}^{N} P_{ij} = 1, \qquad i = 1, \ldots, N$$

A Markov chain is said to be irreducible if for each pair of states i and j there is a positive probability, starting in state i, that the process will ever enter state j. For an irreducible Markov chain, let π_j denote the long-run proportion of time that the process is in state j. (It can be shown that π_j exists and is constant, with probability 1, independent of the initial state.) The quantities π_j, $j = 1, \ldots, N$, can be shown to be the unique solution of the following set of linear equations:

$$\pi_j = \sum_{i=1}^{N} \pi_i P_{ij}, \qquad j = 1, \ldots, N$$

$$\sum_{j=1}^{N} \pi_j = 1$$

(10.1)

Remark The set of equations (10.1) have a heuristic interpretation. Since π_i is the proportion of time that the Markov chain is in state i and since each transition out of state i is into state j with probability P_{ij}, it follows that $\pi_i P_{ij}$ is the proportion of time in which the Markov chain has just entered state j from state i. Hence, the top part of Equation (10.1) states the intuitively clear fact that the proportion of time in which the Markov chain has just entered state j is equal to the sum, over all states i, of the proportion of time in which it has just entered state j from state i. The bottom part of Equation (10.1) says, of course, that summing the proportion of time in which the chain is in state j, over all j, must equal 1. ■

The $\{\pi_j\}$ are often called the *stationary probabilities* of the Markov chain. For if the initial state of the Markov chain is distributed according to the $\{\pi_j\}$ then $P\{X_n = j\} = \pi_j$, for all n and j (see Exercise 1).

An important property of Markov chains is that for any function h on the state space, with probability 1,

$$\lim_{n \to \infty} \frac{1}{n} \sum_{i=1}^{n} h(X_i) = \sum_{j=1}^{N} \pi_j h(j)$$

(10.2)

The preceding follows since if $p_j(n)$ is the proportion of time that the chain is in state j between times $1, \ldots , n$ then

$$\frac{1}{n} \sum_{i=1}^{n} h(X_i) = \sum_{j=1}^{N} h(j)p_j(n) \to \sum_{j=1}^{N} h(j)\pi_j$$

The quantity π_j can often be interpreted as the limiting probability that the chain is in state j. To make precise the conditions under which it has this interpretation, we first need the definition of an aperiodic Markov chain.

Definition   *An irreducible Markov chain is said to be aperiodic if for some* $n \geq 0$ *and some state j,*

$$P\{X_n = j|X_0 = j\} > 0 \quad \text{and} \quad P\{X_{n+1} = j|X_0 = j\} > 0$$

It can be shown that if the Markov chain is irreducible and aperiodic then

$$\pi_j = \lim_{n \to \infty} P\{X_n = j\}, \quad j = 1, \ldots , N$$

There is sometimes an easier way than solving the set of equations (10.1) of finding the stationary probabilities. Suppose one can find positive numbers x_j, $j = 1, \ldots , N$ such that

$$x_i P_{ij} = x_j P_{ji}, \quad \text{for } i \neq j, \quad \sum_{j=1}^{N} x_j = 1$$

Then summing the preceding equations over all states i yields

$$\sum_{i=1}^{N} x_i P_{ij} = x_j \sum_{i=1}^{N} P_{ji} = x_j$$

which, since $\{\pi_j, j = 1, \ldots , N\}$ are the unique solution of (10.1), implies that

$$\pi_j = x_j$$

When $\pi_i P_{ij} = \pi_j P_{ji}$, for all $i \neq j$, the Markov chain is said to be *time reversible*, because it can be shown, under this condition, that if the initial state is chosen according to the probabilities $\{\pi_j\}$, then starting at any time the sequence of states going backwards in time will also be a Markov chain with transition probabilities P_{ij}.

Suppose now that we want to generate the value of a random variable X having probability mass function $P\{X = j\} = p_j, j = 1, \ldots , N$. If we could generate an irreducible aperiodic Markov chain with limiting probabilities p_j, $j = 1, \ldots , N$, then we would be able to approximately generate such a random variable by running the chain for n steps to obtain the value of X_n, where n is large. In addition, if our objective was to generate many random variables distributed according to p_j, $j = 1, \ldots, N$, so as to be able to estimate $E[h(X)] = \sum_{j=1}^{N} h(j)p_j$, then we could also estimate this quantity by using the estimator $\frac{1}{n}\sum_{i=1}^{n} h(X_i)$. However, since the early states of the Markov chain can be strongly influenced by the initial state chosen, it is common in practice to disregard the first k states, for some suitably chosen value of k. That is, the estimator $\frac{1}{n-k}\sum_{i=k+1}^{n}h(X_i)$, is utilized. It is difficult to know exactly how large a value of k should be used (although the advanced reader should see Aarts and Korst (1989) for some useful results along this line) and usually one just uses one's intuition (which usually works fine because the convergence is guaranteed no matter what value is used).

An important question is how to use the simulated Markov chain to estimate the mean square error of the estimator. That is, if we let $\hat{\theta} = \frac{1}{n-k}\sum_{i=k+1}^{n}h(X_i)$, how do we estimate

$$\text{MSE} = E\left[\left(\hat{\theta} - \sum_{j=1}^{N} h(j)p_j\right)^2\right]$$

One way is the *batch means* method, which works as follows. Break up the $n - k$ generated states into s batches of size r, where $s = (n - k)/r$ is integral, and let Y_j, $j = 1, \ldots, s$ be the average of the jth batch. That is,

$$Y_j = \frac{1}{r} \sum_{i=k+(j-1)r+1}^{k+jr} h(X_i), \qquad j = 1, \ldots, s$$

Now, treat the Y_j, $j = 1, \ldots, s$ as if they were independent and identically distributed with variance σ^2 and so use their sample variance $\sum_{j=1}^{s} (Y_j - \bar{Y})^2/(s - 1)$ as the estimator of σ^2. The estimate of MSE is $\hat{\sigma}^2/s$. The appropriate value of r depends on the Markov chain being simulated. The closer X_i, $i \geq 1$, is to being independent and identically distributed, then the smaller should be the value of r.

In the next two sections we will show, for a given set of positive numbers b_j, $j = 1, \ldots, N$, how to construct a Markov chain whose limiting probabilities are $\pi_j = b_j/\sum_{i=1}^{N} b_i$.

10.2   The Hastings–Metropolis Algorithm

Let $b(j)$, $j = 1, \ldots, m$ be positive numbers, and let $B = \sum_{j=1}^{m} b(j)$. Suppose that m is large and B is difficult to calculate, and that we want to simulate a random variable (or a sequence of random variables) with probability mass function

$$\pi(j) = b(j)/B, \qquad j = 1, \ldots, m$$

One way of simulating a sequence of random variables whose distributions converge to $\pi(j)$, $j = 1, \ldots, m$, is to find a Markov chain that is easy to simulate and whose limiting probabilities are the π_j. The *Hastings–Metropolis algorithm* provides an approach for accomplishing this task. It constructs a time-reversible Markov chain with the desired limiting probabilities, in the following manner.

Let **Q** be an irreducible Markov transition probability matrix on the integers $1, \ldots, m$, with $q(i,j)$ representing the row i, column j element of **Q**. Now define a Markov chain $\{X_n, n \geq 0\}$ as follows. When $X_n = i$, a random variable X such that $P\{X = j\} = q(i,j), j = 1, \ldots, m$, is generated. If $X = j$, then X_{n+1} is set equal to j with probability $\alpha(i,j)$ and is set equal to i with probability $1 - \alpha(i, j)$. Under these conditions, it is easy to see that the sequence of states will constitute a Markov chain with transition probabilities $P_{i,j}$ given by

$$P_{i,j} = q(i, j)\alpha(i, j), \quad \text{if } j \neq i$$

$$P_{i,i} = q(i, i) + \sum_{k \neq i} q(i, k)(1 - \alpha(i, k))$$

Now this Markov chain will be time reversible and have stationary probabilities $\pi(j)$ if

$$\pi(i)P_{i,j} = \pi(j)P_{j,i} \qquad \text{for } j \neq i$$

which is equivalent to

$$\pi(i)q(i, j)\alpha(i, j) = \pi(j)q(j, i)\alpha(j, i)$$

It is now easy to check that this will be satisfied if we take

$$\alpha(i, j) = \min\left(\frac{\pi(j)q(j, i)}{\pi(i)q(i, j)}, \ 1\right) = \min\left(\frac{b(j)q(j, i)}{b(i)q(i, j)}, \ 1\right)$$

[To check, note that if $\alpha(i, j) = \pi(j)q(j, i)/\pi(i)q(i, j)$ then $\alpha(j, i) = 1$, and vice versa.]

The reader should note that the value of B is not needed to define the Markov chain, as the values $b(j)$ suffice. Also, it is almost always the case that $\pi(j)$, $j = 1, \ldots, m$, will not only be stationary probabilities but will also be limiting probabilities. (Indeed, a sufficient condition is that $P_{i,i} > 0$ for some i.)

The following sums up the Hastings–Metropolis algorithm for generating a time-reversible Markov chain whose limiting probabilities are $\pi(j) = b(j)/B$, $j = 1, \ldots, m$.

1. Choose an irreducible Markov transition probability matrix $\mathbf{Q}$ with transition probabilities $q(i, j)$, $i, j = 1, \ldots, m$. Also, choose some integer value k between 1 and m.

2. Let $n = 0$ and $X_0 = k$.

3. Generate a random variable X such that $P\{X = j\} = q(X_n, j)$ and generate a random number U.

4. If $U < [b(X)q(X, X_n)]/[b(X_n)q(X_n, X)]$, then $NS = X$; else $NS = X_n$.

5. $n = n + 1$, $X_n = NS$.

6. Go to 3.

Example 10a Suppose that we want to generate a random element from a large complicated "combinatorial" set $\mathscr{S}$. For instance, $\mathscr{S}$ might be the set of all permutations $(x_1, \ldots, x_n)$ of the numbers $(1, \ldots, n)$ for which $\sum_{j=1}^{n} jx_j > a$ for a given constant a; or $\mathscr{S}$ might be the set of all subgraphs of a given graph having the property that for any pair of vertices i and j there is a unique path in the subgraph from i to j (such subgraphs are called trees).

To accomplish our goal we will utilize the Hastings–Metropolis algorithm. We shall start by assuming that one can define a concept of "neighboring" elements of $\mathscr{S}$, and we will then construct a graph whose set of vertices is $\mathscr{S}$ by putting an arc between each pair of neighboring elements in $\mathscr{S}$. For example, if $\mathscr{S}$ is the set of permutations $(x_1, \ldots, x_n)$ for which $\sum_{j=1}^{n} jx_j > a$, then we can define two such permutations to be neighbors if one results from an interchange of two of the positions of the other. That is, $(1, 2, 3, 4)$ and $(1, 2, 4, 3)$ are neighbors, whereas $(1, 2, 3, 4)$ and $(1, 3, 4, 2)$ are not. If $\mathscr{S}$ is a set of trees, then we can say that two trees are neighbors if all but one of the arcs of one of the trees are also arcs of the other tree.

Assuming this concept of neighboring elements, we define the q transition probability function as follows. With $N(s)$ defined as the set of neighbors of s, and $|N(s)|$ equal to the number of elements in the set $N(s)$, let

$$q(s, t) = \frac{1}{|N(s)|}, \qquad \text{if } t \in N(s)$$

That is, the target next state from s is equally likely to be any of its neighbors.

Since the desired limiting probabilities of the Markov chain are $\pi(s) = C$, it follows that $\pi(s) = \pi(t)$, and so

$$\alpha(s, t) = \min(|N(s)|/|N(t)|, 1)$$

That is, if the present state of the Markov chain is s, then one of its neighbors is randomly chosen—say it is t. If t is a state with fewer neighbors than s (in graph theory language, if the degree of vertex t is less than that of vertex s), then the next state is t. If not, a random number U is generated, and the next state is t if $U < |N(s)|/|N(t)|$, and is s otherwise. The limiting probabilities of this Markov chain are $\pi(s) = 1/|\mathscr{S}|$. ∎

Example 10b Suppose in Example 10a that we want to generate a randomly chosen element from the set of all permutations $x = (x_1, \ldots, x_n) \in \mathscr{S}$, where $\mathscr{S} = x : \sum_{j=1}^{n} jx_j > a$. In applying the method detailed in Example 10a, starting with x how do we randomly choose a neighbor permutation in $\mathscr{S}$? Well, if n is small, then we can easily keep track of all the neighbors that are in $\mathscr{S}$ and randomly choose one, call it y, as the target next state. The number of the neighbors of y would then have to be determined, and the next state of the Markov chain would then either be y with probability $\min(1, |N(x)|/|N(y)|)$, or it would remain x. However, if n is large this may be impractical, and a better approach might be to expand the state space to consist of all $n!$ permutations. The desired limiting probability mass function is then

$$\pi(x) = C, \qquad x \in \mathscr{S}$$
$$\pi(x) = 0, \qquad x \notin \mathscr{S}$$

With this setup, each permutation x has $\binom{n}{2}$ neighbors, and one can be randomly chosen by generating a random subset of size two from the set $1, \ldots, n$; if i and j are chosen, then the target next state y is obtained by interchanging the values of x_i and x_j. If $y \in \mathscr{S}$, then y becomes the next state of the chain, and if not, then the next state remains x. ∎

10.3   The Gibbs Sampler

The most widely used version of the Hastings–Metropolis algorithm is the Gibbs sampler. Let $X = (X_1, \ldots, X_n)$ be a random vector with probability mass function (or probability density function in the continuous case) $p(x)$, which may only be specified up to a multiplicative constant, and suppose that we want to generate a random vector whose distribution is that of the conditional distribution of X given that $X \in A$ for some set A. That is, we want to generate a random vector having mass function

$$f(x) = \frac{p(x)}{P\{X \in A\}}, \qquad \text{for } x \in A$$

The Gibbs sampler assumes that for any i, $i = 1, \ldots, n$, and any values x_j, $j \neq i$, we can generate a random variable X having the probability mass function

$$P\{X = x\} = P\{X_i = x | X_j = x_j, j \neq i\}$$

It operates by considering a Markov chain with states $x = (x_1, \ldots, x_i, \ldots, x_n) \in A$ and then uses the Hastings–Metropolis algorithm with Markov transition probabilities defined as follows. Whenever the present state is x, a coordinate that is equally likely to be any of $1, \ldots, n$ is generated. If coordinate i is the one chosen, then a random variable X having probability mass function $P\{X = x\} = P\{X_i = x | X_j = x_j, j \neq i\}$ is generated, and if $X = x$, then the state $y = (x_1, \ldots, x_{i-1}, x, x_{i+1}, \ldots, x_n)$ is considered for transition. In other words, the Gibbs sampler uses the Hastings–Metropolis algorithm with

$$q(x, y) = \frac{1}{n} P\{X_i = x | X_j = x_j, j \neq i\} = \frac{1}{n} \frac{p(y)}{P\{X_j = x_j, j \neq i\}}$$

Since the target mass function is f, the vector y is then accepted as the new state with probability

$$\alpha(x, y) = \min\left(\frac{f(y)q(y, x)}{f(x)q(x, y)}, 1\right)$$

Since, for $x \in A$ and $y \in A$,

$$\frac{f(y)q(y, x)}{f(x)q(x, y)} = \frac{f(y)p(x)}{f(x)p(y)} = 1$$

whereas for $x \in A$ and $y \notin A$

$$\frac{f(y)q(y, x)}{f(x)q(x, y)} = 0$$

we see that either the next state is y if $y \in A$, or it remains x if $y \notin A$.

Summing up, we see that the time-reversible Markov chain with stationary probabilities given by f that is generated by the Gibbs sampler is as follows.

1. Let $x = (x_1, \ldots, x_n)$ be a vector in A for which $p(x) > 0$.
2. Let I be equally likely to be any of the values $1, \ldots, n$.

3. If $I = i$, generate the value of a random variable X such that

$$P\{X = x\} = P\{X_i = x | X_j = x_j, j \neq i\}$$

4. If $X = x$ and $(x_1, \ldots, x_{i-1}, x, x_{i+1}, \ldots, x_n) \in A$, then reset the value of x_i to equal x. Otherwise, leave the value of x_i as is.

5. Return to Step 2.

Thus, at each step one of the variables X_i is randomly chosen, and a random variable having the conditional distribution of X_i given that $X_j = x_j, j \neq i$, is generated. If the new vector, with this value replacing x_i, is in A, then that is the next state of the chain; if this vector is not in A, then the state remains unchanged.

Example 10c Suppose we want to generate n random points in the circle of radius 1 centered at the origin, conditional on the event that no two points are within a distance d of each other, where

$$\beta = P\{\text{no two points are within } d \text{ of each other}\}$$

is assumed to be a small positive number. (If β were not small, then we could just continue to generate sets of n random points in the circle, stopping the first time that no two points in the set are within d of each other.) This can be accomplished by the Gibbs sampler by starting with n points in the circle, $x_1, \ldots, x_n$, such that no two are within a distance d of each other. Then generate a random number U and let $I = \text{Int}(nU) + 1$. Also generate a random point in the circle. If this point is not within d of any of the other $n - 1$ points excluding x_I, then replace x_I by this generated point; otherwise, do not make a change. After a large number of iterations the set of n points will approximately have the desired distribution.   ■

In the next example, the objective is to generate **X**, without any restriction that it must lie in some set of values. (That is, A is taken to be all possible values of **X**.)

Example 10d Queueing Networks. Suppose that r individuals move among $m + 1$ queueing stations, and let, for $i = 1, \ldots, m$, $X_i(t)$ denote the number of individuals at station i at time t. If

$$p(n_1, \ldots, n_m) = \lim_{t \to \infty} P\{X_i(t) = n_i, i = 1, \ldots, m\}$$

then, assuming exponentially distributed service times, it can often be established that

$$p(n_1, \ldots, n_m) = C \prod_{i=1}^{m} P_i(n_i), \qquad \text{if } \sum_{i=1}^{m} n_i \leq r$$

$$p(n_1, \ldots, n_m) = 0, \qquad \text{otherwise}$$

where $P_i(n)$, $n \geq 0$ is a probability mass function for each $i = 1, \ldots, m$. Such a joint probability mass function is said to have a *product form*.

While it is often relatively straightforward both to establish that $p(n_1, \ldots, n_m)$ has the preceding product form and to find the mass functions P_i, it can be difficult to explicitly compute the constant C. For even though

$$C \sum_{n:s(n) \leq r} \prod_{i=1}^{m} P_i(n_i) = 1$$

where $n = (n_1, \ldots, n_m)$ and $s(n) = \sum_{i=1}^{m} n_i$, it can be difficult to utilize this result. This is because the summation is over all nonnegative integer vectors n for which $\sum_{i=1}^{m} n_i \leq r$ and there are $\binom{r+m}{m}$ such vectors, which is a rather large number even when m and r are of moderate size.

Another approach to learning about $p(n_1, \ldots, n_m)$, which finesses the computational difficulties of computing C, is to use the Gibbs sampler to generate a sequence of values having a distribution approximately that of p.

To begin, note that if $N = (N_1, \ldots, N_m)$ has the joint mass function p, then, for $n = 0, \ldots, r - \sum_{k \neq i} n_k$,

$$P\{N_i = n | N_1 = n_1, \ldots, N_{i-1} = n_{i-1}, N_{i+1} = n_{i+1}, \ldots, N_m = n_m\}$$

$$= \frac{p(n_1, \ldots, n_{i-1}, n, n_{i+1}, \ldots, n_m)}{\sum_j p(n_1, \ldots, n_{i-1}, j, n_{i+1}, \ldots, n_m)}$$

$$= \frac{P_i(n)}{\sum_j P_i(j)}$$

where the preceding sum is over all $j = 0, \ldots, r - \sum_{k \neq i} n_k$. In other words, the conditional distribution of N_i given the values of N_j, $j \neq i$, is the same as the conditional distribution of a random variable having mass function P_i given that its value is less than or equal to $r - \sum_{j \neq i} N_j$.

Thus, we may generate the values of a Markov chain whose limiting probability mass function is $p(n_1, \ldots, n_m)$ as follows:

1. Let $(n_1, \ldots, n_m)$ be arbitrary nonnegative integers satisfying $\Sigma_i n_i \leq r$.
2. Generate U and let $I = \text{Int}(mU) + 1$.
3. If $I = i$, let X_i have mass function P_i and generate a random variable N whose distribution is the conditional distribution of X_i given that $X_i \leq r - \Sigma_{j \neq i} n_j$.
4. Let $n_i = N$ and go to 2.

The successive values of $(n_1, \ldots, n_m)$ constitute the sequence of states of a Markov chain with the limiting distribution p. All quantities of interest concerning p can be estimated from this sequence. For instance, the average of the values of the jth coordinate of these vectors will converge to the mean number of individuals at station j, the proportion of vectors whose jth coordinate is less than k will converge to the limiting probability that the number of individuals at station j is less than k, and so on. ∎

In cases where it is easy to generate X_i conditional both on the values of X_j, $j \neq i$, and on the condition that $X \in A$, then such a generation can replace Steps 3 and 4 in the Gibbs sampler. This is illustrated by our next example.

Example 10e Let X_i, $i = 1, \ldots, n$, be independent random variables with X_i having an exponential distribution with rate λ_i, $i = 1, \ldots, n$. Let $S = \Sigma_{i=1}^n X_i$ and suppose we want to generate the random vector $X = (X_1, \ldots, X_n)$ conditional on the event that $S > c$ for some large positive constant c. That is, we want to generate the value of a random vector whose density function is given by

$$f(x_1, \ldots, x_n) = \frac{1}{P\{S > c\}} \prod_{i=1}^n \lambda_i e^{-\lambda_i x_i}, \qquad \text{if } \sum_{i=1}^n x_i > c$$

This is easily accomplished by starting with an initial vector $x = (x_1, \ldots, x_n)$ satisfying $x_i > 0$, $i = 1, \ldots, n$, and $\Sigma_{i=1}^n x_i > c$. Then generate a random number U and set $I = \text{Int}(nU + 1)$. Suppose that $I = i$. Now, we want to generate an exponential random variable X with rate λ_i conditioned on the event that $X + \Sigma_{j \neq i} x_j > c$. That is, we want to generate the value of X conditional on the event that it exceeds $c - \Sigma_{j \neq i} x_j$. Hence, using the fact that an exponential conditioned to be greater than a positive constant is distributed as the constant plus the exponential, we see that we should generate an exponential random variable Y with rate λ_i [say, let $Y = -1/\lambda_i \log U$], and set

$$X = Y + \left(c - \sum_{j \neq i} x_j \right)^+$$

where b^+ is equal to b when $b > 0$ and is 0 otherwise. The value of x_i should then be reset to equal X and a new iteration of the algorithm begun. ∎

Suppose now that we are interested in estimating

$$\alpha = P\{h(X) > a\}$$

where $X = (X_1, \ldots, X_n)$ is a random vector that can be generated by Gibbs sampling, h is an arbitrary function of X, and α is very small. Since a generated value of $h(X)$ will almost always be less than a, it would take a huge amount of time to obtain an estimator whose error is small relative to α if we use a straightforward Gibbs sampler approach to generate a sequence of random vectors whose distribution converges to that of X. Consider, however, the following approach.

To begin, note that for values $-\infty = a_0 < a_1 < a_2 < \cdots < a_k = a$,

$$\alpha = \prod_{i=1}^{k} P\{h(X) > a_i | h(X) > a_{i-1}\}$$

Thus, we can obtain an estimator of α by taking the product of estimators of the quantities $P\{h(X) > a_i | h(X) > a_{i-1}\}$, for $i = 1, \ldots, k$. For this to be efficient, the values $a_i, i = 1, \ldots, k$, should be chosen so that $P\{h(X) > a_i | h(X) > a_{i-1}\}$ are all of moderate size.

To estimate $P\{h(X) > a_i | h(X) > a_{i-1}\}$, we make use of the Gibbs sampler as follows.

1. Set $J = 0$.
2. Choose a vector x such that $h(x) > a_{i-1}$.
3. Generate a random number U and set $I = \text{Int}(nU) + 1$.
4. If $I = k$, generate X having the conditional distribution of X_k given that $X_j = x_j, j \neq k$.
5. If $h(x_1, \ldots, x_{k-1}, X, x_{k+1}, \ldots, x_n) > a_{i-1}$, set $x_k = X$.
6. If $h(x_1, \ldots, x_k, \ldots, x_n) > a_i$, set $J = J + 1$.
7. Go to 3.

The ratio of the final value of J to the number of iterations of this algorithm is the estimator of $P\{h(X) > a_i | h(X) > a_{i-1}\}$.

Example 10f Suppose in the queueing network model of Example 10d that the service times at server i are exponential with rate $\mu_i, i = 1, \ldots, m + 1$, and that when a customer completes service at server i then, independent of all else, that customer then moves over to join the queue (or enter service if the server is free) at server j with probability P_{ij}, where $\sum_{j=1}^{m+1} P_{ij} = 1$. It can then be shown that the limiting probability mass function of the number of customers at servers $1, \ldots, m$ is given, for $\sum_{j=1}^{m} n_j \leq r$, by

$$p(n_1, \ldots, n_m) = C \prod_{j=1}^{m} \left(\frac{\pi_j \mu_{m+1}}{\pi_{m+1} \mu_j} \right)^{n_j}$$

where $\pi_j, j = 1, \ldots, m + 1$, are the stationary probabilities of the Markov chain with transition probabilities P_{ij}. That is, they are the unique solution of

$$\pi_j = \sum_{i=1}^{m+1} \pi_i P_{ij}$$

$$\sum_{j=1}^{m+1} \pi_j = 1$$

If we renumber the servers so that $\max(\pi_j/\mu_j) = \pi_{m+1}/\mu_{m+1}$, then letting $a_j = \pi_j \mu_{m+1}/\pi_{m+1}\mu_j$, we have that for $\sum_{j=1}^{m} n_j \leq r$,

$$p(n_1, \ldots, n_m) = C \prod_{j=1}^{m} (a_j)^{n_j}$$

where $0 \leq a_j \leq 1$. It easily follows from this that the conditional distribution of the number of customers at server i, given the numbers $n_j, j \neq i$, at the other $m - 1$ servers, is distributed as the conditional distribution of -1 plus a geometric random variable with parameter $1 - a_i$, given that the geometric is less than or equal to $r + 1 - \sum_{j \neq i} n_j$.

In the case where the π_j and μ_j are both constant for all j, the conditional distribution of the number of customers at server i, given the numbers $n_j, j \neq i$, at the other servers excluding server $m + 1$, is the discrete uniform distribution on $0, 1, \ldots, r - \sum_{j \neq i} n_j$. Suppose this is the case and that $m = 20$, $r = 100$, and that we are interested in estimating the limiting probability that the number of customers at server 1—call it X_1—is greater than 18. Letting $t_0 = -1$, $t_1 = 5, t_2 = 9, t_3 = 12, t_4 = 15, t_5 = 17, t_6 = 18$, we can use the Gibbs sampler to successively estimate the quantities $P\{X_1 > t_i | X_1 > t_{i-1}\}$, $i = 1, 2, 3, 4, 5$, 6. We would estimate, say $P\{X_1 > 17 | X_1 > 15\}$, by starting with a vector $n_1, \ldots, n_{20}$ for which $n_1 > 15$ and $s = \sum_{i=1}^{20} n_i \leq 100$. We then generate a random number U and let $I = \text{Int}(20U + 1)$. A second random number V is now generated and we set $J = \text{Int}((100 + n_I - s)V + 1)$. If $I \neq 1$, then n_I is reset to equal J. If $I = 1$ and $J > 15$, then n_1 is reset to equal J; otherwise, its value is unchanged and the next iteration of the algorithm begins. The fraction of iterations for which $n_1 > 17$ is the estimate of $P\{X_1 > 17|X_1 > 15\}$. ■

The idea of writing a small probability as the product of more moderately sized conditional probabilities and then estimating each of the conditional probabilities in turn does not require that the Gibbs sampler be employed. Another variant of the Hastings–Metropolis algorithm might be more appropriate. We illustrate by an example that was previously treated, in Example 8u, by using importance sampling.

Example 10g Suppose that we are interested in estimating the number of permutations $x = (x_1, \ldots, x_n)$ for which $t(x) > a$, where $t(x) = \sum_{j=1}^n jx_j$ and where a is such that this number of permutations is very small in comparison to $n!$. If we let $X = (X_1, \ldots, X_n)$ be equally likely to be any of the $n!$ permutations and set

$$\alpha = P\{T(X) > a\}$$

then α is small and the quantity of interest is $\alpha n!$. Letting $0 = a_0 < a_1 < \cdots < a_k = a$, we have that

$$\alpha = \prod_{i=1}^k P\{T(X) > a_i|T(X) > a_{i-1}\}$$

To estimate $P\{T(X) > a_i|T(X) > a_{i-1}\}$ we use the Hastings–Metropolis algorithm as in Examples 10a or 10b to generate a Markov chain whose limiting distribution is

$$\pi(x) = \frac{1}{N_{i-1}}, \qquad \text{if } T(x) > a_{i-1}$$

where N_{i-1} is the number of permutations x such that $T(x) > a_{i-1}$. The proportion of the generated states x of this Markov chain that have $T(x) > a_i$ is the estimate of $P\{T(X) > a_i|T(X) > a_{i-1}\}$. ■

In many applications it is relatively easy to recognize the form of the conditional distributions needed in the Gibbs sampler.

Example 10h Suppose that for some nonnegative function $h(y, z)$ the joint density of the nonnegative random variables $X, Y,$ and Z is

$$f(x, y, z) = Cx^{y-1}(1 - x)^{zy}h(y, z), \qquad \text{for } 0 < x < 0.5$$

Then the conditional density of X given that $Y = y$ and $Z = z$ is

$$f(x|y, z) = \frac{f(x, y, z)}{f_{Y,Z}(y, z)}$$

Since y and z are fixed and x is the argument of this conditional density, we can write the preceding as

$$f(x|y, z) = C_1 f(x, y, z)$$

where C_1 does not depend on x. Hence, we have that

$$f(x|y, z) = C_2 x^{y-1}(1 - x)^{zy}, \qquad 0 < x < 0.5$$

where C_2 does not depend on x. But we can recognize this as the conditional density of a beta random variable with parameters y and $zy + 1$ that is conditioned to be in the interval $(0, 0.5)$. ∎

Rather than always choosing a random coordinate to update on, the Gibbs sampler can also consider the coordinates in sequence. That is, on the first iteration we could set $I = 1$, then set $I = 2$ on the next iteration, then $I = 3$, and so on until the nth iteration, where $I = n$. On the next iteration, we start over. We illustrate this with our next example, which is concerned with modeling the numbers of home runs hit by two of the best hitters in baseball.

Example 10i Let $N_1(t)$ denote the number of home runs hit in the first $100t$ percent of a baseball season, $0 \le t \le 1$, by the San Francisco Giants player Matt Williams; similarly, let $N_2(t)$ be the number hit by the Chicago White Sox player Frank Thomas.

Suppose that there are random variables W_1 and W_2 such that given that $W_1 = w_1$ and $W_2 = w_2$, $\{N_1(t), 0 \le t \le 1\}$ and $\{N_2(t), 0 \le t \le 1\}$ are independent Poisson processes with respective rates w_1 and w_2. Furthermore, suppose that W_1 and W_2 are independent exponential random variables with rate Y, which is itself a random variable that is uniformly distributed between 0.02 and 0.10. In other words, the assumption is that the players hit home runs in accordance with Poisson processes whose rates are random variables from a distribution that is defined in terms of a parameter that is itself a random variable with a specified distribution.

Suppose that Williams has hit 25 and Thomas 18 home runs in the first half of the season. Give a method for estimating the mean number they each hit in the full season.

Solution   Summing up the model, there are random variables Y, W_1, W_2 such that:

1. Y is uniform on $(0.02, 0.10)$.
2. Given that $Y = y$, W_1 and W_2 are independent and identically distributed exponential random variables with rate y.
3. Given that $W_1 = w_1$ and $W_2 = w_2$, $\{N_1(t)\}$ and $\{N_2(t)\}$ are independent Poisson processes with rates w_1 and w_2.

To find $E[N_1(1)|N_1(0.5) = 25, N_2(0.5) = 18]$, start by conditioning on W_1.

$$E[N_1(1)|N_1(0.5) = 25, N_2(0.5) = 18, W_1] = 25 + 0.5W_1$$

Taking the conditional expectation, given that $N_1(0.5) = 25$ and $N_2(0.5) = 18$, of the preceding yields that

$$E[N_1(1)|N_1(0.5) = 25, N_2(0.5) = 18] = 25 + 0.5E[W_1|N_1(0.5) = 25,$$
$$N_2(0.5) = 18]$$

Similarly,

$$E[N_2(1)|N_1(0.5) = 25, N_2(0.5) = 18] = 18 + 0.5E[W_2|N_1(0.5) = 25,$$
$$N_2(0.5) = 18]$$

We can now estimate these conditional expectations by using the Gibbs sampler. To begin, note the joint distribution: For $0.02 < y < 0.10$, $w_1 > 0$, $w_2 > 0$,

$$f(y, w_1, w_2, N_1(0.5) = 25, N_2(0.5) = 18)$$
$$= Cy^2e^{-(w_1+w_2)y}e^{-(w_1+w_2)/2}(w_1)^{25}(w_2)^{18}$$

where C does not depend on any of y, w_1, w_2. Hence, for $0.02 < y < 0.10$,

$$f(y|w_1, w_2, N_1 = 25, N_2 = 18) = C_1y^2e^{-(w_1+w_2)y}$$

which shows that the conditional distribution of Y given w_1, w_2, $N_1 = 25$, $N_2 = 18$, is that of a gamma random variable with parameters 3 and $w_1 + w_2$ that is conditioned to be between 0.02 and 0.10. Also,

$$f(w_1|y, w_2, N_1(0.5) = 25, N_2(0.5) = 18) = C_2e^{-(y+1/2)w_1}(w_1)^{25}$$

from which we can conclude that the conditional distribution of W_1 given y, w_2, $N_1 = 25$, $N_2 = 18$ is gamma with parameters 26 and $y + \frac{1}{2}$. Similarly, the conditional distribution of W_2 given y, w_1, $N_1 = 25$, $N_2 = 18$, is gamma with parameters 19 and $y + \frac{1}{2}$.

Hence, starting with values y, w_1, w_2, where $.02 < y < 0.10$, and $w_i > 0$, the Gibbs sampler is as follows.

1. Generate the value of a gamma random variable with parameters 3 and $w_1 + w_2$ that is conditioned to be between or 0.02 and 0.10 and let it be the new value of y.

2. Generate the value of a gamma random variable with parameters 26 and $y + \frac{1}{2}$, and let it be the new value of w_1.

3. Generate the value of a gamma random variable with parameters 19 and $y + \frac{1}{2}$, and let it be the new value of w_2.

4. Return to Step 1.

The average of the values of w_1 is our estimate of $E[W_1|N_1(0.5) = 25, N_2(0.5) = 18]$, and the average of the values of w_2 is our estimate of $E[W_2|N_1(0.5) = 25, N_2(0.5) = 18]$. One-half of the former plus 25 is our estimate of the mean number of home runs that Matt Williams will hit over the year, and one-half of the latter plus 18 is our estimate of the mean number that Frank Thomas will hit.

It should be noted that the numbers of home runs hit by the two players are dependent, with their dependence caused by their common dependence on the value of the random variable Y. That is, the value of Y (which might relate to such quantities as the average degree of liveliness of the baseballs used that season or the average weather conditions for the year) affects the distribution of the mean number of home runs that each player will hit in the year. Thus, information about the number of home runs hit by one of the players yields probabilistic information about the value of Y that affects the distribution of the number of home runs of the other player. This type of model, where there is a common random variable (Y in this case) that affects the distributions of the conditional parameters of the random variables of interest, is known as an *hierarchical Bayes* model. ∎

When applying the Gibbs sampler, it is not necessary to condition on all but one of the variables. If joint conditional distributions can be generated from, then we may utilize them. For instance, suppose $n = 3$ and that we can generate from the conditional distribution of any two of them given the third. Then, at each iteration we could generate a random number U, set $I = \text{Int}(3U + 1)$, and generate from the joint distribution of the $X_j, X_k, j, k \neq I$, given the present value of X_I. That is, if $I = 2$, we would generate from the joint distribution of X_1, X_3 given the present value of X_2, say $X_2 = x_2$. If this results in the values y_1, y_3, then if the vector (y_1, x_2, y_3) lies in the set A, it becomes the new state vector; otherwise, the state does not change.

Example 10j   Let X_i, $i = 1, 2, 3, 4, 5$, be independent exponential random variables, with X_i having mean i, and suppose we are interested in using simulation to estimate

$$\beta = P\left\{\prod_{i=1}^{5} X_i > 120 \,\middle|\, \sum_{i=1}^{5} X_i = 15\right\}.$$

We can accomplish this by using the Gibbs sampler via a random choice of two of the coordinates. To begin, suppose that X and Y are independent exponentials with respective rates λ and μ, where $\mu < \lambda$, and let us find the conditional distribution of X given that $X + Y = a$, as follows.

$$f_{X|X+Y}(x|a) = C_1 f_{X,Y}(x, a - x), \qquad 0 < x < a$$
$$= C_2 e^{-\lambda x} e^{-\mu(a-x)}, \qquad 0 < x < a$$
$$= C_3 e^{-(\lambda-\mu)x}, \qquad 0 < x < a$$

which shows that the conditional distribution is that of an exponential with rate $\lambda - \mu$ that is conditioned to be less than a.

Using this result, we can estimate β by letting the initial state $(x_1, x_2, x_3, x_4, x_5)$ be any five positive numbers that sum to 15. Now randomly choose two elements from the set 1, 2, 3, 4, 5; say $I = 2$ and $J = 5$ are chosen. Then the conditional distribution of X_2, X_5 given the other values is the conditional distribution of two independent exponentials with means 2 and 5, given that their sum is $15 - x_1 - x_3 - x_4$. But, by the preceding, the values of X_2 and X_5 can be obtained by generating the value of an exponential with rate $\frac{1}{2} - \frac{1}{5} = \frac{3}{10}$ that is conditioned to be less than $15 - x_1 - x_3 - x_4$, then setting x_2 equal to that value and resetting x_5 to make $\sum_{i=1}^{5} x_i = 15$. This process should be continually repeated, and the proportion of state vectors $\mathbf{x}$ having $\prod_{i=1}^{5} x_i > 120$ is the estimate of β.   ∎

Remarks

1. The same argument can be used to verify that we obtain the appropriate limiting mass function when we consider the coordinates in sequence and apply the Gibbs sampler (as in Example 10i), or when we use it via conditioning on less than all but one of the values (as in Example 10j). These results are proven by noticing that if one chooses the initial state according to the the mass function f, then, in either case, the next state

also has mass function f. But this shows that f satisfies the equations (10.1), implying by uniqueness that f is the limiting mass function.

2. Suppose you are using the Gibbs sampler to estimate $E[X_i]$ in a situation where the conditional means $E[X_i|X_j, j \neq i]$ are easily computed. Then, rather than using the average of the successive values of X_i as the estimator, it is usually better to use the average of the conditional expectations. That is, if the present state is x, then take $E[X_i|X_j = x_j, j \neq i]$ rather than x_i as the estimate from that iteration. Similarly, if you are trying to estimate $P\{X_i = x\}$, and $P\{X_i = x|X_j, j \neq i\}$ is easily computed, then the average of these quantities is usually a better estimator than is the proportion of time in which the the ith component of the state vector equals x.

3. The Gibbs sampler shows that knowledge of all the conditional distributions of X_i given the values of the other $X_j, j \neq i$, determines the joint distribution of X. ∎

10.4   Simulated Annealing

Let $\mathscr{A}$ be a finite set of vectors and let $V(\mathbf{x})$ be a nonnegative function defined on $\mathbf{x} \in \mathscr{A}$, and suppose that we are interested in finding its maximal value and at least one argument at which the maximal value is attained. That is, letting

$$V^* = \max_{x \in \mathscr{A}} V(\mathbf{x})$$

and

$$\mathscr{M} = \{x \in \mathscr{A} : V(x) = V^*\}$$

we are interested in finding V^* as well as an element in $\mathscr{M}$. We will now show how this can be accomplished by using the methods of this chapter.

To begin, let $\lambda > 0$ and consider the following probability mass function on the set of values in $\mathscr{A}$:

$$p_\lambda(\mathbf{x}) = \frac{e^{\lambda V(\mathbf{x})}}{\sum_{\mathbf{x} \in \mathscr{A}} e^{\lambda V(\mathbf{x})}}$$

By multiplying the numerator and denominator of the preceding by $e^{-\lambda V^*}$, and letting $|\mathscr{M}|$ denote the number of elements in $\mathscr{M}$, we see that

$$p_\lambda(\mathbf{x}) = \frac{e^{\lambda(V(\mathbf{x}) - V^*)}}{|\mathscr{M}| + \sum_{\mathbf{x} \notin \mathscr{M}} e^{\lambda(V(\mathbf{x}) - V^*)}}$$

However, since $V(\mathbf{x}) - V^* < 0$ for $\mathbf{x} \notin \mathcal{M}$, we obtain that as $\lambda \to \infty$,

$$p_\lambda(\mathbf{x}) \to \frac{\delta(\mathbf{x}, \mathcal{M})}{|\mathcal{M}|}$$

where $\delta(\mathbf{x}, \mathcal{M}) = 1$ if $\mathbf{x} \in \mathcal{M}$ and is 0 otherwise.

Hence, if we let λ be large and generate a Markov chain whose limiting distribution is $p_\lambda(\mathbf{x})$, then most of the mass of this limiting distribution will be concentrated on points in $\mathcal{M}$. An approach that is often useful in defining such a chain is to introduce the concept of neighboring vectors and then use a Hastings–Metropolis algorithm. For instance, we could say that the two vectors $\mathbf{x} \in \mathcal{A}$ and $\mathbf{y} \in \mathcal{A}$ are neighbors if they differ in only a single coordinate or if one can be obtained from the other by interchanging two of its components. We could then let the target next state from $\mathbf{x}$ be equally likely to be any of its neighbors, and if the neighbor $\mathbf{y}$ is chosen, then the next state becomes $\mathbf{y}$ with probability

$$\min\left\{1, \frac{e^{\lambda V(\mathbf{y})}/|N(\mathbf{y})|}{e^{\lambda V(\mathbf{x})}/|N(\mathbf{x})|}\right\}$$

or remains $\mathbf{x}$ otherwise, where $|N(\mathbf{z})|$ is the number of neighbors of $\mathbf{z}$. If each vector has the same number of neighbors (and if not already so, this can almost always be arranged by increasing the state space and letting the V value of any new state equal 0), then when the state is $\mathbf{x}$, one of its neighbors, say $\mathbf{y}$, is randomly chosen; if $V(\mathbf{y}) \geq V(\mathbf{x})$, then the chain moves to state $\mathbf{y}$, and if $V(\mathbf{y}) < V(\mathbf{x})$, then the chain moves to state $\mathbf{y}$ with probability $\exp\{\lambda(V(\mathbf{y}) - V(\mathbf{x}))\}$ or remains in state $\mathbf{x}$ otherwise.

One weakness with the preceding algorithm is that since λ was chosen to be large, if the chain enters a state $\mathbf{x}$ whose V value is greater than that of each of its neighbors, then it might take a long time for the chain to move to a different state. That is, whereas a large value of λ is needed for the limiting distribution to put most of its weight on points in $\mathcal{M}$, such a value typically requires a very large number of transitions before the limiting distribution is approached. A second weakness is that since there are only a finite number of possible values of $\mathbf{x}$, the whole concept of convergence seems meaningless since we could always, in theory, just try each of the possible values and so obtain convergence in a finite number of steps. Thus, rather than considering the preceding from a strictly mathematical point of view, it makes more sense to regard it as a heuristic approach, and in doing so it has been found to be useful to allow the value of λ to change with time.

A popular variation of the preceding, known as *simulated annealing,* operates as follows. If the nth state of the Markov chain is **x**, then a neighboring value is randomly selected. If it is **y**, then the next state is either **y** with probability

$$\min\left\{1, \frac{e^{\lambda_n V(\mathbf{y})}/|N(\mathbf{y})|}{e^{\lambda_n V(\mathbf{x})}/|N(\mathbf{x})|}\right\}$$

or it remains **x**, where λ_n, $n \geq 1$, is a prescribed set of values that start out small (thus resulting in a large number of changes in state) and then grow.

A computationally useful choice of λ_n (and a choice that mathematically results in convergence) is to let $\lambda_n = C \log(1 + n)$, where $C > 0$ is any fixed positive constant (see Besag *et al.,* 1995; Diaconis and Holmes, 1995). If we then generate m successive states $X_1, \ldots, X_m$, we can then estimate V^* by $\max_{i=1 \ldots, m} V(X_i)$, and if the maximum occurs at X_{i*} then this is taken as an estimated point in $\mathcal{M}$.

Example 10k The Traveling Salesman Problem. One version of the traveling salesman problem is for the salesman to start at city 0 and then sequentially visit all of the cities $1, \ldots, r$. A possible choice is then a permutation $x_1, \ldots, x_r$ of $1, \ldots, r$ with the interpretation that from 0 the salesman goes to city x_1, then to x_2, and so on. If we suppose that a nonnegative reward $v(i, j)$ is earned whenever the salesman goes directly from city i to city j, then the return of the choice $\mathbf{x} = (x_1, \ldots, x_r)$ is

$$V(\mathbf{x}) = \sum_{i=1}^{r} v(x_{i-1}, x_i)$$

By letting two permutations be neighbors if one results from an interchange of two of the coordinates of the other, we can use simulated annealing to approximate the best path. Namely, start with any permutation **x** and let $X_0 = \mathbf{x}$. Now, once the nth state (that is, permutation) has been determined, $n \geq 0$, then generate one of its neighbors at random [by choosing I, J equally likely to be any of the $\binom{r}{2}$ values $i \neq j$, $i, j = 1, \ldots, r$ and then interchanging the values of the Ith and Jth elements of X_n]. Let the generated neighbor be **y**. Then if $V(\mathbf{y}) \geq V(X_n)$, set $X_{n+1} = \mathbf{y}$. Otherwise, set $X_{n+1} = \mathbf{y}$ with probability $(1 + n)^{(V(\mathbf{y})-V(X_n))}$, or set it equal to X_n otherwise. [Note that we are using $\lambda_n = \log(1 + n)$.] ∎

10.5   The Sampling Importance Resampling Algorithm

The sampling importance resampling, or SIR, algorithm is a method for generating a random vector X whose mass function

$$f(x) = C_1 f_o(x)$$

is specified up to a multiplicative constant, by simulating a Markov chain whose limiting probabilities are given by a mass function

$$g(x) = C_2 g_o(x)$$

that is also specified up to a multiplicative constant. It is similar to the acceptance–rejection technique, where one starts by generating the value of a random vector Y with density g and then, if $Y = y$, accepting this value with probability $f(y)/cg(y)$, where c is a constant chosen so that $f(x)/cg(x) \leq 1$, for all x. If the value is not accepted, then the process begins anew, and the eventually accepted value X has density f. However, as f and g are no longer totally specified, this approach is not available.

The SIR approach starts by generating m successive states of a Markov chain whose limiting probability mass function is g. Let these state values be denoted as $y_1, \ldots, y_m$. Now, define the "weights" w_i, $i = 1, \ldots, m$, by

$$w_i = \frac{f_o(y_i)}{g_o(y_i)}$$

and generate a random vector X such that

$$P\{X = y_j\} = \frac{w_j}{\sum_{i=1}^m w_i}, \qquad j = 1, \ldots, m$$

We will show that when m is large, the random vector X has a mass function approximately equal to f.

Proposition   *The distribution of the vector X obtained by the SIR method converges as $m \to \infty$ to f.*

Proof   Let Y_i, $i = 1, \ldots, m$, denote the m random vectors generated by the Markov chain whose limiting mass function is g, and let $W_i = f_o(Y_i)/g_o(Y_i)$ denote their weights. For a fixed set of vectors $\mathscr{A}$, let $I_i = 1$ if $Y_i \in \mathscr{A}$ and let it equal 0 otherwise. Then

$$P\{X \in \mathscr{A} | Y_i, i = 1, \ldots, m\} = \frac{\sum_{i=1}^m I_i W_i}{\sum_{i=1}^m W_i} \qquad (10.3)$$

Now, by the Markov chain result of Equation (10.2), we see that as $m \to \infty$,

$$\sum_{i=1}^{m} I_i W_i / m \to E_g[IW] = E_g[IW|I = 1] P_g\{I = 1\} = E_g[W|Y \in \mathcal{A}] P_g\{Y \in \mathcal{A}\}$$

and

$$\sum_{i=1}^{m} W_i / m \to E_g[W] = E_g[f_o(Y)/g_o(Y)] = \int \frac{f_o(y)}{g_o(y)} g(y) dy = C_2/C_1$$

Hence, dividing numerator and denominator of (10.3) by m shows that

$$P\{X \in \mathcal{A}|Y_i, i = 1, \ldots, m\} \to \frac{C_1}{C_2} E_g[W|Y \in \mathcal{A}] P_g\{Y \in \mathcal{A}\}$$

But,

$$\frac{C_1}{C_2} E_g[W|Y \in \mathcal{A}] P_g\{Y \in \mathcal{A}\} = \frac{C_1}{C_2} E_g\left[\frac{f_o(Y)}{g_o(Y)}\Big|Y \in \mathcal{A}\right] P_g\{Y \in \mathcal{A}\}$$

$$= \int_{y \in \mathcal{A}} \frac{f(y)}{g(y)} g(y) dy$$

$$= \int_{y \in \mathcal{A}} f(y) dy$$

Hence, as $m \to \infty$,

$$P\{X \in \mathcal{A}|Y_i, i = 1, \ldots, m\} \to \int_{y \in \mathcal{A}} f(y) dy$$

which implies, by a mathematical result known as Lebesgue's dominated convergence theorem, that

$$P\{X \in \mathcal{A}\} = E[P\{X \in \mathcal{A}|Y_i, i = 1, \ldots, m\}] \to \int_{y \in \mathcal{A}} f(y) dy$$

and the result is proved. ∎

The sampling importance resampling algorithm for approximately generating a random vector with mass function f starts by generating random variables with a different joint mass function (as in *importance sampling*) and then *resamples* from this pool of generated values to obtain the random vector.

Suppose now that we want to estimate $E_f[h(X)]$ for some function h. This can be accomplished by first generating a large number of successive states of a Markov chain whose limiting probabilities are given by g. If these states are

$y_1, \ldots, y_m$, then it might seem natural to choose k vectors $X_1, \ldots, X_k$ having the probability distribution

$$P\{X = y_j\} = \frac{w_j}{\sum_{i=1}^{m} w_i}, \qquad j = 1, \ldots, m$$

where k/m is small and $w_i = f_o(y_i)/g_o(y_i)$, and then use $\sum_{i=1}^{k} h(X_i)/k$ as the estimator. However, a better approach is not to base the estimator on a sampled set of k values, but rather to use the entire set of m generated values $y_1, \ldots, y_m$. We now show that

$$\frac{1}{\sum_{i=1}^{m} w_i} \sum_{j=1}^{m} w_j h(y_j)$$

is a better estimator of $E_f[h(X)]$ than is $\sum_{i=1}^{k} h(X_i)/k$. To show this, note that

$$E[h(X_i)|y_1, \ldots, y_m] = \frac{1}{\sum_{i=1}^{m} w_i} \sum_{j=1}^{m} w_j h(y_j)$$

and thus

$$E\left[\frac{1}{k} \sum_{i=1}^{k} h(X_i)|y_1, \ldots, y_m\right] = \frac{1}{\sum_{i=1}^{m} w_i} \sum_{j=1}^{m} w_j h(y_j)$$

which shows that $\sum_{j=1}^{m} h(y_j)w_j/\sum_{i=1}^{m} w_i$ has the same mean and smaller variance than $\sum_{i=1}^{k} h(X_i)/k$.

The use of data generated from one distribution to gather information about another distribution is particularly useful in Bayesian statistics.

Example 10l   Suppose that X is a random vector whose probability distribution is specified up to a vector of unknown parameters θ. For instance, X could be a sequence of independent and identically distributed normal random variables and $\theta = (\theta_1, \theta_2)$ where θ_1 is the mean and θ_2 is the variance of these random variables. Let $f(x|\theta)$ denote the density of X given θ. Whereas in classical statistics one assumes that θ is a vector of unknown constants, in Bayesian statistics we suppose that it, too, is random and has a specified probability density function $p(\theta)$, called the prior density.

If X is observed to equal x, then the conditional, also known as the posterior, density of θ is given by

$$p(\theta|x) = \frac{f(x|\theta)p(\theta)}{\int f(x|\theta)p(\theta)d(\theta)}$$

However, in many situations $\int f(x|\theta)p(\theta)d(\theta)$ cannot easily be computed, and so the preceding formula cannot be directly used to study the posterior distribution.

One approach to study the properties of the posterior distribution is to start by generating random vectors θ from the prior density p and then use the resulting data to gather information about the posterior density $p(\theta|x)$. If we suppose that the prior density $p(\theta)$ is completely specified and can be directly generated from, then we can use the preceding with

$$f_o(\theta) = f(x|\theta)p(\theta)$$

$$g(\theta) = g_o(\theta) = p(\theta)$$

$$w(\theta) = f(x|\theta)$$

To begin, generate a large number m of random vectors from the prior density $p(\theta)$. Let their values be $\theta_1, \ldots, \theta_m$. We can now estimate any function of the form $E[h(\theta)|x]$ by the estimator

$$\sum_{j=1}^{m} \alpha_j h(\theta_j), \qquad \text{where } \alpha_j = \frac{f(x|\theta_j)}{\sum_{i=1}^{m} f(x|\theta_i)}$$

For instance, for any set $\mathcal{A}$ we would use

$$\sum_{j=1}^{m} \alpha_j I\{\theta_j \in \mathcal{A}\} \qquad \text{to estimate } P\{\theta \in \mathcal{A}|x\}$$

where $I\{\theta_j \in \mathcal{A}\}$ is 1 if $\theta_j \in \mathcal{A}$ and is 0 otherwise.

In cases where the dimension of θ is small, we can use the generated data from the prior along with their weights to graphically explore the posterior. For instance, if θ is two-dimensional, then we can plot the prior generated values $\theta_1, \ldots, \theta_m$ on a two-dimensional graph in a manner that takes the weights of these points into account. For instance, we could center a dot on each of these m points, with the area of the dot on the point θ_j being proportional to its weight $f(x|\theta_j)$. Another possibility would be to let all the dots be of the same size but to let the darkness of the dot depend on its weight in a linear additive fashion. That is, for instance, if $m = 3$ and $\theta_1 = \theta_2$, $f(x|\theta_3) = 2f(x|\theta_1)$, then the colors of the dots at θ_1 and θ_3 should be the same.

If the prior density p is only specified up to a constant, or if it is hard to directly generate random vectors from it, then we can generate a Markov chain having p as the limiting density, and then continue as before. ∎

Remark The estimator of $E[h(\theta)|x]$ presented in Example 10l could also have been derived by an importance sampling type argument. Since

$$p(\theta|x) = \frac{f(x|\theta)p(\theta)}{C}$$

where

$$C = \int f(x|\theta)p(\theta)d\theta = E[f(x|\theta)]$$

we have that

$$E[h(\theta)|x] = \int \frac{h(\theta)p(\theta|x)}{p(\theta)} p(\theta)d\theta = E\left[\frac{h(\theta)p(\theta|x)}{p(\theta)}\right]$$
$$= \frac{E[f(x|\theta)h(\theta)]}{C} = \frac{E[f(x|\theta)h(\theta)]}{E[f(x|\theta)]}$$

But the preceding suggests the estimator

$$\frac{\sum_{j=1}^{m} f(x|\theta_j)h(\theta_j)}{\sum_{i=1}^{m} f(x|\theta_i)}$$

which is precisely the one given in Example 10l. ∎

Exercises

1. Let $\pi_j, j = 1, \ldots, N$, denote the stationary probabilities of a Markov chain. Show that if $P\{X_0 = j\} = \pi_j, j = 1, \ldots, N$, then

$$P\{X_n = j\} = \pi_j, \qquad \text{for all } n, j$$

2. Let Q be a symmetric transition probability matrix, that is $q_{ij} = q_{ji}$ for all i, j. Consider a Markov chain which, when the present state is i, generates the value of a random variable X such that $P\{X = j\} = q_{ij}$, and if $X = j$, then either moves to state j with probability $b_j/(b_i + b_j)$, or remains in state i otherwise, where $b_j, j = 1 \ldots, N$, are specified positive numbers. Show that the resulting Markov chain is time reversible with limiting probabilities $\pi_j = Cb_j, j = 1, \ldots, N$.

3. Let S be the set of all $n \times n$ matrices A whose elements are either 0 or 1. (Thus, there are 2^{n^2} matrices in S.) The pair of elements $a_{i,j}$ and $a_{r,s}$ of the matrix A are said to be neighbors if $|r - i| + |s - j| = 1$. (Thus, for instance, the neighbors of $a_{2,2}$ are $a_{1,2}, a_{2,1}, a_{2,3}$, and $a_{3,2}$.) Let $\mathcal{N}$ denote

all the pairs of neighboring elements of A. The "Ising energy" of the matrix A is defined by

$$H(A) = -\sum_{\mathcal{N}} a_{i,j} a_{r,s}$$

where the sum is over all the pairs of neighboring elements. Give a method for randomly choosing such a matrix A according to the probability mass function

$$P(A) = \frac{\exp\{-\lambda H(A)\}}{\sum_{A \in S} \exp\{-\lambda H(A)\}}, \quad A \in S$$

where λ is a specified positive constant.
Hint: Let the matrices A and B be neighbors if $A - B$ has only one nonzero element.

4. Consider a system of 20 independent components, with component i being functional with probability $0.5 + i/50$, $i = 1, \ldots, 20$. Let X denote the number of functional components. Use simulation to estimate the conditional probability mass function $P\{X = i | X \le 5\}$, $i = 1, 2, 3, 4, 5$.

5. Suppose that the random variables X and Y both take on values in the interval $(0, B)$. Suppose that the joint density of X given that $Y = y$ is

$$f(x|y) = C(y)e^{-xy}, \quad 0 < x < B$$

and the joint density of Y given that $X = x$ is

$$f(y|x) = C(x)e^{-xy}, \quad 0 < y < B$$

Give a method for approximately simulating the vector X, Y. Run a simulation to estimate (a) $E[X]$ and (b) $E[XY]$.

6. Give an efficient method for generating nine uniform points on $(0, 1)$ conditional on the event than no two of them are within 0.1 of each other. (It can be shown that if n points are independent and uniformly distributed on $(0, 1)$, then the probability that no two of them are within d of each other is, for $0 < d < 1/(n - 1)$, $[1 - (n - 1)d)]^n$.)

7. In Example 10d, it can be shown that the limiting mass function of the number of customers at the $m + 1$ servers is

$$p(n_1, \ldots, n_m, n_{m+1}) = C \prod_{i=1}^{m+1} P_i(n_i), \quad \sum_{i=1}^{m+1} n_i = r$$

where for each $i = 1, \ldots, m + 1$, $P_i(n)$, $n = 0, \ldots, r$, is a probability mass function. Let e_k be the $m + 1$ component vector with a 1 in the kth position and zeros elsewhere. For a vector $\mathbf{n} = (n_1, \ldots, n_{m+1})$, let

$$q(\mathbf{n}, \mathbf{n} - \mathbf{e}_i + \mathbf{e}_j) = \frac{\mathbf{I}(\mathbf{n}_i > 0)}{(\mathbf{m} + 1) \sum_{j=1}^{m+1} \mathbf{I}(\mathbf{n}_j > 0)}$$

In words, q is the transition probability matrix of a Markov chain that at each step randomly selects a nonempty server and then sends one of its customers to a randomly chosen server. Using this q function, give the Hastings–Metropolis algorithm for generating a Markov chain having $p(n_1, \ldots, n_m, n_{m+1})$ as its limiting mass function.

8. Let X_i, $i = 1, 2, 3$, be independent exponentials with mean 1. Run a simulation study to estimate

   (a) $E[X_1 + 2X_2 + 3X_3 | X_1 + 2X_2 + 3X_3 > 15]$.
   (b) $E[X_1 + 2X_2 + 3X_3 | X_1 + 2X_2 + 3X_3 < 1]$.

9. Let $X_1, \ldots, X_{20}$ be a random permutation of $1, \ldots, 20$. Estimate $P\{\sum_{j=1}^{20} jX_j > 2500\}$ by a Markov chain Monte Carlo technique.

10. Suppose the joint density of X, Y, Z is given by

$$f(x, y, z) = Ce^{-(x+y+z+axy+bxz+cyz)}, \qquad x > 0, y > 0, z > 0$$

where a, b, c are specified nonnegative constants, and C does not depend on x, y, z. Explain how we can simulate the vector X, Y, Z, and run a simulation to estimate $E[XYZ]$ when $a = b = c = 1$.

11. Suppose that for random variables X, Y, N

$$P\{X = i, y \le Y \le y + dy, N = n\}$$
$$\approx C\binom{n}{i} y^{i+\alpha-1}(1 - y)^{ni+\beta-1} e^{-\lambda} \frac{\lambda^n}{n!} \, dy$$

where $i = 0, \ldots, n$, $n = 0, 1, \ldots$, $y \ge 0$, and where α, β, λ are specified constants. Run a simulation to estimate $E[X]$, $E[Y]$, and $E[N]$ when $\alpha = 2, \beta = 3, \lambda = 4$.

12. Use the SIR algorithm to generate a permutation of $1, 2, \ldots, 100$ whose distribution is approximately that of a random permutation $X_1, \ldots, X_{100}$ conditioned on the event that $\sum_j jX_j > 285,000$.

13. Let $\mathbf{X}^1, \mathbf{X}^2, \ldots, \mathbf{X}^n$ be random points in $\mathscr{C}$, the circle of radius 1 centered

at the origin. Suppose that for some r, $0 < r < 1$, their joint density function is given by

$$f(\mathbf{x}_1, \ldots, \mathbf{x}_n) = K \exp\{-\beta t(r : \mathbf{x}_1, \ldots, \mathbf{x}_n)\},$$
$$\mathbf{x}_i \in \mathscr{C}, \, i = 1, \ldots, n$$

where $t(r : \mathbf{x}_1, \ldots, \mathbf{x}_n)$ is the number of the $\binom{n}{2}$ pairs of points $\mathbf{x}_i$, $\mathbf{x}_j$, $i \neq j$, that are within a distance r of each other, and $0 < \beta < \infty$. (Note that $\beta = \infty$ corresponds to the case where the $\mathbf{X}^i$ are uniformly distributed on the circle subject to the constraint that no two points are within a distance r of each other.) Explain how you can use the SIR algorithm to approximately generate these random points. If r and β were both large, would this be an efficient algorithm?

14. Generate 100 random numbers $U_{0,k}$, $k = 1, \ldots, 10$, $U_{i,j}$, $i \neq j$, $i, j = 1, \ldots, 10$. Now, consider a traveling salesman problem in which the salesman starts at city 0 and must travel in turn to each of the 10 cities $1, \ldots, 10$ according to some permutation of $1, \ldots, 10$. Let U_{ij} be the reward earned by the salesman when she goes directly from city i to city j. Use simulated annealing to approximate the maximal possible return of the salesman.

References

Aarts, E., and J. Korst, *Simulated Annealing and Boltzmann Machines*, Wiley, New York, 1989.

Besag, J., "Towards Bayesian Image Analysis," *Journal of Applied Statistics,* **16,** 395–407, 1989.

Besag, J., P. Green, D. Higdon, and K. Mengersen, "Bayesian Computation and Stochastic Systems (with Discussion)," *Statistical Science,* **10,** 3–67, 1995.

Diaconis, P., and S. Holmes, "Three Examples of Monte-Carlo Markov Chains: At the Interface between Statistical Computing, Computer Science, and Statistical Mechanics," *Discrete Probability and Algorithms* (D. Aldous, P. Diaconis, J. Spencer, and J. M. Steele, eds.), Springer-Verlag, pp. 43–56, 1995.

Gelfand, A. E., S. E. Hills, A. Racine-Poon, and A. F. Smith, "Illustration of Bayesian Inference in Normal Data Models using Gibbs Sampling," *Journal of the American Statistical Association,* **85,** 972–985, 1990.

Gelfand, A. E., and A. F. Smith, "Sampling Based Approaches to Calculating Marginal Densities," *Journal of the American Statistical Association,* **85,** 398–409, 1990.

Gelman, A., and D. B. Rubin, "Inference from Iterative Simulation (with Discussion)," *Statistical Science,* **7,** 457–511, 1992.

Geman, S., and D. Geman, "Stochastic Relaxation, Gibbs Distributions, and the Bayesian Restoration of Images," *IEEE Transactions on Pattern Analysis and Machine Intelligence,* **6,** 721–724, 1984.

Geyer, C. J., "Practical Markov Chain Monte Carlo (with Discussion)," *Statistical Science,* **7,** 473–511, 1992.

Gidas, B., "Metropolis-type Monte Carlo Simulation Algorithms and Simulated Annealing," in *Trends in Contemporary Probability* (J. L. Snell, ed), CRC Press. Boca Raton, 1995.

Hajek, B., "Cooling Schedules for Optimal Annealing," *Math. of Operations Research,* **13,** 311–329, 1989.

Hammersley, J. M., and D. C. Handscomb, *Monte Carlo Methods,* Methuen, London, 1965.

Ripley, B., *Stochastic Simulation,* Wiley, New York, 1987.

Rubin, D. R., "Using the SIR Algorithm to Simulate Posterior Distributions," in *Bayesian Statistics 3* (J. M. Bernardo, M. H. DeGroot, D. V. Lindley, and A. F. M. Smith, eds.), Oxford University Press, pp. 395–402, 1988.

Rubinstein, R. R., *Monte Carlo Optimization, Simulation, and Sensitivity of Queueing Networks,* Wiley, New York, 1986.

Sinclair, A., *Algorithms for Random Generation and Counting,* Birkhauser, Boston, 1993.

Smith, A. F., and G. O. Roberts, "Bayesian Computation via the Gibbs Sampler and Related Markov Chain Monte Carlo Methods (with Discussion)," *Jour. of Royal Statistical Society, Series B,* **55,** 3–23, 1993.

Chapter 11 | Some Additional Topics

Introduction

In this chapter we present some additional topics that are somewhat more specialized than those considered in earlier chapters. In Section 11.1 we present a highly efficient technique, called the alias method, for generating discrete random variables. In Section 11.2 we define and then present a method for simulating a two-dimensional Poisson process. In Section 11.3 we present a probability identity concerning the sum of Bernoulli random variables and show how its use can lead to dramatic variance reductions when estimating small probabilities. Finally, Section 11.4 considers how to efficiently estimate probabilities and expectations relating to first passage times of Markov processes by making use of the total hazard variable.

11.1 The Alias Method for Generating Discrete Random Variables

In this section we study a technique for generating discrete random variables which, although requiring some setup time, is very fast to implement.

In what follows, the quantities $\mathbf{P}, \mathbf{P}^{(k)}, \mathbf{Q}^{(k)}, k \leq n - 1$, represent probability mass functions on the integers $1, 2, \ldots, n$—that is, they are n-vectors of nonnegative numbers summing to 1. In addition, the vector $\mathbf{P}^{(k)}$ has at most k nonzero components, and each of the $\mathbf{Q}^{(k)}$ has at most two nonzero components. We show that any probability mass function $\mathbf{P}$ can be represented as an equally weighted mixture of $n - 1$ probability mass functions $\mathbf{Q}$ (each having at most two nonzero components). That is, we show, for suitably defined $\mathbf{Q}^{(1)}, \ldots, \mathbf{Q}^{(n-1)}$, that $\mathbf{P}$ can be expressed as

$$\mathbf{P} = \frac{1}{n - 1} \sum_{k=1}^{n-1} \mathbf{Q}^{(k)} \tag{11.1}$$

As a prelude to presenting the method for obtaining this representation, we need the following simple lemma whose proof is left as an exercise.

Lemma *Let $P = \{P_i, i = 1, \ldots, n\}$ denote a probability mass function. Then*

(a) *there exists an i, $1 \le i \le n$, such that $P_i < 1/(n - 1)$, and*

(b) *for this i there exists a j, $j \ne i$, such that $P_i + P_j \ge 1/(n - 1)$.*

Before presenting the general technique for obtaining the representation (11.1), let us illustrate it by an example.

Example 11a Consider the three-point distribution $\mathbf{P}$ with $P_1 = \frac{7}{16}$, $P_2 = \frac{1}{2}$, $P_3 = \frac{1}{16}$. We start by choosing i and j satisfying the conditions of the preceding lemma. Since $P_3 < \frac{1}{2}$ and $P_3 + P_2 > \frac{1}{2}$, we can work with $i = 3$ and $j = 2$. We now define a two-point mass function $\mathbf{Q}^{(1)}$, putting all its weight on 3 and 2 and such that $\mathbf{P}$ is expressible as an equally weighted mixture between $\mathbf{Q}^{(1)}$ and a second two-point mass function $\mathbf{Q}^{(2)}$. In addition, all the mass of point 3 is contained in $\mathbf{Q}^{(1)}$. As we have

$$P_j = \frac{1}{2}(Q_j^{(1)} + Q_j^{(2)}), \qquad j = 1, 2, 3 \tag{11.2}$$

and, by the above, $Q_3^{(2)}$ is supposed to equal 0, we must therefore take

$$Q_3^{(1)} = 2P_3 = \frac{1}{8}, \qquad Q_2^{(1)} = 1 - Q_3^{(1)} = \frac{7}{8}, \qquad Q_1^{(1)} = 0$$

To satisfy (10.2), we must then set

$$Q_3^{(2)} = 0, \qquad Q_2^{(2)} = 2P_2 - \frac{7}{8} = \frac{1}{8}, \qquad Q_1^{(2)} = 2P_1 = \frac{7}{8}$$

Hence we have the desired representation in this case. Suppose now that the original distribution was the following four-point mass function:

$$P_1 = \frac{7}{16}, \qquad P_2 = \frac{1}{4}, \qquad P_3 = \frac{1}{8}, \qquad P_4 = \frac{3}{16}$$

Now $P_3 < \frac{1}{3}$ and $P_3 + P_1 > \frac{1}{3}$. Hence our initial two-point mass function—$\mathbf{Q}^{(1)}$—concentrates on points 3 and 1 (giving no weight to 2 and 4). Because the final representation gives weight $\frac{1}{3}$ to $\mathbf{Q}^{(1)}$ and in addition the other $\mathbf{Q}^{(j)}$, $j = 2, 3$, do not give any mass to the value 3, we must have that

$$\frac{1}{3} Q_3^{(1)} = P_3 = \frac{1}{8}$$

Hence

$$Q_3^{(1)} = \frac{3}{8}, \qquad Q_1^{(1)} = 1 - \frac{3}{8} = \frac{5}{8}$$

Also, we can write

$$\mathbf{P} = \frac{1}{3} \mathbf{Q}^{(1)} + \frac{2}{3} \mathbf{P}^{(3)}$$

where $\mathbf{P}^{(3)}$, to satisfy the above, must be the vector

$$\mathbf{P}_1^{(3)} = \frac{3}{2} \left(P_1 - \frac{1}{3} Q_1^{(1)} \right) = \frac{11}{32}$$

$$\mathbf{P}_2^{(3)} = \frac{3}{2} P_2 = \frac{3}{8}$$

$$\mathbf{P}_3^{(3)} = 0$$

$$\mathbf{P}_4^{(3)} = \frac{3}{2} P_4 = \frac{9}{32}$$

Note that $\mathbf{P}^{(3)}$ gives no mass to the value 3. We can now express the mass function $\mathbf{P}^{(3)}$ as an equally weighted mixture of two-point mass functions $\mathbf{Q}^{(2)}$ and $\mathbf{Q}^{(3)}$, and we end up with

$$\mathbf{P} = \frac{1}{3} \mathbf{Q}^{(1)} + \frac{2}{3} \left(\frac{1}{2} \mathbf{Q}^{(2)} + \frac{1}{2} \mathbf{Q}^{(3)} \right)$$

$$= \frac{1}{3} (\mathbf{Q}^{(1)} + \mathbf{Q}^{(2)} + \mathbf{Q}^{(3)})$$

(We leave it as an exercise for the reader to fill in the details.) ∎

The above example outlines the following general procedure for writing the n-point mass function $\mathbf{P}$ in the form (11.1), where each of the $\mathbf{Q}^{(i)}$ are mass functions giving all their mass to at most two points. To start, we choose i and j satisfying the conditions of the lemma. We now define the mass function $\mathbf{Q}^{(1)}$ concentrating on the points i and j and which contain all the mass for point i by noting that in the representation (10.1) $Q_i^{(k)} = 0$ for $k = 2, \ldots, n - 1$, implying that

$$Q_i^{(1)} = (n - 1)P_i \quad \text{and so} \quad Q_j^{(1)} = 1 - (n - 1)P_i$$

Writing

$$\mathbf{P} = \frac{1}{n - 1} \mathbf{Q}^{(1)} + \frac{n - 2}{n - 1} \mathbf{P}^{(n-1)} \tag{11.3}$$

where $\mathbf{P}^{(n-1)}$ represents the remaining mass, we see that

$$P_i^{(n-1)} = 0$$

$$P_j^{(n-1)} = \frac{n - 1}{n - 2} \left(P_j - \frac{1}{n - 1} Q_j^{(1)} \right) = \frac{n - 1}{n - 2} \left(P_i + P_j - \frac{1}{n - 1} \right)$$

$$P_k^{(n-1)} = \frac{n - 1}{n - 2} P_k, \quad k \neq i \quad \text{or} \quad j$$

That the above is indeed a probability mass function is easily checked—for example, the nonnegativity of $P_j^{(n-1)}$ follows from the fact that j was chosen so that $P_i + P_j \geq 1/(n - 1)$.

We may now repeat the above procedure on the $(n - 1)$ point probability mass function $\mathbf{P}^{(n-1)}$ to obtain

$$\mathbf{P}^{(n-1)} = \frac{1}{n - 2} \mathbf{Q}^{(2)} + \frac{n - 3}{n - 2} \mathbf{P}^{(n-2)}$$

and thus from (11.3) we have

$$\mathbf{P} = \frac{1}{n - 1} \mathbf{Q}^{(1)} + \frac{1}{n - 1} \mathbf{Q}^{(2)} + \frac{n - 3}{n - 1} \mathbf{P}^{(n-2)}$$

We now repeat the procedure on $P^{(n-2)}$ and so on until we finally obtain

$$\mathbf{P} = \frac{1}{n - 1} (\mathbf{Q}^{(1)} + \cdots + \mathbf{Q}^{(n-1)})$$

In this way we are able to represent $\mathbf{P}$ as an equally weighted mixture of $n - 1$ two-point mass functions. We can now easily simulate from $\mathbf{P}$ by first generating a random integer N equally likely to be either $1, 2, \ldots, n - 1$. If the resulting value N is such that $\mathbf{Q}^{(N)}$ puts positive weight only on the points i_N and j_N, we can set X equal to i_N if a second random number is less than $Q_{i_N}^{(N)}$ and equal to j_N otherwise. The random variable X will have probability mass function **P**. That is, we have the following procedure for simulating from **P**.

STEP 1:   Generate U_1 and set $N = 1 + \text{Int}[(n - 1)U_1]$.

STEP 2:   Generate U_2 and set

$$X = \begin{cases} i_N & \text{if } U_2 < Q_{i_N}^{(N)} \\ j_N & \text{otherwise} \end{cases}$$

Remarks

1. The above is called the alias method because by a renumbering of the **Q**'s we can always arrange things so that for each k, $Q_k^{(k)} > 0$. (That is, we can arrange things so that the kth two-point mass function gives positive weight to the value k.) Hence, the procedure calls for simulating N, equally likely to be 1, 2, . . . , $n - 1$, and then if $N = k$ it either accepts k as the value of X, or it accepts for the value of X the "alias" of k (namely, the other value that $\mathbf{Q}^{(k)}$ gives positive weight).

2. Actually, it is not necessary to generate a new random number in Step 2. Because $N - 1$ is the integer part of $(n - 1)U_1$, it follows that the remainder $(n - 1)U_1 - (N - 1)$ is independent of N_1 and is uniformly distributed on $(0, 1)$. Hence, rather than generating a new random number U_2 in Step 2, we can use $(n - 1)U_1 - (N - 1)$.   ∎

11.2   Simulating a Two-Dimensional Poisson Process

A process consisting of randomly occurring points in the plane is said to constitute a two-dimensional Poisson process having rate λ, $\lambda > 0$, if

1. The number of points occurring in any given region of area A is Poisson distributed with mean λA.

2. The numbers of points occurring in disjoint regions are independent.

For a given fixed point **0** in the plane, we now show how to simulate points, according to a two-dimensional Poisson process with rate λ, that occur in a circular region of radius r centered at **0**.

Let $C(a)$ denote the circle of radius a centered at **0**, and note that, from Condition 1, the number of points in $C(a)$ is Poisson distributed with mean $\lambda \pi a^2$.

Let R_i, $i \geq 1$, denote the distance from the origin $\mathbf{0}$ to its ith nearest point (Figure 11.1). Then

$$P\{\pi R_1^2 > x\} = P\{R_1 > \sqrt{x/\pi}\}$$

$$= P\left\{\text{no points in } C\left(\sqrt{\frac{x}{\pi}}\right)\right\}$$

$$= e^{-\lambda x}$$

where the last equality uses the fact that the area of $C(\sqrt{x/\pi})$ is x. Also, with $C(b) - C(a)$ denoting the region between $C(b)$ and $C(a)$, $a < b$, we have

$$P\{\pi R_2^2 - \pi R_1^2 > x | R_1 = a\} = P\left\{R_2 > \sqrt{\frac{x + \pi R_1^2}{\pi}} \bigg| R_1 = a\right\}$$

$$= P\left\{\text{no points in } C\left(\sqrt{\frac{x + \pi a^2}{\pi}}\right) - C(a) | R_1 = a\right\}$$

$$= P\left\{\text{no points in } C\left(\sqrt{\frac{x + \pi a^2}{\pi}}\right) - C(a)\right\} \qquad \text{by Condition 2}$$

$$= e^{-\lambda x}$$

In fact, the same argument can be repeated continually to obtain the following proposition.

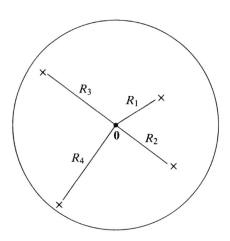

Figure 11.1

Proposition   *With $R_0 = 0$, $\pi R_i^2 - \pi R_{i-1}^2$, $i \geq 1$, are independent exponential random variables each having rate λ.*

In other words, the amount of area that need be traversed to encounter a Poisson point is exponential with rate λ. Since, by symmetry, the respective angles of the Poisson points are independent and uniformly distributed over $(0, 2\pi)$, we thus have the following algorithm for simulating the Poisson process over a circular region of radius r about **0**.

STEP 1:   Generate independent exponentials with rate λ, $X_1, X_2, \ldots$, stopping at

$$N = \text{Min}\{n: X_1 + \cdots + X_n > \pi r^2\}$$

STEP 2:   In $N = 1$ stop; there are no points in $C(r)$. Otherwise, for $i = 1$, $\ldots, N - 1$, set

$$R_i = \sqrt{\frac{X_1 + \cdots + X_i}{\pi}}$$

(that is, $\pi R_i^2 = X_1 + \cdots + X_i$).

STEP 3:   Generate random numbers $U_1, \ldots, U_{N-1}$.

STEP 4:   The polar coordinates of the $N - 1$ Poisson points are

$$(R_i, 2\pi U_i), \qquad i = 1, \ldots, N - 1$$

The above algorithm can be considered as the fanning out from a circle centered at **0** with a radius that expands continuously from 0 to r. The successive radii at which points are encountered are simulated by using the result that the additional area necessary to explore until one encounters another point is always exponentially distributed with rate λ. This fanning-out technique can also be used to simulate the process over noncircular regions. For example, consider a nonnegative function $f(x)$ and suppose that we are interested in simulating the Poisson process in the region between the **x**-axis and the function f (Figure 11.2) with x going from 0 to T. To do so, we can start at the left-hand edge and fan vertically to the right by considering the successive areas encountered. Specifically, if $X_1 < X_2 < \cdots$ denote the successive projections on the Poisson process on the x-axis, it follows in exactly the same manner as before that (with $X_0 = 0$)

$$\int_{X_{i-1}}^{X_i} f(x)\,dx, \qquad i = 1, \ldots, \text{ are independent exponentials with rate } \lambda$$

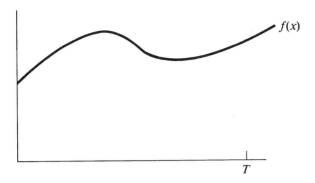

Figure 11.2

Hence, we can simulate the above by generating independent exponential random variables with rate λ, W_1, W_2, . . . , stopping at

$$N = \text{Min}\left\{n : W_1 + \cdots + W_n > \int_0^T f(x)\, dx\right\}$$

We should now determine X_1, . . . , X_{N-1} by using the equations

$$\int_0^{X_1} f(x)\, dx = W_1$$

$$\int_{X_1}^{X_2} f(x)\, dx = W_2$$

$$\vdots$$

$$\int_{X_{N-2}}^{X_{N-1}} f(x)\, dx = W_{N-1}$$

Because the projection on the y-axis of the point whose x-coordinate is X_i is clearly uniformly distributed over $(0, f(X_i))$, it thus follows that if we now generate random numbers U_1, . . . , U_{N-1}, then the simulated Poisson points are, in rectangular coordinates, $(X_i, U_i f(X_i))$, $i = 1$, . . . , $N - 1$.

The above procedure is most useful when f is regular enough so that the above equations can be efficiently solved for the values of X_i. For example, if $f(x) = c$ (and so the region is a rectangle), we can express X_i as

$$X_i = \frac{W_1 + \cdots + W_i}{c}$$

and the Poisson points are

$$(X_i, cU_i), \qquad i = 1, \ldots, N - 1$$

11.3   Simulation Applications of an Identity for Sums of Bernoulli Random Variables

Let $X_1, \ldots, X_m$ be Bernoulli random variables such that

$$P\{X_i = 1\} = \lambda_i = 1 - P\{X_i = 0\}.$$

Also, let $S = \sum_{i=1}^{m} X_i$, and set $\lambda = E[S] = \sum_{i=1}^{m} \lambda_i$. Let R be an arbitrary random variable, and suppose that I, independent of $R, X_1, \ldots, X_m$, is such that

$$P\{I = i\} = 1/m, \qquad i = 1, \ldots, m$$

That is, I is a discrete uniform random variable on $1, \ldots, m$ that is independent of the other random variables.

The following identity is the key to the results of this section.

Proposition

(a) $P\{I = i \,|\, X_I = 1\} = \lambda_i / \lambda$

(b) $E[SR] = \lambda E[R | X_I = 1]$

(c) $P\{S > 0\} = \lambda E\,[1/S | X_I = 1]$

Proof   To prove part (a), note that

$$P\{I = i | X_I = 1\} = \frac{P\{X_I = 1 | I = i\} P\{I = i\}}{\sum_i P\{X_I = 1 | I = i\} P\{I = i\}}$$

Now,

$$P\{X_I = 1 | I = i\} = P\{X_i = 1 | I = i\}$$

$$= P\{X_i = 1\} \qquad \text{by independence}$$

$$= \lambda_i$$

which completes the proof of Part (a). To prove Part (b), reason as follows:

$$E[SR] = E\left[R \sum_i X_i\right]$$

$$= \sum_i E[RX_i] \tag{11.4}$$

$$= \sum_i \{E[RX_i | X_i = 1]\lambda_i + E[RX_i | X_i = 0](1 - \lambda_i)\}$$

$$= \sum_i \lambda_i E[R | X_i = 1]$$

Also,

$$E[R|X_I = 1] = \sum_i E[R|X_I = 1, I = i]P\{I = i|X_I = 1\}$$

$$= \sum_i E[R|X_i = 1, I = i]\lambda_i/\lambda \qquad \text{by Part (a)} \qquad (11.5)$$

$$= \sum_i E[R|X_i = 1]\lambda_i/\lambda$$

Combining Equations (11.4) and (11.5) proves Part (b).

To prove (c), define R to equal 0 if $S = 0$ and to equal $1/S$ if $S > 0$. Then,

$$E[SR] = P\{S > 0\} \quad \text{and} \quad E[R|X_I = 1] = E\left[\frac{1}{S}\bigg|X_I = 1\right]$$

and so (c) follows directly from (b). ■

We will now use the preceding proposition to estimate (a) the failure probability of a system, and (b) the probability that a specified pattern occurs within a given time frame.

Example 11b Consider the model of Example 8b, which is concerned with a system composed of n independent components, and suppose that we want to estimate the probability that the system is failed, when this probability is very small. Now, for any system of the type considered in Example 8b there will always be a unique family of sets $\{C_1, \ldots, C_m\}$, none of which is a subset of another, such that the system will be failed if and only if all the components of at least one of these sets are failed. These sets are called the *minimal cut sets* of the system.

Let $Y_j, j = 1, \ldots, n$ equal 1 if component j is failed and let it equal 0 otherwise, and let $q_j = P\{Y_j = 1\}$ denote the probability that component j is failed. Now, for $i = 1, \ldots, m$, let

$$X_i = \prod_{j \in C_i} Y_j$$

That is, X_i is the indicator for the event that all components in C_i are failed. If we let $S = \Sigma_i X_i$, then θ, the probability that the system is failed, is given by

$$\theta = P\{S > 0\}$$

We will now show how to make use of the proposition to efficiently estimate θ.

First, let $\lambda_i = E[X_i] = \prod_{j \in C_i} q_j$, and let $\lambda = \Sigma_i \lambda_i$. Now, simulate the value of J, a random variable that is equal to i with probability λ_i/λ, $i = 1 \ldots, m$. [It follows from Part (a) of the proposition that J has the same distribution as the conditional distribution of I, given that $X_I = 1$.] Then set Y_i equal to 1 for all $i \in C_J$, and simulate the value of all of the other Y_i, $i \notin C_J$, by letting them equal 1 with probability q_i and 0 otherwise. Let S^* denote the resulting number of minimal cut sets that have all their components down, and note that $S^* \geq 1$. From Part (c) of the proposition, it follows that λ/S^* is an unbiased estimator of θ. Since $S^* \geq 1$, it also follows that

$$0 \leq \lambda/S^* \leq \lambda$$

and so when λ, the mean number of minimal cut sets that are down, is very small the estimator λ/S^* will have a very small variance.

For instance, consider a 3-of-5 system that fails if at least 3 of the 5 components are failed, and suppose that each component independently fails with probability q. For this system, the minimal cut sets will be the $\binom{5}{3} = 10$ subsets of size 3. Since all the component failures are the same, the value of I will play no role. Thus, the preceding estimate can be obtained by supposing that components 1, 2, and 3 are all failed and then generating the status of the other two. Thus, by considering the number of components 4 and 5 that are failed, it follows since $\lambda = 10q^3$ that the distribution of the estimator is

$$P\{\lambda/S^* = 10q^3\} = (1 - q)^2$$
$$P\{\lambda/S^* = 10q^3/4\} = 2q(1 - q)$$
$$P\{\lambda/S^* = q^3\} = q^2$$

Hence, with $p = 1 - q$,

$$\text{Var}(\lambda/S^*) = E[(\lambda/S^*)^2] - (E[\lambda/S^*])^2$$
$$= 100q^6[p^2 + pq/8 + q^2/100 - (p^2 + pq/2 + q^2/10)^2]$$

The following table gives the value of θ and the ratio of $\text{Var}(I)$ to the variance of the estimator λ/S^* for a variety of values of q, where $\text{Var}(I) = \theta(1 - \theta)$ is the variance of the raw simulation estimator.

q	θ	$\text{Var}(I)/\text{Var}(\lambda/S^*)$
0.001	9.985×10^{-9}	8.896×10^{10}
0.01	9.851×10^{-6}	8,958,905
0.1	0.00856	957.72
0.2	0.05792	62.59
0.3	0.16308	12.29

Thus, for small q, $\text{Var}(\lambda/S^*)$ is roughly of the order θ^2, whereas $\text{Var}(I) \approx \theta$. ∎

Example 11c Waiting for a Pattern. Let Y_i, $i \geq 1$, be a sequence of independent and identically distributed discrete random variables with probability mass function $P_j = P\{Y_i = j\}$. Let $s_1, \ldots, s_k$ be a fixed sequence of possible values of these random variables and define

$$N = \min\{i{:}i \geq k, \, Y_{i-j} = s_{k-j}, j = 0, 1, \ldots, k - 1\}$$

That is, N is the first time the pattern $s_1, \ldots, s_k$ occurs. We are interested in using simulation to estimate $\theta = P\{N \leq n\}$, in cases where θ is small. Whereas the usual simulation estimator is obtained by simulating the sequence of random variables until either the pattern occurs or it is no longer possible for it to occur by time n (and letting the estimator for that run be 1 in the former case and 0 in the latter), we will show how the preceding proposition can be applied to obtain a more efficient simulation estimator.

To begin, generate the n random variables $Y_1, \ldots, Y_n$, and for $i \geq k$ let

$$X_i = 1 \quad \text{if} \quad Y_i = s_k, \quad Y_{i-1} = s_{k-1}, \ldots, Y_{i-k+1} = s_1$$

and let it be 0 otherwise. In other words, X_i is equal to 1 if the pattern occurs (not necessarily for the first time) at time i. Let

$$S = \sum_{i=k}^{n} X_i$$

denote the number of times the pattern has occurred by time n and note that

$$\theta = P\{N \leq n\} = P\{S > 0\}$$

Since, for $k \leq i \leq n$

$$\lambda_i = P\{X_i = 1\} = P_{s_1} P_{s_2} \cdots P_{s_k}$$

it follows from the proposition that

$$\theta = (n - k + 1)\left(\prod_{i=1}^{k} P_{s_i}\right) E\left[\frac{1}{S}\middle| X_I = 1\right]$$

where I, independent of the Y_j, is equally likely to be any of the values $k, \ldots, n$. Thus, we can estimate θ by first simulating J, equally likely to be any of the values $k, \ldots, n$, and setting

$$Y_J = s_k, \quad Y_{J-1} = s_{k-1}, \ldots, \quad Y_{J-k+1} = s_1$$

We then simulate the other $n - k$ values Y_i according to the mass function P and let $S*$ denote the number of times the pattern occurs. The simulation estimator of θ from this run is

$$\hat{\theta} = \frac{n - k + 1}{S*} \prod_{i=1}^{k} P_{s_i}$$

For small values of $(n - k + 1)(\Pi_{i=1}^{k} P_{s_i})$, the preceding will be a very efficient estimator of θ. ∎

11.4   Estimating Probabilities and Expected First Passage Times by Using Random Hazards

Consider a process that moves from state to state in the following manner. If the present state is x, then, independent of the sequence of previous states, the next state is chosen according to the distribution function F_x. Such a process is called a Markov process (if the state space is discrete, it is called a Markov chain).

For a given initial state—call it 0—and a fixed set of states A, suppose we are interested in estimating the expected number of transitions needed for the process to enter the set $\mathscr{A}$. That is, if X_n is the state at time n, then we are interested in $E[N]$, where

$$N = \text{Min}\{n: X_n \in \mathscr{A}\}$$

In many cases of interest A is a "rare set of states" in the sense the process has a tendency to be drawn to the initial state 0 with visits to A occurring infrequently. Hence, in such cases, $E[N]$ is relatively large. In addition, since the process has this tendency to revert back to 0, it follows, by the memoryless property, that N will roughly have an exponential distribution (see Example 8a of Chapter 8 for a more detailed discussion of this latter point). But if such is the case, we have that $\text{Var}(N) \approx (E[N])^2$, implying that $\sqrt{\text{Var}(N)}$, the standard deviation of N, is also large; thus, the raw simulation approach to estimate $E[N]$ requires a huge number of runs.

A powerful variance reduction technique makes use of the so-called observed hazards, also called the predictable projections, as control variates. It works as follows. Consider a simulation run that results in the sequence of states $X_0, \ldots,$ X_N and define the observed hazards, $\lambda_n, n \geq 0$, by

$$\lambda_n = P\{N = n | X_0, \ldots, X_{n-1}\}$$

In words, if A has not yet been entered before time n, then λ_n is the probability, given the state at time $n - 1$, that the next state will be in the set $\mathcal{A}$. Now let Y denote the sum of these hazards—that is,

$$Y = \sum_{n=1}^{N} \lambda_n$$

Proposition

$$E\left[\sum_{n=1}^{N} \lambda_n\right] = P\{N < \infty\}.$$

Proof Let

$$I_n = \begin{cases} 1 & \text{if } N = n \\ 0 & \text{otherwise} \end{cases}$$

and note that

$$E[I_n|X_0, \ldots, X_{n-1}] = P\{N = n|X_0, \ldots, X_{n-1}\} = \lambda_n$$

Now

$$\sum_{n=1}^{\infty} I_n = \begin{cases} 1 & \text{if } N < \infty \\ 0 & \text{otherwise} \end{cases}$$

and so, by taking expectations,

$$P\{N < \infty\} = E\left[\sum_{n=1}^{\infty} I_n\right]$$

$$= \sum_{n=1}^{\infty} E[I_n]$$

$$= \sum_{n=1}^{\infty} E[E[I_n|X_0, \ldots, X_{n-1}]]$$

$$= E\left[\sum_{n=1}^{\infty} E[I_n|X_0, \ldots, X_{n-1}]\right]$$

$$= E\left[\sum_{n=1}^{\infty} \lambda_n\right]$$

$$= E\left[\sum_{n=1}^{N} \lambda_n\right]$$

■

Suppose now that the situation is such that $\mathcal{A}$ is eventually entered with probability 1, and so the expected sum of the random hazards has mean 1. Since runs having large values of N often result from many missed opportunities to enter A, it follows that Y is a natural candidate for a control variable since it gives a way of gauging whether a given value of N is much larger or smaller than normal. Therefore, we should simulate until the process enters A and then use the output estimator

$$N + c(Y - 1)$$

The best value of c, given by

$$c = -\frac{\text{Cov}(N, Y)}{\text{Var}(Y)}$$

can be approximated from the simulated data.

Example 11d Cumulative Sum Control Chart for Exponential Random Variables. Let $X_1, X_2, \ldots$ denote a sequence of independent exponential random variables each with mean 1. Let $S_0 = 0$ and define

$$S_n = \text{Max}\{0, S_{n-1} + X_n - 2\}, \qquad n \geq 1$$

We are interested in estimating $E[N]$, where

$$N = \text{Min}\{n: S_n > 4\}$$

The above sequence S_n, $n \geq 1$, is called a cumulative sum control chart. The idea is that the quantities X_n represent the successive values of items produced in a given process. When the process is in control, these values are assumed to have an exponential distribution with mean 1, whereas when the process goes out of control, these values tend to become larger. The quantities S_n are cumulative sums of the successive quantities $X_n - 2$, which are not allowed to become negative—that is, the value of the cumulative sum is reset to 0 whenever it would fall negative. Since the values $X_n - 2$ have a negative mean when the process is in control, the cumulative sum usually has a small value in this case and so a large value is an indicator that the process may have gone out of control. However, since large values eventually occur even when the process remains in control, we are interested in $E[N]$, the expected time until the process is mistakenly declared out of control when in fact it remains in control throughout.

Since the values S_n tend to be near 0, excursion to a value as large as 4 tends to be a rare event whose distribution is approximately exponential. Thus, the raw simulation estimator has a large standard deviation. The random hazard is given by

$$\lambda_n = P\{S_{n-1} + X_n - 2 > 4|S_{n-1}\}$$
$$= P\{X_n > 6 - S_{n-1}|S_{n-1}\}$$
$$= \exp\{S_{n-1} - 6\}$$

Hence, the use of the controlled estimator

$$N + c[Y - 1]$$

where

$$Y = \sum_{n=1}^{N} \exp\{S_{n-1} - 6\}$$

is recommended. Indeed, a small simulation study revealed to the author that the variance of the controlled estimator is smaller than that of the raw estimator by a factor of roughly 1/30. In addition, it was seen that $E[N] \approx 243$. ∎

Example 11e Expected Length of a Busy Period in a Queueing System. Consider a single-server queue in which the times between arriving customers are independent random variables having a common distribution F. (In other words, the arrival process is a renewal process: see Section 8.3 of Chapter 8.) There is a single server that takes a random time to serve a customer. An arrival finding the server idle immediately enters service, whereas one finding the server busy joins the waiting queue. Upon a service completion, one of the waiting customers, if there are any, enters service. Each service is assumed to take a random time, independent of the past, having distribution G.

Such a system as described above alternates between times when the server is busy and times when he is idle. Suppose we are interested in determining $E[N]$, the expected number of customers served in an arbitrary busy period.

Let W_n denote the total amount of work that remains in the system—that is, the sum of the service times of those customers waiting plus the remaining service time of the customer in service—immediately after the arrival of the nth customer. Also, let X_n denote the number of customers in the system found by the nth arrival, so that $X_1 = 0$ and

$$N = \text{Min}\{n > 1: X_n = 0\} - 1$$

Now consider the process whose state at time n is the pair W_n, X_n and define the random hazards by

$$\lambda_n = P\{N = n | W_1, X_1, \ldots, W_n, X_n\}$$

Now given that the workload immediately after the nth arrival is w, it follows that the next arrival will find the system empty—implying that $N = n$—if the next interarrival time is greater than w. Hence, for $n \leq N$,

$$\lambda_n = 1 - F(W_n) = \bar{F}(W_n)$$

Thus, we recommend using the estimator

$$N + c\left[\sum_{n=1}^{N} \bar{F}(W_n) - 1\right]$$

where the value of c can be determined from the simulation.

If the queueing system contained more than one server, we could still proceed as above, except we would now define W_n as the time until the system becomes empty of all customers presently in the system at the moment immediately after the nth customer arrives, provided there are no additional arrivals. The estimator would then be as given above.

If we wanted to estimate $E[T]$, the mean time of a busy period, we could either estimate $E[N]$ and use the identity

$$E[T] = E[N]\mu_F$$

where μ_F is the mean time between arrivals, or we could directly use the estimator T—again with the above as a control. That is, we could use

$$T + c\left[\sum_{n=1}^{N} \bar{F}(W_n) - 1\right]$$

with c now equal to the negative of the covariance between T and the control divided by the variance of the control. Whereas it is not immediately clear which of these approaches is best (either estimating $E[N]$ and then using $E[N]\mu_F$ or directly estimating $E[T]$), the author expects that the former method is usually better. ∎

Since

$$E\left[\sum_{n=1}^{N} \lambda_n\right] = P\{N < \infty\}$$

we can also use the sum of the hazards as an estimator of $P\{N < \infty\}$ in cases where this probability is less than 1. For instance, if N represents the first time that the process enters a state in $\mathcal{A}$, then

$$P\{N \leq m\} = E\left[\sum_{n=1}^{\min(N,m)} \lambda_n\right]$$

and so we can estimate $P\{N \leq m\}$ by $\sum_{n=1}^{\min(N,m)} \lambda_n$. If there is a set of states $\mathcal{B}$ such that if the process enters $\mathcal{B}$ then it is impossible for it to ever enter $\mathcal{A}$ from then on, then

$$P\{\text{ever enter } \mathcal{A}\} = E\left[\sum_{n=1}^{\min(N_\mathcal{A}, N_\mathcal{B})} \lambda_n\right]$$

where $N_\mathcal{A}$ and $N_\mathcal{B}$ are, respectively, the first times that the process enters states $\mathcal{A}$ and $\mathcal{B}$.

Example 11f Another approach to using simulation to estimate $E[N]$ in Example 11d is to define a cycle to occur either when S_n exceeds 4 or when it returns to 0. Let C denote the time of a cycle. Then it is easy to see that

$$E[N] = \frac{E[C]}{p}$$

where p is the probability that the random walk exceeds 4 before it goes negative. Since p tends to be small, it would seem that we could efficiently estimate it by using the sum of the hazards of N during a cycle as the estimator. That is, we could use the estimator

$$\hat{p} = \sum_{n=1}^{C} \exp\{S_{n-1} - 6\}$$

In addition, because $E[C]$ is probably relatively small, it can be estimated by using C along with the sum of the hazards as a control. That is, we can estimate $\mu_C = E[C]$ by an estimator of the form

$$\hat{\mu}_C = C + c\left[\sum_{n=1}^{C} (\exp\{S_{n-1} - 6\} + 1 - \exp\{S_{n-1} - 2\}) - 1\right]$$

The ratio $\hat{p}/\hat{\mu}_C$ can then be used to estimate $E[N]$. ∎

The total hazard estimator of $P\{N < \infty\}$ can be improved by using stratified sampling ideas. Letting $H = \sum_{n=1}^{N} \lambda_n$, we can write

$$H = \lambda_1 + H_R$$

with H_R being the remaining total hazard after the initial transition. By conditioning on whether $X_1 \in \mathcal{A}$, we obtain

$$E[H] = \lambda_1 + (1 - \lambda_1)E[H_R | X_1 \notin \mathcal{A}]$$

Hence, if H_1 has the conditional distribution of H_R given that $X_1 \notin \mathcal{A}$, then $\lambda_1 + (1 - \lambda_1)H_1$ has the same mean and a smaller variance than does H. The variable H_1 can be generated by simulating the initial transition of the process, and if it leads to a state in $\mathcal{A}$ then this step is repeated until it results in a state that is not in $\mathcal{A}$. The quantity H_1 is then the sum of the remaining hazards from this point on. However, rather than directly using H_1, we can further improve by repeating the argument. Continual repetition thus leads to the following algorithm for generating an unbiased estimator of $P\{N < \infty\}$ whose variance is less than or equal to that of H.

1. $n = 0$, $X = 0$.
2. $X_n = X$.
3. Output X_n.
4. Generate X having distribution F_{X_n}.
5. If $X \in \mathcal{A}$, go to 4.
6. $n = n + 1$.
7. Go to 2.

The algorithm should be programmed to stop whenever it either becomes impossible to ever enter $\mathcal{A}$ within the time frame of interest, or whenever a state is reached that goes to $\mathcal{A}$ with probability 1. If X_n, $n \geq 0$, are the successive values outputted in the preceding algorithm, then the estimate of $p = P\{N < \infty\}$ is

$$\hat{p} = \lambda_1 + \sum_{i \geq 2} \lambda_i \prod_{j=1}^{i-1} (1 - \lambda_j)$$

where

$$\lambda_i = F_{X_{i-1}}(\mathcal{A}) = \int_{x \in \mathcal{A}} dF_{X_{i-1}}(x)$$

Exercises

1. Set up the alias method for generating a binomial with parameters (5, 0.4).

2. Explain how we can number the $Q^{(k)}$ in the alias method so that k is one of the two points to which $Q^{(k)}$ gives weight.

3. Complete the details of Example 11a.

4. Write a program to generate the points of a two-dimensional Poisson process within a circle of radius R, and run the program for $\lambda = 1$ and $R = 5$. Plot the points obtained.

5. Use simulation to estimate the probability that the bridge structure given in Figure 8.1 will fail if components 1, 2, and 3 all, independently, fail with probability 0.05, and 4 and 5 with probability 0.01. Also, compare the variance of your estimator with that of the raw simulation estimator.

6. Use simulation to estimate the probability that a run of 10 consecutive heads occurs within the first 100 flips of a fair coin. Also, compare the variance of your estimator with that of the raw simulation estimator.

7. Use simulation to estimate the probability that the pattern HTTHT occurs within the first 20 flips of a coin whose probability of coming up heads on flip i is $(i + 10)/40$, $i = 1, \ldots , 20$. Assume independence.

8. Explain how the variance of the simulation estimator in Example 11b can be further reduced by using antithetic variables.

9. In Exercise 5, determine the additional variance reduction obtained by also using antithetic variables.

10. Let X_i be Bernoulli random variables with means λ_i, $i = 1, \ldots , m$, and let $S = \Sigma_i a_i X_i$, where the a_i are positive constants. Let R be an arbitrary random variable, and let I, independent of the other variables, have mass function $P\{I = i\} = a_i / \Sigma_i a_i$, $i = 1, \ldots , m$. Set $\lambda = \Sigma_i a_i \lambda_i$.
    (a) Find $P\{I = i | X_I = 1\}$.
    (b) Show that $E[SR] = \lambda E[R | X_I = 1]$.
    (c) Show that $P\{S > x\} = \lambda E[I(S > x)/S | X_I = 1]$, where $I(S > x)$ is 1 if $S > x$ and 0 otherwise.

11. Suppose that a set of n components, with component j independently functioning with probability p_j, $j = 1, \ldots , n$, is available. There are m experiments that we want to perform. However, in order to perform

experiment i, all of the components in the set $\mathscr{A}_i$, $i = 1, \ldots, m$, must function. If experiment i can be performed, then we earn an amount a_i. With the total return being the sum of the returns from all m experiments, suppose that we are interested in estimating the probability that the total return exceeds x. Assuming that this probability is small, give an efficient simulation procedure for estimating it.

12. Let $Z_1, Z_2, \ldots$ denote a sequence of independent unit normals. Let

$$M_n = \frac{Z_n + Z_{n-1} + Z_{n-2} + Z_{n-3}}{4}, \qquad n \geq 4$$

and define N by

$$N = \text{Min}\left\{n: |M_n| > \frac{3}{2}\right\}$$

We want to use simulation to find $E[N]$. Determine the variance of the raw simulation estimator and then of the one that uses the sum of the random hazards as a control. (The above is called a moving-average control chart and is used to determine when the distribution has shifted from the unit normal.)

13. Let $X_1, X_2, \ldots$ be independent geometric random variables with parameter $p = \frac{1}{100}$. Let

$$N = \min\{n : X_n = X_k, \qquad \text{for some } k = 1, \ldots, n - 1\}$$

denote the first time a random variable is observed to have a value equal to one of its predecessors.

(a) Use simulation to estimate $\text{Var}(N)$.

(b) Estimate the variance of the estimator of $E[N]$ that uses the sum of the random hazards as a control variate.

References

El Khadiri, M., and H. Cancela, "An Improvement to the Total Hazard Method for System Reliability Simulation," *Probability in the Engineering and Informational Sciences,* **10**, 2, 1996.

Kronmal, R. A., and A. V. Peterson, Jr., "On the Alias Method for Generating Random Variables from a Discrete Distribution," *American Statistician,* **33**, 214–218, 1979.

Peterson, A. V., Jr., and R. A. Kronmal, "On Mixture Methods for the Computer Generation of Random Variables," *American Statistician, 36,* 184–191, 1982.

Ross, S. M., "Variance Reduction in Simulation via Random Hazards," *Probability in the Engineering and Informational Sciences, 4,* 299–310, 1990.

Ross, S. M., "A New Simulation Estimator of System Reliability," *Journal of Applied Mathematics and Stochastic Analysis, 7,* 331–336, 1994.

Appendix of Programs

Program 4-1

```
 10  PRINT "THIS PROGRAM WILL SIMULATE N IID POISSON RAN-
         DOM VARIABLES"
 20  PRINT "ENTER THE MEAN"
 30  INPUT L
 40  PRINT "ENTER N"
 50  INPUT N
 60  RANDOMIZE
 70  I = INT (L)
 80  B = 1/L
 90  FOR K = 1 TO I
100  S = S + LOG (K)
110  NEXT
120  S = - S - L + I * LOG (L)
```

```
130  PP = EXP (S)
140  F = 1
150  FOR K = 1 TO I
160  F = F * (I + 1 - K) * B
170  CUM = CUM + F
180  NEXT
190  CUM = (CUM + 1) * PP
200  FOR J = 1 TO N
210  I = INT (L)
220  A = CUM
230  P = PP
240  U = RND
250  IF U < A GOTO 310
260  I = I + 1
270  P = L * P/I
280  A = A + P
290  IF U < A THEN GOTO 360
300  GOTO 260
310  A = A - P
320  IF U > A GOTO 360
330  P = I * P * B
340  I = I - 1
350  GOTO 310
360  PRINT I
370  NEXT
380  END
```

Program 9-0

```
10  PRINT "THIS PROGRAM COMPUTES THE PROBABILITY THAT A
        UNIT NORMAL RANDOM VARIABLE IS LESS THAN X"
20  PRINT "ENTER THE DESIRED VALUE OF X"
30  INPUT X
40  U = ABS (X)
50  IF U > 4 GOTO 180
60  Y = U ^ 2
70  I = U
80  FOR J = 1 TO 40
90  U = -U * Y * (2 * J - 1)/(2 * J * (2 * J + 1))
```

```
100  I = I + U
110  NEXT
120  I = I/SQR (2 * 3.14159)
130  IF X < 0 GOTO 160
140  PRINT "THE PROBABILITY IS" .5 + I
150  GOTO 220
160  PRINT "THE PROBABILITY IS" .5 - I
170  GOTO 220
180  IF X < 0 GOTO 210
190  PRINT "THE PROBABILITY IS GREATER THAN" 1 - 10 ^ - 4
200  GOTO 220
210  PRINT "THE PROBABILITY IS LESS THAN" 10 ^ - 4
220  END
```

Program 9-1

```
 10  PRINT "THIS PROGRAM COMPUTES THE PROBABILITY THAT A
       CHI-SQUARE RANDOM VARIABLE WITH N DEGREES OF FREE-
       DOM IS LESS THAN X"
 20  PRINT "ENTER THE DEGREE OF FREEDOM PARAMETER"
 30  INPUT N
 40  S = (N - 1)/2
 50  PRINT "ENTER THE DESIRED VALUE OF X"
 60  INPUT X
 70  M = X/2
 80  D = X/2 - N/2 + 1/3
 90  D = D - .04/N
100  IF N = 1 GOTO 160
110  IF S = M GOTO 180
120  H = S/M
130  X = (1 - H * H + 2 * H * LOG (H))/(1 - H) ^ 2
140  X = D * SQR ((1 + X)/M)
150  GOTO 190
160  X = D * SQR (2/M)
170  GOTO 190
180  X = D/SQR (M)
190  U = ABS (X)
200  IF U > 4 GOTO 330
210  Y = U ^ 2
```

```
220   I = U
230   FOR J = 1 TO 40
240   U = −U * Y * (2 * J − 1)/(2 * J * (2 * J + 1))
250   I = I + U
260   NEXT
270   I = I/SQR (2 * 3.14159)
280   IF X < 0 GOTO 310
290   PRINT "THE PROBABILITY IS" .5 + I
300   GOTO 370
310   PRINT "THE PROBABILITY IS" .5 − I
320   GOTO 370
330   IF X < 0 GOTO 360
340   PRINT "THE PROBABILITY IS GREATER THAN" 1 − 10 ^ − 4
350   GOTO 370
360   PRINT "THE PROBABILITY IS LESS THAN" 10 ^ − 4
370   END
```

Program 9-2

```
 10   PRINT "THIS PROGRAM USES SIMULATION TO APPROXIMATE
        THE p-VALUE IN THE GOODNESS OF FIT TEST"
 20   RANDOMIZE
 30   PRINT "ENTER THE NUMBER OF POSSIBLE VALUES"
 40   INPUT N
 50   DIM P (N)
 60   DIM Q (N)
 66   Q (0) = 0
 70   PRINT "ENTER THE PROBABILITIES ONE AT A TIME"
 80   FOR I = 1 TO N
 90   INPUT P (I)
100   Q (I) = Q (I − 1) + P (I)
110   NEXT I
120   PRINT "ENTER THE SAMPLE SIZE"
130   INPUT D
140   DIM B (N)
150   DIM C (N)
160   FOR J = 1 TO N
170   B (J) = D * P (J)
180   C (J) = 1/B (J)
```

```
190  NEXT
200  DIM X (N)
210  PRINT "ENTER THE DESIRED NUMBER OF SIMULATION RUNS"
220  INPUT R
230  PRINT "ENTER THE VALUE OF THE TEST STATISTIC"
240  INPUT W
250  FOR K = 1 TO R
260  FOR L = 1 TO N
270  X (L) = 0
280  NEXT L
290  FOR J = 1 TO D
300  U = RND
310  I = 1
320  IF U < Q (I) THEN GOTO 350
330  I = I + 1
340  GOTO 320
350  X (I) = X (I) + 1
360  NEXT J
370  S = 0
380  FOR L = 1 TO N
390  S = S + (X(L) − B(L)) ^ 2 * C (L)
400  NEXT L
410  IF S > = W THEN C = C + 1
420  NEXT K
430  PRINT "THE ESTIMATE OF THE p-VALUE IS" C/R
440  END
```

Program 9-3

```
10  PRINT "THIS PROGRAM USES SIMULATION TO APPROXIMATE
        THE p-VALUE OF THE KOLMOGOROV-SMIRNOV TEST"
20  RANDOMIZE
30  PRINT "ENTER THE VALUE OF THE TEST QUANTITY"
40  INPUT D
50  PRINT "ENTER THE SAMPLE SIZE"
60  INPUT N
70  A = 1/N
80  PRINT "ENTER THE DESIRED NUMBER OF SIMULATION RUNS"
90  INPUT R
```

```
100  DIM T(N)
110  FOR I = 1 TO R
120  S = 0
130  T (0) = 0
140  FOR J = 1 TO N
150  U = RND
160  Y = -LOG (U)
170  T J) = T (J - 1) + Y
180  S = S + Y
190  NEXT
200  S = S -LOG (RND)
210  C = 1/S
220  J = 1
230  X = T (J) * C
240  IF J * A - X > D THEN GOTO 290
250  IF X - (J - 1) * A > D THEN GOTO 290
260  IF J = N GOTO 300
270  J = J + 1
280  GOTO 230
290  CC = CC + 1
300  NEXT I
310  PRINT "THE APPROXIMATE p-VALUE IS" CC/R
320  END
```

Program 9-4

```
 10  PRINT "THIS PROGRAM COMPUTES THE p-VALUE FOR THE
     TWO-SAMPLE RANK SUM TEST"
 20  PRINT "THIS PROGRAM WILL RUN FASTEST IF YOU DESIGNATE
     AS THE FIRST SAMPLE THE SAMPLE HAVING THE SMALLER
     SUM OF RANKS"
 30  PRINT "ENTER THE SIZE OF THE FIRST SAMPLE"
 40  INPUT N
 50  PRINT "ENTER THE SIZE OF THE SECOND SAMPLE"
 60  INPUT M
 70  PRINT "ENTER THE SUM OF THE RANKS OF THE FIRST SAM-
     PLE"
 80  INPUT T
 90  DIM P(N, M, T + 1)
```

```
100   FOR I = 1 TO N
110   FOR K = I * (I + 1)/2 TO T
120   P (I, O, K) = 1
130   NEXT
140   NEXT
150   FOR K = 1 TO T + 1
160   FOR J = 1 TO M
170   P (O, J, K - 1) = 1
180   NEXT
190   NEXT
200   FOR I = 1 TO N
210   FOR J = 1 TO M
220   FOR K = 1 TO T
230   IF K < (I + J) THEN P(I, J, K) = (J/(I + J)) * P(I, J - 1, K)
        ELSE P(I, J, K) = (I/(I + J)) * P(I - 1, J, K - I - J) + (J/(I
        + J)) * P(I, J - 1,K)
240   NEXT
250   NEXT
260   NEXT
270   IF P(N, M, T) < 1 - P(N, M, T - 1) THEN V = P(N, M, T) ELSE
        V = 1 - P(N, M, T - 1)
280   PRINT "THE p-VALUE IS" 2 * V
290   END
```

Program 9-5

```
 10   PRINT "THIS PROGRAM APPROXIMATES THE p-VALUE IN THE
        TWO-SAMPLE RANK SUM TEST BY A SIMULATION STUDY"
 20   RANDOMIZE
 30   PRINT "ENTER THE SIZE OF THE FIRST SAMPLE"
 40   INPUT N (1)
 50   PRINT "ENTER THE SIZE OF THE SECOND SAMPLE"
 60   INPUT N (2)
 70   PRINT "ENTER THE SUM OF THE RANKS OF THE FIRST SAM-
        PLE"
 80   INPUT T
 90   PRINT "ENTER THE DESIRED NUMBER OF SIMULATION RUNS"
100   INPUT M
110   N = N(1) + N(2)
```

```
120  DIM X(N)
130  NUM = NUM + 1
140  S = 0
150  FOR I = 1 TO N
160  X (I) = I
170  NEXT I
180  FOR I = 1 TO N(1)
190  R = INT((N + 1 - I) * RND) + 1
200  S = S + X(R)
210  X(R) = X(N + 1 - I)
220  NEXT I
230  IF S < = T THEN C(1) = C(1) + 1
240  IF S > = T THEN C(2) = C(2) + 1
250  IF NUM < M GOTO 130
260  IF C(1) > C(2) THEN C(1) = C(2)
270  PRINT "THE APPROXIMATE p-VALUE IS" 2 * C(1)/M
280  END
```

Index

Statistical Modeling and Decision Science

Gerald J. Leiberman and Ingram Olkin, editors

ISBN 0-12-598410-3